Dr Josephine Perry is a Chartered Sport and Exercise Psychologist whose purpose is to help people accomplish more than they had previously believed possible. She integrates expertize in sport psychology and communications to support athletes, stage performers and business leaders to develop the approaches, mental skills and strategies which will help them achieve their ambitions.

The TEN PILLARS of SUCCESS

Secret Strategies of High Achievers

DR JOSEPHINE PERRY

ALLEN&UNWIN

Published in trade paperback in Great Britain in 2022 by
Allen & Unwin, an imprint of Atlantic Books Ltd.

10 9 8 7 6 5 4 3 2 1

A CIP catalogue record for this book is available from the British Library.

Trade paperback ISBN: 978 1 83895 773 5
E-book ISBN: 978 1 83895 774 2

Printed in Great Britain

Allen & Unwin
An imprint of Atlantic Books Ltd
Ormond House
26–27 Boswell Street
London
WC1N 3JZ

www.allenandunwin.com/uk

Contents

Introduction   1

1   A Sense of Belonging   7
2   Developing Mastery   37
3   Autonomy   65
4   A Powerful Purpose   93
5   Cultivated Confidence   119
6   Process-Driven   147
7   Courage   177
8   Pragmatic Optimism   207
9   Internal Insight   235
10   Gratitude   269

Conclusion   297
Acknowledgements   301
Index   305

Introduction

One of the first activities I do with my sport and performance psychology clients is give them a pack of fifty cards. On each card is written a value; not a numerical value, but a word – 'ambitious', 'family', 'spirituality', 'courage'; the type of values we can live our lives by. Clients sort the cards into three piles: 'not me', 'a little me', 'definitely me'. We usually end up with about twenty cards in the 'definitely me' pile. Then I get mean. I make them filter and filter until they have three cards left – three words which get to the core of who they are and what matters most to them. One card which is almost always in those three is... Success.

It was this realization that we all have a similar desire for success that prompted me to explore just what it is that makes us successful. Each individual client I see has their own unique way of trying to get there – their own approaches, their own background, their own environment, their own talents – but there do seem to be some psychological characteristics that many of them share.

Success is clearly something that many of us crave and yet achieving it is so difficult. To try, we often look to learn from others. We are told to surround ourselves with those we want to be like, in order for their skills and approaches to rub off on us. In doing so, we want to understand what allows those who seem successful to hit their goals. What is it that medal-winning athletes, spellbinding performers and captivating CEOs do differently? How do their minds work? And what can we learn from them, so that those of us who have yet to become exceptional can get closer to achieving our ambitions?

The truth is, though they may not realize it, these successful people do share some ingrained psychological 'pillars'. They have, purposely or inadvertently, developed an understanding of what success looks like in their world and use the benefits which come from those pillars to move towards it. By contrast, most of us have yet to locate our version of success. The feeling is something we all crave, but if we struggle to grasp that tangible 'what' we want and 'why' we want it, how will we know when we have achieved it?

We can start by being clear on what success is *not*. Success is not winning. Winning might feel great for a moment or two, but such moments are fleeting and don't help us feel satisfied when we are looking back or give us a sense of wellbeing. The idea of winning is divisive, implying that there is a loser, but there doesn't always have to be. Take driving tests for example. Our ego feels good if we pass first time when others haven't – but, surely, we all do better when more people pass and the roads become safer.

Winning is also problematic because so much of what we achieve in life depends on the cards we are dealt; we do not all start out on a level playing field. Even when we do win it is often down to luck, such as picking the right lottery numbers, and, even in that, case studies have found that winners are often no happier a year after their jackpot. We need to stop obsessing about results, and concentrate less on winning and more on making long-term positive impacts.

As a Chartered Sport Psychologist I have worked with children as young as eight up to athletes in their eighties and I combine skills in sport psychology with a background in communications to support athletes, stage performers and business leaders in developing the approaches, mental skills and strategies that will help them achieve their ambitions. In all the work I do with these high-achieving performers, whether it is in the dressing room with athletes, the green room with actors, the court room with lawyers or the boardroom with CEOs, those who have risen highest and feel happiest understand that success is about much more than just winning – in fact, it is rarely the win itself that matters, but why they wanted to win. What does it mean to them? Where does that win take them? Notable athletes want to be brilliant at what they do; winning is a great side effect.

If success does involve any sort of winning, it is winning at being the best version of who you are. This is not about being macho and mentally tough – those are outdated and harmful concepts. Rather, it is about being flexible and authentic, shaping who you already are into the ideal version of yourself and giving yourself the best possible chance of making your 'why' happen. Success – and this book – is about finding who you are, rather than who you or anyone else thinks you *should* be. After all, what would be the point in finding that you are successful, only to realize that it is someone else's version of success that you are living?

Following our own version of success is not easy. True success is rarely measured in terms of who was first across the line or how much money was made. Instead, we need to measure what matters and create meaningful metrics that resonate with our own values. This is within our control, but it takes work to learn to focus on the endeavour and the effort, rather than the triumph and the trophy.

In *The Ten Pillars of Success*, we will journey through the principles of success. By the end of this book, you will understand what will give you the best possible chance of attaining whatever goal you set yourself. You will be supported through the use of cutting-edge evidence in the fields of psychology, education and medicine.

These pillars are not innate personality traits. Some of us may be lucky enough to be born with one or more, but anyone can learn them. And when we have all ten, we possess the building blocks that help to shape and maintain a successful life. Academic studies have shown that these positive psychological interventions foster not only potential outward success, but also inner well-being. All the evidence suggests that possessing these ten pillars will lead to a happier, healthier and more successful life.

So what *are* the ten pillars and why do we need to focus on them?

- **Belonging, mastery** and **autonomy**: together, these create the sense of self-determination that is needed to be motivated to stretch ourselves.

- **Purpose**: without this, we don't know where we are heading.

- **Confidence**: even with strong motivation and a destination, it is confidence which gets us to the starting point.

- **Process**: when we set out to achieve something, the outcome provides the motivation but it is the processes which facilitate it. These need to be kept front of mind.

- **Courage, optimism** and a large amount of **internal insight**: to keep ourselves focused on the process and not the outcome.

- **Gratitude**: without appreciating who and what we have in our lives, we will never make a true success of them. Though this is the final pillar, it is arguably the most important.

In each chapter we will consider the evidence for a pillar's inclusion, highlighting its benefits and telling the stories of those who have used it. In examining how each pillar is incorporated by various high achievers, we will learn how we might use that pillar ourselves. It is the success stories that bring each chapter to life, following those who utilized a pillar until it became integral to their approach. Whether it brings a sense of belonging, mastery, autonomy, purpose, confidence, process, courage, optimism, internal insight or gratitude, each pillar has been fundamental in helping them to overcome setbacks to succeed.

We will learn about the importance of collaboration from a double Olympic champion. An award-winning actress will tell us how she became successful by tenaciously developing her mastery. An endurance adventurer will reveal that his world record attempts have been successful because he thrives on the sense of autonomy that his challenges offer.

We will meet an ultra-runner who uses strategically placed acorns to fuel his achievements and remind him of his purpose, and a paracanoeist who cultivated her own style of confidence and has achieved multiple world and Paralympic titles. A poker player will explain how understanding the process-driven nature of his game led him to success in Vegas, and a movie stuntman will share how he used the courage required for death-defying manoeuvres to recover from what might have been career-ending surgery.

We will also meet a choreographer and director whose optimism encouraged him to step up to challenges rather than remain hidden in the wings, and a comedian who used her internal insight to find the perfect career. Finally, we will learn about the importance of gratitude from an oncologist and Ironman athlete who achieved a top-ten finish at the World Championships only eight weeks after breaking her collarbone.

In each of our success stories, their pillar has become their superpower.

This book first came out as an audiobook. Listeners got in touch to ask for a physical copy because they wanted to be able to take notes and underline key messages; they wanted guidance on how to do some of the techniques discussed. As a result, *The Ten Pillars of Success* has been updated and a toolkit has been added to the end of each chapter, so you can access some of the tools in a much more visual way. There are thirty-nine tools in total. You don't need to use them all, but if you find a few which work for you then get stuck in and you should feel more equipped to take the next moves towards finding your personal success.

So, as you read, think about what superpower you would like. Notice the pillars you need, the techniques which will help embed them and enjoy the journey of securing your personal success. Let's get going.

1

A Sense of Belonging

You have an innate need to belong. When you don't belong, your physical and mental health diminishes and your opportunities for success reduce. When you feel like you belong, you are far more likely to succeed.

It might seem a little odd to start a book about how to be successful in the twenty-first century with a quote by a metaphysical poet who died in 1631. And yet when John Donne wrote 'No man is an island...', he was expressing the idea that humans rarely thrive when they are isolated from others. That remains true, nearly four hundred years later.

The idea is perfectly embodied by one infamous – possibly somewhat apocryphal – example of true teamwork, quoted by leadership courses all over the world. The story goes that when John F. Kennedy was touring NASA for the first time after becoming president, he got talking to a man mopping the floor. When he asked the cleaner what he did, the man replied, 'I'm helping to put a man on the moon.' That cleaner had a true sense of belonging; he felt part of a big organization and knew how to play his role. It is that sense of belonging, of feeling like you play a purposeful role and that you have value to others, that makes us open to success.

In this chapter we meet our first success story: Colonel Dame Kelly Holmes, MBE (mil). She probably doesn't need much introduction as so many of us will remember seeing her wide-eyed with excitement and pride when she realized that she'd won a gold medal in the 800 m – the first of two – at the Athens Olympics in 2004. As well as her Olympic medals, she spent nine years in the army, is an author, a global speaker and founder of three organizations: the Dame Kelly Holmes Trust, Elf at Work (an Employee Lifestyle and Fitness platform) and Military in Motion (a fitness and motivation platform).

Kelly's story in getting to the Olympics, and beyond, illustrates all the benefits of having a sense of belonging and utilizing social connection. It is this social connection that powered so much of her success on the track and afterwards.

'I love to connect people. All the things I've done have given me a great basis for understanding how to connect people. It is about finding connections in areas that you are passionate about. You will find some real gems. When you find those gems, don't let them go, because they are the people that you can do everything with.'

The Importance of Belonging

As humans, we have a fundamental need to feel connected and to relate to others. Evolution shows the ways in which being part of something bigger is beneficial. Being a member of a group allows us to pool effort, resources, skills and knowledge. Groups diffuse risk – we feel safer, less threatened and more able to focus on what we do best, bringing our strengths together. We can cooperate more and maximize our own protection against rivals. This need is so strong that, when we cut ourselves off and don't feel we belong, we feel pain. Because of this need to preserve a sense of belonging, we tend to stay in toxic relationships far longer than is healthy. If you send holiday cards you might continue to send them to people you haven't spoken to for years because not doing so might signify the end of that fragile bond with them. It is for a similar reason that getting retweets and 'likes' on social media can feel so addictive – the bigger the response to our statements and photos, the more we feel we belong. Feeling accepted and welcomed prompts positive emotions; being rejected and ignored hurts.

Our need for acceptance begins at birth. Attachment theory suggests that the bonds established between a newborn and its parents exert great influence on the child's sense of belonging in later life. Children may experience insecure attachment through inconsistency in the way they are parented and lack of validation, and they may be left with the constant fear that they might have to fend for themselves. By contrast, strong attachment creates a lasting connectedness that makes children feel secure and gives them a solid base from which to go out and explore. Children with secure attachments function well in adolescence, get on better with their peers, perform well academically and are able to build strong relationships. They know that there is always a safe haven, and that gives them the freedom to explore. Their attachment acts as a buffer when facing obstacles, which provides the confidence to work towards success. Without that safe haven, nothing feels quite so accessible and there is no freedom, only fear.

The attachment style we develop with those early bonds – whether secure, resistant or avoidant – follows us into all areas of adulthood. Secure individuals have high self-esteem and a strong sense of belonging. They are able to be caring, intimate, supportive and understanding. Resistant adults feel far more emotional instability and may have a preoccupation with physical attractiveness, leading them to form relationships with the 'wrong' people. Avoidant adults have a fear of intimacy and may stay away from relationships altogether. They may have low self-esteem and be hesitant, shy and afraid of rejection. Others who are avoidant might seem dismissive, overly confident and critical. These attachment styles impact our work and education, and influence the relationships we have with family, friends and colleagues.

We are all keen to form social attachments and unwilling to dissolve existing bonds; we spend our lives trying to maintain a number of lasting, significant and positive relationships. The sense of belonging that we seek out as a result of these needs creates an internal model of our beliefs and values; of whether we feel lovable and whether the social world is trustworthy. This model influences how we connect with others. If we build a secure attachment in childhood, we have a greater chance of enjoying a sense of high self-esteem, being more self-reliant, having calmer romantic relationships and enjoying the confidence to share feelings. We may also experience lower levels of depression and anxiety. We will look at how to manage the attachment style we do have in the toolkit at the end of this chapter (see page 31).

Kelly has a really interesting take on this as her childhood was less secure than that of many others. She spent time in a children's home and, as a result, she has had to proactively learn how to use her attachment style to her advantage.

'My mother basically had me when she was seventeen and was told by her parents – my nan and granddad – that she couldn't look after me until she could look after herself, so I was actually put into a children's home. When the adoption services came to pick me up, she refused to sign the final papers and said, "No." So her strength of character obviously was very, very strong. I suppose I get a bit of that strength of character from her. But equally, I suppose, what happened was a bit of detachment as well. Because when you are fearful that somebody is not going to come back for you, when you are left on your own – like I was then – you get a sense of worry that somebody is always going to leave you so you pre-empt that.'

As Kelly indicates, that powerful need to belong can also come with fear, and this can impact our motivation. We need to forge close relationships if we are to enhance our drive and determination. It makes sense that, in order to be successful, we require positive relationships with people who can support us in the pursuit of our goals and that we should offer the same support and feedback to others. Motivational theories suggest that we can only push ourselves forward if we feel a strong sense of connection or rapport with others.

In sport, belonging is expressed in the power of teams, the importance of specialist support around athletes and the use of technology that can connect athletes in meaningful ways. In schools, pupils who feel fully integrated in their environment achieve high results and develop an innate love of learning. And in workplaces, united teams are able to achieve far more than individuals ever can.

You don't have to be in a team to feel that you belong though. You may work, play a sport or parent alone and enjoy that solitude. But solitude only helps us within a context of security – knowing that if we choose to reach out to others, they will be there. You don't have to be connected all the time, but you need to know that there are people who understand you and who you can relate to. Spending time alone because we have no choice is very different. A weekend alone to re-energise because you have had a busy week at work and been out playing sport most nights is very different to a weekend alone after a dull week because no one has asked to spend it with you.

Belonging comes from having high-quality social interaction and a special bond with a few people who really matter.

We need both these things and, without them, we tend to feel lonely and disconnected. We see it in young children for whom having a 'best friend' is so important. We see it in sport when a coach becomes incredibly influential. Without these, there is a disconnect which can feel isolating and hard to fix. And quality is more important than quantity. Studies into whether people prefer having lots of friends or deeper connections with fewer, closer friends have suggested that we have a clear preference for the latter.

For Kelly, it was her first coach, Dave Arnold, who gave her the connection and sense of belonging she needed: 'He started with me when I was twelve. He was a person who I would always fall back to if things weren't going so well, even if I wasn't with him directly, I was training away or training with other coaches. And I think that was a real kind of secure place to have.'

As Kelly shows, belonging can be about choice. We lose some of the positive benefits of a group or community if we are forced to belong, because our autonomy has been removed. Here we do not 'belong', but we are trying to fit in. This is disempowering and we become resentful and uncomfortable. It does not improve our chances of success at all. It is when we *choose* to belong and genuinely feel we do, that we get great results.

Belonging supports success

The support we get from others improves our chances of success. We often hear about the 'bystander effect' – the more people who are present when someone is in trouble, the fewer come forward to help. The sheer number of people present means that the bystanders, as a group, feel that it is not their responsibility to offer assistance and, in fact, fear the possibility of the negative consequences of helping. However, in a cohesive group, this changes. When you are with people you know and feel you belong with, everyone wants to help. The mere realization that we might, in the future, be with this group of bystanders again is enough to make us more likely to come to each other's aid.

In big groups of people in which we don't feel any sense of connection, we naturally put our own self-interest ahead of the needs of others. We may do as little as we can get away with in the hope that others will make up the deficit, a tendency known as 'social loafing'. When we are in a group in which we feel that we belong, we have a much stronger sense of duty that is highlighted through the bystander effect – particularly if we have some way of making a unique contribution. We might go on a group holiday and know that we are rubbish at cooking so offer to do the cleaning instead. In team sport we see it clearly – we get given a position based on our skills and expertise; the goal attack in netball uses their shooting skills, in contrast to the skills of the defender. We can see that a sense of belonging can help us overcome even thoroughly ingrained, self-interested patterns of behaviour – all for the good of the wider group.

Within groups in which members feel a sense of belonging, there is also a sense of purpose – and this, as we will learn later in the book, is another pillar of success (see Chapter 4). In an experiment at the Wharton School, the business school of the University of Pennsylvania, a university fundraising team was split into two groups: one spent five minutes with a beneficiary, learning about the school's impact on his life, while the other continued to make calls. The funds raised by the team that met the beneficiary increased by over 170 per cent in the following months, while the other group's fundraising remained at the same level. The simple act of connecting employees to those who benefitted from their work had yielded a huge business advantage.

Although Kelly won two Olympic gold medals in 2004, she went on to realize that this was not where her sense of purpose lay. She felt far more successful when she motivated, mentored and helped others connect, something she did through a project called On Camp with Kelly. She decided early in 2004 that if she didn't achieve her dream of becoming an Olympic champion she could still pass on her knowledge and experience of elite sport to help young teenage girls with real potential.

'The whole outlook was to take them away for a month, to South Africa where I had been living, to teach them what it takes to be a world-class athlete because, at that stage, those young girls were going through disordered eating patterns, lack of self-esteem, lack of confidence. I ended up having sixty-three international athletes in my group.' Her goal was to teach them that there is way more to being an elite athlete than just running fast. 'It is all about your attitude, the extra work you do, the rehabilitation, your focus, your belief, your preparation, your mental, as well as your physical, attitude to your performance as well as your physical, your tactical awareness... It is all of those things, even if you are just running twice around a track.'

In each girl she helped embed a sense of belonging. 'I ran all these programmes and projects and training camps, and they all became friends, even though a lot of them were rivals and competitors. I was really proud of them. I was this shoulder to cry on, best friend, mentor and kind of like teacher. I was all of them together really.'

As the On Camp with Kelly girls found, belonging means knowing that there are always people on your side, cheering you on. In many sports, hearing the cheers from supporters can boost the players' ability. This is why sports fans are often talked about as part of the team – the sixth player in a basketball team or that twelfth person in football.

When you find a team or group in which you feel comfortable, you have psychological safety. You can bounce ideas off each other, discuss how to do things better and enhance each other's work, making your group greater than the sum of its parts. When you know that you belong, your success links to the success of your team; this can make you a better team player, further increasing your sense of belonging.

Our need for belonging spreads into the type of success we pursue, in that we prefer achievements that can be easily validated and recognized by others: a degree; a football score; a time for running a mile; a place in the New Year Honours List. Achievements that are valued by others can sometimes seem more important than those we alone value. They give an easy metric that others can comprehend and, as a result, we want to belong to the communities that award them – to be a graduate, a Manchester City fan, a member of the British Milers Club or of the British Empire. Our sense of our own credibility and the confidence that comes from it all relates to this sense of belonging.

Kelly understood this, and for her final Olympics used the knowledge to maximize her chances of success. At different stages she had a coach, training partners, physio and massage therapist. She wouldn't have daily interactions with them all, but the knowledge that they were on her side was vital in the build-up to Athens in 2004. 'I knew that the only way that I could achieve my twenty-year dream was to ensure that the people around me had the same vision and outlook as me, to be the best version of themselves, whatever job they had, and to bring a team of people connected together for one purpose. That team became so connected that we were able to be on the same page, and that was to only think of one thing – that we were going to win. It just felt brilliant. Because all the people around me were just giving me 100 per cent confidence in my ability.'

It is not just personal success that is improved by belonging; businesses also do better. A study of nearly one thousand eight hundred people in the US found that when people feel like they belong at work, company performance increases by 56 per cent, turnover of staff decreases and 75 per cent fewer employees take sick days. Staff are also more likely to spread the news, making their company more popular with potential employees and customers. According to the study, this would save a 10,000-person company £42 million each year.

In all these situations, it is not just that belonging provides a foundation for success, but that it makes the whole process of attaining success more enjoyable. The psychological safety we gain from membership of a group has huge value, both because of the feeling that others have our back and the confidence that if we fail we can climb up again. When we are successful in a group, we have people to share that success with; whether that be celebrating a contract won, an exam passed or a big presentation nailed. Being with other people validates the success and makes it more fun.

A good way to highlight how this works is to examine a specific environment. Schools are ideal communities to study as they provide a natural laboratory with regular testing; we can examine the pupils' sense of belonging to groups that include teachers, peers, the school community as a whole and their parents.

Numerous studies have shown that if a child feels liked, respected and valued by their teacher, they will develop a love of learning and perform at a higher level. How teachers rate their closeness with students is another good predictor of how well those students will perform academically. Those who are deemed to have a close relationship with their teacher will show greater levels of engagement, take part in more school activities, develop a genuine love of learning and feel fewer negative emotions. A study looking at the attitudes towards reading of 820 six-year-olds found that the more the children were able to engage with their teachers, the greater their love of reading and the higher their confidence in their reading ability, which then positively influenced their ability to learn and develop.

In 189 studies of children, from nursery through to high school, a positive relationship was identified between how teachers related to their class and the students' own engagement and achievement. In fact, studies have found that pupils' relationships to their teachers are linked to a host of motivational outcomes, such as the ability to achieve goals, the effort and persistence they put into their work and how well they regulate themselves. It has even been found to influence a student's confidence to tackle academic tasks. Of 138 factors linked to academic achievement, how well the child felt they related to their teacher has been ranked the eleventh most important.

How children engage with their peers is also hugely influential. When children learn to cooperate with classmates at school, they develop social competence, which is vital to their sense of belonging as they go through life. A sense of social competence increases the number of groups or communities they feel comfortable engaging with and thus increases their sense of belonging. In education, this social competence can help them transition to new classes or schools more easily, help them feel more secure among their peers, improving their motivation, engagement and academic performance, and it boosts their self-esteem. It can even influence their physical health as they tend to be more active at break times.

The Harm of 'Anomie'

A sense of belonging is fundamental to success itself, something which becomes clear when we examine the negative impact of feeling as if we don't belong. The effect of isolation and loneliness is powerful. When we don't feel like we have strong and meaningful connections, the pain can be acute. The term 'anomie' refers to the sense of not belonging to a community.

Evolutionary psychologists have long stated that humans are designed to live in small communities that enhance a sense of belonging and support the social bonds required for survival: cooperation to find food and shelter, communication to engage and procreation to pass down our genes. Our current way of life in the West is not well suited to belonging. In the UK, 8 million people live alone and, for those people, mixing with others can require significant effort. We may work at home and shop and socialize online. Even if we do work away from home and live with a family, we may have long commutes, meaning that members of an immediate family spend lots of time apart.

In addition, the Western world in the twenty-first century has become so focused on productivity that we have engineered an environment in which we struggle to live in the moment. Work takes precedence over play, even though it is in play that many of our most valuable relationships develop. The relationships that we build at work can feel transient compared to the bonds we build in our social lives.

This focus on productivity means that we miss out on social bonds. We have fewer opportunities to bump into others, meaning that we may not feel particularly connected to our immediate community. We may feel more secure if we own our house, but data from the UK government's 2021 English Housing Survey found that 36 per cent of householders are renters – and a quarter of those have moved in the previous year – suggesting a significant number of people will not feel it worthwhile to invest in building strong relationships with those around them when they may soon have to move on.

A sense of belonging can also come from sharing a passion or hobby or having something in common with others. We can then feel that we belong to a number of different communities, whether they be clubs or groups based on shared interests that link to our background, identity, hobbies or faith.

It is possible to belong to groups but to still feel alone. Those who are lonely and those who are not spend similar amounts of time with other people, demonstrating that the experience of loneliness is not necessarily a result of *being* alone, but of *feeling* alone. We can feel lonely when our experiences of social engagement don't match up to our expectations. Anomie comes from both a mixture of feeling socially isolated and of feeling lonely within those relationships that we do have.

When we feel a sense of being related but are without the other important elements of belonging – such as the feeling of being cared about – we can really struggle. Isolation can be both social and emotional. We feel social isolation when we have a weak social network with few family or friend relationships and little connection to society on a wider level. Emotional isolation is the perception of social isolation – the experience of being lonely. We might have a strong social network and enjoy membership of outside groups and yet still feel socially isolated, lonely and disconnected.

What each of us finds isolating can be very different. Neuroscientists have suggested that we develop our expectations of belonging from our upbringing and those we socialize with as young children. For some people, a close romantic relationship and a few friends is all they need; other people may expect to be surrounded by a wide number of family members and to be part of multiple groups. If either of their realities falls outside of these expectations, they feel uncomfortable and will begin to feel lonely.

The gap between the expectations and the reality of belonging seems to have become more acute because our society has become so digitalized. Technology plays a complicated role in our sense of belonging. On the positive side, it allows us to work more flexibly and to connect with those who live a long distance away. It can also help us find our own communities based on what we love, allowing us to engage with others, unhindered by logistics or location. It can start virtual alliances which develop into real-life friendships.

The downside is that technology limits our opportunities to interact meaningfully with others, not just in the sense that time online takes us away from face-to-face activities, but also in that spending time on social media sites can undermine our social skills. Over 90 per cent of our communication is thought to be non-verbal and we need to keep practising reading body language in our interactions in the physical world.

Sending an email or tweet is simple; meeting with someone face to face is far more complex, requiring physiological responses, cognitive engagement and the production of a neuro-peptide (which is a chemical messenger in our brain) called oxytocin. This is the hormone produced by mothers when they give birth that helps them bond with their children. It also helps in social situations, helping us to bond with each other. We don't get this hormonal stimulation behind a screen.

Anomie impacts our behaviours, our physical health, our productivity and our self-esteem. Its impact on our physical health is huge; when we lose our sense of belonging, the results can be devastating. A team that ran a meta-analysis of seventy studies looking at social isolation, loneliness and risk of mortality found that people who said they felt lonely had a 26 per cent higher risk of death. The increase was 29 per cent for those who were socially isolated and 32 per cent for those who lived on their own.

Loneliness makes it harder to control and regulate our habits and behaviour. When we feel isolated, we are more likely to drink more alcohol, have an unhealthier diet, take illegal drugs or do less exercise. It's harder to instil habits that lead to better health. A lack of social connection makes for health outcomes that are detrimental; people who feel lonely have an increased risk of high blood pressure, coronary heart disease, stroke, lung disease, depression, dementia, arthritis and poorer immune functioning. The health risk of loneliness is thought to be the equivalent of smoking fifteen cigarettes a day. And, according to psychologists at the University of California, Los Angeles (UCLA) who used neuroimaging to measure changes in brain activity, the process of social exclusion hurts physically as well as mentally. Our reactions to rejection are mediated in the brain by our pain system and we feel it acutely.

Suicide is also higher in those who are lonely. More than a hundred years ago, the theorist Émile Durkheim described loneliness as a failure of social integration and many others have since proposed that those who are well integrated into society are less likely to contemplate suicide. Study after study finds that suicide rates are highest in those with a reduced sense of belonging: single, divorced and widowed people, those who are unemployed and those in shrinking cultural or employment groups.

Kelly's story highlights the harm that can come when we feel disconnected even when, theoretically, we have people close to us. Early in 2004 she suffered from depression when she went through a long period of injury, but at the time she didn't realize and so wasn't able to reach out to those who could have helped. Without the support in place or knowing why she was feeling that way, Kelly found an unhealthy coping mechanism.

'When I first self-harmed I was in a training camp and, basically, I saw some scissors on the side in the toilets and I ended up trying to cut myself for every day that I had been injured.

And that was almost like telling off my body. Telling my body that "You are letting me down." Cutting myself was sort of a release. I hated myself. I mean, I literally hated myself at that point. So every time I was cutting was more, just like evidence of things that make me hate myself.'

Kelly realized that something needed to change. She was still depressed and having anxiety attacks and occasionally self-harming, but she realized that it wasn't just the injury which had caused her to hit rock bottom, but the lack of connection, so she took decisive action. She had to make a tough decision. Should she stick with her current coach, training partner and set-up or move over to the team GB set-up? Which connections would help her belong and give the greatest chance of success?

She made the decision to train with the British team. 'That gave me a sense of "we are all in this together", rather than a detachment from those people who I really trusted and really believed in. By doing that, it gave this kind of weight off my shoulders that the expectations of conforming to one way of training were gone. And I could just do what I knew was right throughout my whole career, with the people I absolutely knew I could trust and absolutely were in it for one reason – and that was for me to win a gold medal and for them to be that best version of themselves and, you know, well, I won two gold medals, so it clearly worked.'

While economics is far less important individually than wellbeing, there is an economic cost to anomie. Those who are lonely require a greater number of GP consultations, have higher rates of hospital admissions, spend more nights in nursing homes, are off work more often, have lower productivity and move jobs more frequently. One study has estimated that the annual cost to the UK economy of this disconnection in our communities is £32 billion.

More than anything though, loneliness can also make us feel angry, sad, depressed, worthless, resentful, empty, vulnerable and pessimistic. When we feel like this, we tend to separate ourselves from others, expecting and fearing rejection. We are less likely to confide in others about how we are feeling and miss out on reassurance. As a result, we become trapped in a vicious circle – the more we withdraw, the less support we receive and the more isolated we get. We feel even less like we belong.

Who belongs?

Everyone has the ability to find their tribe and feel that sense of belonging, but some of us find it harder than others. Current figures suggest that over 9 million people in the UK are either always or often lonely, while other studies have suggested that the figure is even higher. According to a 2019 YouGov poll, 31 per cent of us find it difficult to make friends. A meta-analysis of 345 studies published in 2022 in *Psychological Bulletin* found that between 1976 and 2012, loneliness increased and since then has levelled off, suggesting that more of us than ever before feel lonely. A 2019 study from life insurance company Cigna questioned over twenty thousand people and suggested that loneliness levels are highest in the younger generations: 48 per cent of Generation Z (born after 1997 and into the early 2010s) say they sometimes or often feel lonely.

There is a strand of thinking that suggests that some of us are genetically predisposed to feel lonely. A 2005 study at the University of Chicago found a hereditary element to the way we process social interactions. Those who are lonely also tend to have low self-esteem and to look for instant gratification. This may be because they don't feel that they are worthy of feeling that sense of belonging or because they are unwilling to spend the time building a community, knowing how they will feel if they fail.

Happily married people tend to be much healthier than people in unsupportive social relationships. In the latter group, the lack of a satisfying relationship contributes to a sense of vulnerability. Many common emotional problems and behaviours result from a failure to belong in some way and come from an array of unhelpful coping mechanisms, such as avoidance, shutting ourselves down emotionally, ghosting people if we can't face giving them bad news and often just not asking for support when we need it most.

Teenagers are thought to be particularly vulnerable to loneliness because their brains are still developing and are not fully able to deal with rational judgement until the age of twenty-five. They process a greater proportion of information than adults through the amygdala which, as we shall discover in Chapter 6, is our emotional, irrational and threat-focused brain. An adult would dismiss the lack of immediate response to a Snapchat message with a, 'Well, they are probably busy', but the same delayed reply is interpreted by a teen as rejection. A missed invitation to a party doesn't mean that there was a number limit for a teen – it means that those not invited are disliked and unworthy. The emotional, threat-focused responses mean that they have a higher risk of misreading social cues or other people's emotions and respond far too quickly in kind.

Teens are also trying to develop their own identity away from their parents, which can be overwhelming. The feeling of being ostracized is often acute among young people, and we can see this in teenagers who leave home for their first year at university. A ThinkImpact report found that 30 per cent of those who start at American universities don't make it to the end of their first year and, in the UK, at some of the newer universities, a drop-out rate of over 20 per cent was identified.

Another particularly vulnerable group consists of those who move abroad for education, work, relationships or their own safety; cultural and language barriers can mean that they feel isolated and have trouble fitting in. Asylum seekers and refugees have these issues and may feel unable to engage with communities of their own diaspora without being reminded of the horrors they have witnessed. The only group to which they feel that they belong also feels as if it is toxic.

Being in a situation that alienates us from what we see as mainstream society can accentuate our sense of a lack of belonging. We are at risk of loneliness through becoming unemployed, having a chronic health condition or disability, retiring, developing an addiction, dealing with trauma or becoming involuntary carers.

Specific trigger points also put us at risk of becoming lonely. These include such life-changing events as moving house, the death of a loved one, the arrival of a new baby or the reverse – an empty nest – and divorce. The acute loneliness that such events cause is to be expected, but when it becomes chronic loneliness, we should worry. Chronic loneliness might be identified as:

- You feel unable to connect with others on a deep, intimate level.

- You have friends, but they feel more like acquaintances than people you can fully be yourself with.

- You might be surrounded by others but still be disengaged.

- Your sense of self-worth is low.

- When you reach out to others your efforts don't feel reciprocated.

- You feel exhausted after engaging with others.

That long-term lack of belonging can be hard to escape if we get stuck in a cycle of unhelpful habits: pushing others away, focusing only on transient contact such as one-night stands or risky actions that increase the feeling of isolation. A study in Poland found that when we are lonely we are more likely to put on a facade for others and feel that we can't display our real character. This is mentally fatiguing and, in hiding our authenticity, further reduces our chances of creating a sense of belonging with those who, if they only knew the real person, would like us for who we really are. The paradox of loneliness is that it leaves us less able to establish the relationships we crave. When it becomes chronic and persistent, we need to find ways to increase our sense of belonging and to become proactive about attaining the feeling that we belong.

Developing a Stronger Sense of Belonging

In an ideal world, we would glide through life with a loving family, close friends, welcoming and supportive clubs, a workplace that enables constructive teamwork and a fabulous local community. We would know our roles within each group, and feel comfortable and authentic when we performed them. In every relationship in this perfect scenario, we would always be able to see the big picture and see where we, our values and our purpose fit in. However, such situations are not realistic. We all need to proactively work on developing our sense of belonging and, to do this, we need to work on our social connectivity, our social strengths and our social competence.

The good news is that we don't need to work that hard. There is a limit to the number of connections that bring us benefit. British anthropologist Robin Dunbar has estimated that we cannot maintain more than 150 social relationships in our life. We might feel well connected with 1,000 Facebook friends or 500 connections on LinkedIn but, once we have more than 150 connections, each becomes far less meaningful. It is more useful to have fewer friends who you nurture, rather than hundreds of barely known acquaintances.

Improve your social connectivity

The easiest way to develop your social connectivity is to join groups. These usually have a shared purpose and that means that all members start off with a common interest, say a hobby or craft, a sport or an academic subject. If you are going through a period of transition such as retirement or being a new parent, groups focused on those particular needs can be valuable in establishing new friendships and cementing your identity. If you are struggling with a specific problem, such as mental health or addiction, group therapy and support sessions may help. You are able to realize that you are not alone in your struggles when you meet other people who are in the same position and understand what you are going through. Groups such as Alcoholics Anonymous help to sustain people in the long term through establishing a connection, understanding and taking responsibility for each other. It might not be a connectivity that you would ideally want, but in your situation it can become a connectivity that you need.

Technology may also help to solve the problem of anomie. A number of apps claim to enhance social wellness by helping us to develop genuine and meaningful relationships beyond those of dating apps. For example, Peanut – for new mums – helps to find other new parents in the locality, while Friender is designed, as it suggests, to find new friends. These apps have search functions that identify people with similar interests or hobbies who are nearby. The beauty of starting off online is that we can take baby steps towards putting ourselves out there without having to jump in at the deep end and walk into a room full of strangers.

Kelly discovered the power of tech to connect in the 2020 COVID-19 lockdown when she found herself stuck at home, cut off from her usual speaking engagements. She began using Instagram to show off her alpacas and cheer people up, which turned into seven months of free core and abs workouts to anyone who wanted to join in. These morning exercises developed into 'Military in Motion', a community of people from all over the world, with different backgrounds, ages, abilities, sizes, shapes, fitness and journeys. 'A lot of them have ended up becoming friends. People getting to know each other and, when they were able to meet up, meeting up as friends. I love the fact that it connects people from wherever, whoever, no matter what you have got – or haven't got – to make every single individual feel valued, and I think that is so important.'

Volunteering is a regularly suggested route to developing a wider circle of connections, and for very good reasons. From an evolutionary perspective, altruism is an essential part of human nature. People who are engaged in helping others tend to be happier. And when we study the feelings of volunteers, they often talk about the sense of satisfaction they feel and how it enhances their social capital. In volunteering, you not only help others, but you also get to engage meaningfully with more people and build your own social network. A group called GoodGym is an excellent example of this in practice. Runners sign up to help others – they might run to work in someone's garden or to the supermarket to buy essentials for an elderly person. The runners connect with each other through their passion for running and with those they help through the good deed. Everyone wins.

Strengthen your connections

Social groups tend to form quite quickly. Even over short-term engagements, such as training courses, people tend to swap details and aim to stay in touch. But while the allegiances seem to come about quickly, the numbers that actually keep in touch and build long-term contacts tends to be small. Once we have developed a connection, the key is to strengthen it, and for this we need regular personal contact or interaction. This should be free of conflict and we need to feel stable enough within those relationships that we can relax and be ourselves. We are not just seeking affiliations – the connections need to be stronger.

If we end up in relationships in which we feel that we have to play by the other person's rules and try to be someone we are not, the sense of belonging will be void – it is not just about being connected, but about feeling close. When we feel intimate, our motivation and wellbeing are nurtured, helping us grow.

It is important to learn how to build strong connections because the skill of it can help our success. We see this in the government minister who starts every local radio interview by referencing the local football team result from the weekend; in the PR person who keeps a spreadsheet noting the favourite foods and hobbies of each journalist and client; and in the manager at work who remembers every employee's birthday and their children's names. Such small details build connections and make people feel special; they get rewarded by loyalty and the strength of relatedness. From this, we can learn that, in building relationships, the acts of listening and remembering – noticing the details of people's lives and hearing what they have to say – are vital. It helps others feel that they belong and becomes especially valuable when reciprocated. We can show how much we notice about others through compliments – offering a genuine compliment to someone each day will not only make the recipient feel great, but, over time, will build closer and more enduring relationships.

One nice trick to try is mirroring the body language of those you are developing relationships with. A study from Linköping University in Sweden found that doing this improves the quality of communication and helps both parties feel emotionally closer, speeding up the bonding process.

Foster social competence

To gain the skills for fostering a sense of belonging, we need to develop social competence – the ability to interact positively with others – and for this we can turn to studies on the import-ance of belonging in school. Teachers build their students' social competence through peer-mediated learning – projects that require teamwork or collaboration. This gives children social support and the chance to benefit from the knowledge of others, as well as a supported way of establishing peer rela-tionships. It can, however, become counterproductive when peers choose their own groups. Anyone who isn't brilliant at sports will remember that moment in PE lessons when team captains chose their teams. Recalling the sensation of being last to be picked is something that still fills many of us with dread. Successful peer-mediated learning requires us to create groups that are socially engineered rather than allowed to develop holistically.

Encouraging ownership of social competence can also be effective. Getting team members to consider what changes could be made to boost their group's enjoyment and inclusivity makes people think about what could improve things for every-one. Similarly, asking people how they would coach someone else who felt left out and isolated has been found to help prompt that person to put some of those strategies into place themselves.

Building good-quality social networks and relationships through connectivity, strength and competence improves your physical and mental wellbeing and increases happiness, comfort and resilience. When these things are in place, society improves because there is less crime, lower levels of loneliness and a far better quality of life. All this means that, when you have a sense of belonging, success becomes so much easier to reach.

BELONGING TOOLKIT

Connect with purpose

We have a fundamental need to feel connected, to relate to others and be part of groups. This allows us to pool effort, resources, skills and knowledge; diffuse risks; increase our own protection; and feel a sense of intrinsic motivation. It is important to remember this when you start on any new project and consider who you will be surrounding yourself with. You should ask yourself four questions:

1. How can I help them?
2. How can they help me?
3. Who else do we need?
4. How can we be stronger together?

Attachment style awareness

Our need to belong begins at birth as early attachments can have a lifetime of influence on our self-esteem, resilience and mental health. An awareness of our attachment style is valuable as it helps us see through that lens and consider if we are making choices freely or because of our prior environment.

There are four types of attachment style. The most common (studies suggest between 50 and 62 per cent of us have this style) is secure. This is where you have mutual trust and respect, so you feel able to maintain healthy, lasting relationships while still feeling confident and valued in yourself. You know that you deserve love and affection and have a positive view of yourself and others. With this style, a sense of belonging can be fairly easy to develop and maintain. There are three other types of attachment style, though, and here a sense of belonging is harder to develop:

- Anxious/Preoccupied: A craving for love, intimacy and relationships. May struggle to be single, but will fear rejection or become jealous when in a relationship. May put the needs of others well before their own and blame themselves for things that go wrong. Can come across as needy. As parents, they may be hypervigilant and set strict expectations so the child struggles to develop their own character or autonomy.

- Avoidant/Dismissive: Very independent, assertive and self-sufficient. This group found out fairly early in life that some people may not be able to fulfil their needs so learned to look after themselves. May struggle to connect deeply with people as they can seem aloof and detached as their brain protects them from getting too close for fear of rejection. As parents, they may struggle to show affection and can be very inflexible.

- Disorganized or Fearful/Avoidant: These people seem confident and keen to connect with others, but struggle to open up. They can seem inconsistent as they move between clinginess and needing reassurance and being totally distanced. They crave attention, but are also terrified of receiving it. Parents with this style can come across as inconsistent – sometimes dismissing and other times overly involved, and this can create fear.

If you feel one of these insecure types describes you, some steps you can take include:

1. Stop beating yourself up. You are not a failure – you have just been born into an environment that required you to adapt in order to survive. These adaptations do not help us thrive as adults so we need to learn some different behaviours.

2. Find some role models. List those in your life who seem to have a secure attachment style. What do they do that makes you feel loved, calm or confident? Write down some actions you could take that would mirror those.

3. Explain the attachment style you have to those close to you. And then explain how this may sometimes make you behave and how they can help. Offering scenarios can help here: 'When X happens my response is often Y. This is because Z.' If someone doesn't understand why you may come across as needy, they may push back. When they get why, they may support that need instead.

4. Acceptance. If you feel your natural attachment style coming out in your behaviours, notice it, label it and accept it. We might say to ourselves, 'I can see that I am currently being avoidant. I do this because I feel safer not relying on others. It isn't ideal so I will work on it.' Labelling and accepting helps us get more distance from the pain of it so we can switch to healthier coping mechanisms.

Circle of safety

Belonging comes from having high-quality social interactions and a special bond with a few people who really matter. This doesn't just provide a foundation for success, but also makes the process of attaining success more enjoyable. When you find a team or group in which you feel comfortable, you have psychological safety which allows you to take risks and explore, secure that if something goes wrong you have a safety net. Hunt out that crowd. Allow yourself to be vulnerable with them and see what feedback you get. Look for the signs of psychological safety:

- Seeing mistakes as learning opportunities which are celebrated rather than punished.
- People taking risks.
- An atmosphere of openness and honesty.
- A sense of trust; each person in the group has the others' back.

Relationship building

We can only effectively maintain around 150 social relationships, so it is more useful to have fewer friends who you nurture, rather than hundreds of barely known acquaintances. Look through Facebook, Twitter and Instagram and write a list of who matters to you and who you would like to build a deeper sense of belonging with. Perhaps see this as a project to stay in touch with those people much more.

Shared purpose

Groups with a shared purpose are the easiest way to develop your social connectivity. As we shall discover in Chapter 4, a purpose is essential for feeling we have lived a successful life, but it needs to be a purpose that feels authentic; something we really care about. When we identify this purpose (which could be around the environment, how we support others, a campaign we work on or an expertise we have developed), engaging with others who hold similar aims can help us to make strong connections and build a sense of belonging to the shared ambition. Below, list three areas of your life where joining a group or connecting more with people sharing that passion could be beneficial:

1. _____

2. _____

3. _____

2

Developing Mastery

When you have mastered what matters and you own what you know, you have more confidence to go out and succeed in style.

We begin this chapter by heading back over a hundred years, to the time when Thomas Edison – now mainly known as the inventor of the modern light bulb – was working in his lab.

Edison started working on his key invention at the age of thirty-one and went on to conduct thousands of experiments, trying to make a filament hot enough to glow when heated by electricity. When asked about this huge number of attempts, he is said to have replied, 'I have not failed, I have just found ten thousand ways that won't work.' Once he had eventually found a solution, he was asked about his exacting process. His response was, 'None of my inventions came by accident. I see a worthwhile need to be met and I make trial after trial until it comes. What it boils down to is 1 per cent inspiration and 99 per cent perspiration... accordingly, a "genius" is often merely a talented person who has done all of his or her homework.' This is a beautiful way of highlighting why we need to focus on mastery if we are to be successful.

If we are to succeed at something, we first require competency, followed by mastery over time. Competency grants us the skills required to achieve our chosen goal and mastery gives us the confidence that we can use them when necessary. The latter skill is deemed essential in a number of motivational theories, including those which aim to internalize how much we want to achieve something. This is because it can reduce the amount by which we compare ourselves to others and helps us work through our development in stages so we build our self-esteem. Proactively developing mastery means that, rather than waiting for opportunities to arise, you have the confidence to go out and find them for yourself.

Someone who achieves mastery is actress and writer Maxine Peake. We know her for appearing as Martha Costello in the drama *Silk* and Veronica in the iconic show *Shameless*. She acted alongside Julie Walters and Victoria Wood in the comedy *Dinnerladies* and, on the stage, she was the first female in the UK to play Hamlet for over thirty years. Looking at her career from the outside, it could be assumed that mastery came easily to her and opportunities just flew her way. However, this was not the case. She says she really had to hunt for work, for years and years.

'I went to Salford College of Technology when I was sixteen and I had a terrible time. Two weeks in they said, "You are not an actor. You should consider leaving", and I just remember thinking, "I can't. I don't want to leave", even though it was painful. And it was two years. So I stuck at it and I think that's the best thing I ever did – to hang on in there – 'cos it gave me resilience. It gave me resilience when they wouldn't cast me, give me parts in shows. They said, "Well, you can do props." We did a play, a version of *Lysistrata*, and they made me go to the sex shop and buy twenty dildos – really humiliating things. And then it took me three years to get into drama school. The more I got rejected, the more I wanted to do it. I kept pushing and pushing.'

Maxine didn't see those rejections as evidence to stop, but she certainly saw them as setbacks and was worn down by them. 'I auditioned for RADA [the Royal Academy of Dramatic Art] and didn't expect to get in, but I just thought this will be fun, auditioning for RADA – see how the other half live – and it worked out.' Mastery was the last thing on Maxine's mind at that point. 'I was very rough around the edges. You know, when I look back at early work, I think, wow, wow, I'm really surprised they took me on. I always thought if I was given the opportunities, I could be a good actor. I didn't go in going, "I'm a good actor – take me." I just, I felt, as well, there was something, if I honed my craft, I could be.' In fact, the rejections were helpful to her mastery as she felt she had a Greek chorus telling her that she couldn't, making her work harder to prove that she could.

What Is Mastery?

Mastery is not a destination; it is a journey that we are all on, continually, and that is part of its beauty – the idea that we have a knowledge base that we can always refine and expand. And as a master consolidates their mastery, its content changes and evolves. The types of moves achieved by the Romanian gymnast Nadia Comaneci in the 1976 Montreal Olympics, when she was the first gymnast to be awarded a perfect score – 10.0 – would now not even be enough to win her a place on the modern-day GB or US national teams. The equipment she used has evolved. It has become more difficult, and the skills required to use it are trickier to master too. From this, we can see that mastery is not a smooth or direct journey. It is best described as 'lumpy'. Some days you will make leaps of understanding, while on others it will feel like everything you have learned is beginning to unravel. However, with hindsight, you may perceive that the journey is always progressing in the right direction.

True mastery requires repeated trial and error; those who achieve it will experience more failures than many are willing to bear. The basketball player Michael Jordan was a master on the court. Many people might imagine that this was because he scored with every shot, but he has been clear that this was not the case when he was featured in a Nike commercial saying: 'I've missed more than nine thousand shots in my career. I've lost almost three hundred games. Twenty-six times, I've been trusted to take the game-winning shot and missed. I've failed over and over and over again in my life. And that is why I succeed.' It is this openness to the possibility of failure that allows us to become a master. As the experiences of both Jordan and Edison highlight, we can only develop a profound understanding of something when we understand all the things that can go wrong.

Those who are most successful are able to channel their goals positively, rather than keep their many failures in mind; they look to achieve success rather than avoid failure. We can see that both Jordan and Edison accepted failure as part of their journey, but, rather than trying to avoid it, they still focused on trying to do well. The distinction may seem a matter of semantics, but the approach is very different. An engaged and opportunistic mindset is far more effective than the restrictive and narrow one that comes from trying not to screw up. It also tends to ensure that we approach a situation by keeping as much control over it as possible, playing well or writing in a way we can be proud of. However, outcomes are not controllable; if we are not focused on them and if we don't accept these inevitable failures along the way, how will we know if we have obtained mastery?

Michael Jordan could tell he had mastered basketball because he was continually praised by the media for his huge contribution and because of the trophies he won. But how do we judge mastery in other walks of life? Most of us can usually distinguish competence from incompetence, but mastery requires something much more distinctive. It is hard to detect mastery in oneself. If we are overconfident, we tend to assume that we are showing mastery when we are still at a basic level of competency, and if we lack confidence, we may well downplay everything we do.

Mastery is elusive. Do others judge it in us? Is our mastery decided in the hallowed halls of a professional society, in the corridors of our workplace or by our friends or adversaries commenting on our achievements? We have institutionalized mastery by creating paraphernalia where there are specific boxes that we must tick; we have developed degrees, certificates, surveys, professional societies and continuing professional development points. Some people are simply skilled at taking tests. However, taking exams demonstrates competence, but does not indicate mastery. In fact, when we cram we might retain the information for the exam the next day, but it will soon be forgotten. Instead, mastery should perhaps be thought of as a portfolio of knowledge, skills and techniques.

For Maxine, on the stage or in front of the camera, mastery is about effort and the energy which comes with that effort. 'To me, mastery is about work. It's about working, it's about passion, it's about an understanding of your chosen craft. It's something that never stops. It's about pushing yourself. But it's going further, isn't it? It is about constant learning, it's about expressing, it's about trying, it's about failing. But I think, for me, it is just an energy thing. You just see somebody and it's like there is like a halo around them. You can feel, there is a force field.'

Mastery may be hard to measure, but, like Maxine, we all know it when we see it – watching the best athletes in the world play their sport at the Olympics; hearing an accomplished musician on stage; even being subjected to the patter of an award-winning salesperson – all of these things can elicit a feeling that you are witnessing something special. If you follow a master's development over a long period of time, you can observe how they display their mastery in different conditions and environments. This is the true sign of mastery: depth of knowledge allowing for adaptation to every situation.

Focusing on our own strengths can remind us of our skills and of what we should do more of. It helps us develop what we can do, rather than encouraging us to listen to the voice inside our head that tells us what we can't.

Maxine is clear in this strength focus: 'I think for mastery, in the acting world, your individuality is your strength. That's what I always say to young actors when they ask me about, you know, how they should proceed. I always say, "You have to tap into what you've got."'

So what is it that Maxine's got – what is her strength? She said hers was highlighted to her by one of her long-term col-laborators, the director Sarah Frankcom. 'I always remember Sarah saying to me, "The audience want to go with you, especially in theatre." She said you have this capacity; an audience warm to you and they will go with you. I remember watching a production of WIT at the Royal Exchange, and Julie Hesmondhalgh was in the lead. And I went, "She has got that – I get it." Whatever she did, you would go with her. If she said, "Right, audience, strip off and we are all going to run round St Ann's Square naked", we would all be, "OK, OK." I've been told when I'm on stage that is my strength – of being able to say to an audience, "Come with me" and they will trust me to take them on that story in an interesting and complex way.'

We usually think of mastery as sector-specific. For example, Michael Jordan can certainly shoot a basketball, but he probably isn't so skilled in a scientific laboratory. Thomas Edison was a whizz with inventions but, conversely, he probably wasn't great at basketball. However, there are times and places when people are able to develop a central component of mastery that can move between disciplines. Achieving mastery of such central skills means that we are set up for success in whatever we put our minds to.

We can observe a great example of this if we look up to space. Kathy Sullivan is an American geologist and former NASA astronaut. She has been a crew member on three separate space shuttle missions and, on 11 October 1984, she became the first American woman to walk in space. Over three and a half hours, she did what was called a trial fluid transfer, to demonstrate that it was feasible to refuel satellites while they were in orbit. She found another reason to enter the history books in 2020 when, at the age of sixty-eight, she became the first woman to travel the 11 km down to the bottom of the Mariana Trench, the deepest known oceanic trench on Earth. While her two records initially seem entirely opposite, taking her from space to the deepest part of the sea, they are linked by Sullivan's craving to understand as much as possible about the world around her. The skills and the mindset she gained going into space assisted with her preparation to dive to the bottom of the sea. Her mastery is around developing the skills and dedication that help bring her curiosity to reality. Her mastery is in exploration.

We can see from Sullivan, Edison and Jordan that having this area of mastery provides a solid foundation for life. As long as you continue to top up your knowledge and practise your skills, you will always have something to fall back on. That provides a huge amount of confidence and can make you feel more in control. Competence and mastery, and the confidence that comes with them, have been linked to increased wellbeing and better emotional states. In the workplace, mastery helps us adjust to work and achieve higher performance, leaving us less anxious and less prone to depression. That competence gives you your toolbox to handle whatever is thrown at you.

The toolbox is something Maxine feels she was given at RADA, alongside an appreciation that mastery takes time, lots of time. 'Nick Barter, who was our principal, said, "Don't try and endgame while you are here." And it is so true. Things have come to me that I learned at RADA which at the time I couldn't understand why I was doing them; they didn't really make sense. You know, sort of, ten years later things fall into place and it is about constantly striving. It's about striving to be the best.'

When we feel competent, we tend to switch on our motivation; we engage better and put in more effort for a longer period of time and are more likely to attempt more difficult tasks. The passion for what we are working on comes from within us. We are not aiming to win awards, get pay rises or beat others – we are looking to become excellent and to recognize this excellence in ourselves. This is a powerful force as it gives us the enthusiasm to do whatever is necessary and we are more likely to enjoy the process itself. We self-regulate more effectively and don't need to be pushed, encouraged, monitored or supervised. We don't need threats or punishments – we just get on with it. An added bonus is that we feel more autonomous and take more ownership of what we do. The effect is cyclical: the more intrinsically motivated we are to do something, the greater our curiosity and interest, which maintain that motivation.

Mastery makes the magic

We cannot be a master of everything. There are many sayings that remind us of this, but one is regularly used to direct people back towards mastery: 'Jack of all trades, master of none.' We need to pick what we love to give us passion and purpose. With this, we can focus on developing a 'mastery mindset', which we use to create the right climate for success. This is about more than just ensuring you are competent; it is about developing an environment that inspires you to strive for more and to do whatever it takes to be excellent. Once the basic competence is in place, we can offer ourselves realistic but stretching challenges, positive and constructive feedback, clear goals, support and an acceptance that we will make mistakes along the way.

We already know that belonging helps us in our quest for success and it helps when we try to develop mastery too. When we have others on side to help us through this process we tend to feel greater psychological safety so we feel able to stretch. Maxine had Sarah Frankcom, who was then running the Royal Exchange. 'I had that mastery with Sarah, constantly being able to push myself in parts. And I felt secure and safe. I always, you know, I always wonder if anybody else offered me Hamlet, would I have done it? Probably not. I just feel, I feel this complete security when I'm with Sarah. I mean, she doesn't give me an easy ride by any means. But she knows I will get there.'

This mastery mindset sets the tone for focusing on what we know, understand and can do, and takes our attention away from comparing ourselves to others. The goals we create for ourselves when we have such a mindset tend to cover our desire to improve our competence through learning new skills and developing a depth of understanding. We expect to have to put in lots of effort and to collaborate, which means that we focus on the process of learning. Understanding as much as possible or performing to the best of our ability becomes our goal. Helpfully, we tend to use better strategies when we are trying to master skills rather than just learning to perform them. And when we are not comparing ourselves with others, we can more helpfully judge ourselves. This helps us feel more confident at taking on challenges, working harder for longer and learning more.

Maxine has become well attuned to the importance of keeping her focus internal. 'The only person I can compete with is myself,' she says. 'It is about pushing myself to be better, to be braver, to be freer and to keep learning. That, for me, is what mastery is: an ongoing relationship with your work.' She does admit it is hard though. 'There is a feeling when you have seen a master at work. Usually, it is envy – or jealousy.' But when she makes it about mastery, she chooses to turn that jealousy into curiosity. 'I'm constantly learning. And a lot of the time learning from younger actors because they bring in new techniques and they have got a different attitude, finding different ways of tackling a character, of being on stage, of filming. Constantly going. "That's great. What are they doing? How can I tap into that?"'

The 'mastery climate' also makes cheating less likely. If you are only cheating yourself, why would you bother? After all, you know the truth. In fact, opponents doing well can actually be helpful, as they push you to work harder. A review covering over thirty-four thousand people across 104 studies found that being in a mastery climate improves how competent we feel, increases our self-esteem and persistence, makes us feel happier and even improves our morality – all things that can contribute to improved performance.

By contrast, a 'performance climate', say a workplace culture driven by sales figures, is focused on how we do by comparison with others, which is more about social status. Here, everything works towards a single event or activity. It has an end point, and the joy of learning for its own sake is replaced by a focus on 'learn to impress'. The joy is sucked away. If we focus on performance goals – always with an eye on outperforming others – our mastery ceases to be subject to our control and our motivation changes. We are no longer learning about a subject or developing skills because they make us more able; we are reacting to what someone else has achieved.

This sort of performance-driven environment tends to be accompanied by negative side effects: anxiety, avoidance and poor coping strategies. We can find that we fall into self-sabotage or avoidance because we are working to someone else's agenda. This is when we might well handicap ourselves in order to avoid things that could be difficult, because who wants to risk failing? We adopt unhelpful coping mechanisms, such as ranting and raving about our frustrations. And cheating is more prevalent in these circumstances; if everything is about winning, then foul play helps us to get closer to our goals, whether that means claiming credit for someone else's work or injecting performance-enhancing drugs. It is unethical, of course, but, if it is aligned with our goals, it feels easier to brush aside.

All this means that, if we are to develop mastery, we should adopt mastery goals and try to set up a mastery climate. This applies in all areas of life except one – and it might surprise you to learn that the odd one out is education. Despite it seeming counter-intuitive, 'skim-learning' brings greater success than actually aiming to master a subject. Education is largely tested by exam and this environment supports a 'learn to the test' process. We may have developed mastery in a subject, but if an exam question does not look to that depth and does not use the more abstract knowledge that comes from such an understanding, we will not perform so well. This is simply a function of how the education system works. By contrast, if students were evaluated by observation and over a long period of time, mastery would be a more effective method of learning. But with exams and qualifications in secondary education moving towards digital marking, multiple choice and narrow marking frameworks, students need to be aware that learning superficially and ensuring that they pass is better than seeking mastery.

Mastery Undermined

The greatest pitfall that can undermine our mastery is trying to win. It is ironic, but when we focus on performance goals – as so many of us do naturally – our mastery gets lost and we end up doing worse. Performance goals focus on a specific outcome, which might be to get a new personal best in sport, to win a business pitch, to receive a prize or to get an A for an essay. They are the moments we remember, the ones we list on our CVs and record on social media profiles, but they are driven by our ego and by how we compare ourselves to others. This makes these goals less about us and more about whether we match or beat the competition.

This drive to win, based on living by the standards of others, gives us lots of reasons to feel anxious and focus on the wrong things. It doesn't give us feedback on how to improve or a deep knowledge of anything. Such achievements make us feel amazing for a short amount of time, but the irony is that, the more we focus on mastery goals, the better our performance becomes. When we focus on becoming a brilliant runner, we run better and set new personal bests. When we focus on delivering a mind-blowing pitch, we are more likely to win the contract. But the focus must always be on mastery rather than on performance, and that can feel unnatural.

We only develop great processes and the mastery from them if we are given space to fail. This is easier in some areas than others. In sport, we can fail time and time again in practice until we master a skill, but on the stage, 'How do you train if you are not doing it?' questions Maxine. 'The best actors, the actors with the mastery, are also the actors who have been fortunate enough to be given the jobs. I struggled at the beginning, but when I look at my early work, crikey, some of my early telly performances are shocking. But it's how I learned. Back in the day, I just used to watch myself and go into a depression for weeks. But it is about going, "Get over that. What didn't you like, what wasn't working – move on with it." I've been very fortunate to be able to keep working at my craft and working at my mastery. But a lot of actors don't get that.' Actors need to be working on stage or in TV to get the practice and build their mastery. 'Can you do it in your living room? Can you? You can't! You need an audience. You need other actors.'

Pay is an interesting element in motivation. We often think that rewarding people for the level of performance they attain keeps them hungry and encourages them to work harder. Performance-related pay usually comes from earning commission, which is easy to measure, or from meeting high standards, which is much harder to measure. But what makes a company successful? Hundreds of people who are all out for themselves or a few brilliant salespeople who are supported by a team of experts? A study of the telecommunications industry found that, in an organization where staff worked entirely on commission, after two months spent learning the ropes, 75 per cent of employees had left within a year.

Michael Phelps provides another example of why performance-related pay isn't as beneficial as we might imagine. In 2003, he agreed to a contract with his sponsors, Speedo, that dangled a bonus of US$1 million if he won seven gold medals at an Olympic Games. Did this inspire him to achieve mastery at swimming? It would surely have been a nice motivator during those wintery, cold 5 a.m. training sessions, but, in his autobiography, he wrote that his push to develop mastery was not about the money – it was about his sense of purpose. He wanted the PR value that the bonus would give him in order to create a story and get swimming on the front pages of all the newspapers, where he felt it belonged. Winning such a newsworthy bonus would give swimming a media platform and get more kids in the pool. The mastery came from a specific purpose beyond the huge payout. And hundreds of studies show that we work hard and strive for mastery – particularly when we are focused on the quality rather than the quantity of achievement – because we have an underlying intrinsic motivation to do so.

Impostor syndrome

Millions of high achievers have achieved mastery and are successful on paper, but fail to internalize these successes. They are continually fighting self-doubt, expecting at any moment to be unmasked and exposed as a fraud. Believing that other people perceive you to be more capable than you are is known as impostor syndrome, and it can be very harmful.

Sufferers of impostor syndrome tend to be ambitious, high-achieving individuals who become paralysed by a fear of failure. They have limited self-confidence and, as a result, spend too much time feeling under threat. When something goes well, instead of attributing it to their own competence, they attribute it to external elements such as luck, a mistake or the efforts of other people. Compliments get pooh-poohed, dismissed as the words of people merely being polite or, worse, pitying the recipient. A win in a race, they tell themselves, only happened because no one really fast turned up. Even a personal best can be dismissed as a fluke. Those suffering from impostor syndrome feel uncomfortable owning their success, so they don't – but they do, of course, own any failures or setbacks.

Even headlining actors are not immune. 'I always have impostor syndrome. You know, I don't speak to many actors who don't think they've got impostor syndrome,' reassures Maxine. She has developed a strategy for it though – to be upfront that it won't be great to begin with. 'I always go into the rehearsal room and say, "Look, I'm telling you now, this is going to be messy for a while"', and, for Maxine, and many others using a similar strategy, it all comes good in the end.

Impostor syndrome is more common than we might expect. Physicist Albert Einstein thought of himself as a swindler. Former First Lady Michelle Obama has talked of crippling self-doubt. I have worked with award-winning actors who can no longer step on stage as they feel they cannot live up to their reputation. If Nobel laureates, bestselling writers and award-winners can feel like impostors, is it therefore any surprise that so many of the rest of us do too?

When we understand something called the 'Dunning-Kruger effect', we can see that some level of impostor syndrome is to be expected. The Dunning-Kruger effect comes from a paper published in 1999 by two psychologists at Cornell University in the US, David Dunning and Justin Kruger. They identified that, when we start doing something, we are quite rightly aware that we are not very good at it. After a while, we will still be pretty bad, but have so little experience that we can't yet see how far it is to excellence, so we start to feel that we are getting good. It is only once we have done lots of training that we actually become more expert, but our expertise simply highlights how much we don't know. It is this gap – between where we are and where we think mastery lies – that makes us feel like we don't deserve our position. We may have officially 'made it', but we can still see that there is much further to go. What Dunning-Kruger suggests is that the more of an impostor you feel, the less likely you are to be one.

Maxine says that, when she was at RADA, a teacher told her that it takes at least ten years to feel competent as an actor. With hindsight, she agrees. 'After about ten years I felt I am an actor now. I can say I'm an actor in the back of a taxi without feeling embarrassed or that I'd have to get my CV out. I thought, I've done the work now. There is still a lot more to gain, but I've got strong basic tools in my toolkit that will now get me through.'

Since impostor syndrome was first recognized in 1978, studies have identified it in people from all walks of life, of all genders and all ethnicities. In fact, an analysis of sixty-two studies covering over fourteen thousand participants found that as many as 82 per cent of adults have felt it at some point in their careers. The studies found that it is often social factors that reinforce feelings of fraudulence, particularly among those working in a profession that hasn't traditionally been accessible to other people from their culture or background. Such fears are triggered every time a female doctor is assumed to be a nurse, a working-class student is asked to show their university ID or, at the entrance to a court, a black barrister is directed towards the area reserved for defendants.

Those who are most at risk from impostor syndrome tend to have lower self-worth and self-esteem, lack social support and have higher levels of pessimism, perfectionism and neuroticism. Impostor syndrome is usually fear-driven, deriving from worries about social standing or competence. However, such fears do not have a valid basis. When the condition is studied in students, there is no difference between the exam grades of those who do not feel like an impostor and those who do, even though the latter group expect to do worse and are more likely to be anxious about the exam.

Impostor syndrome holds us back in three ways. First, it can make us feel dreadful. When we live with it, we might feel intimidated and insecure. It can make us feel constantly apprehensive, which is utterly exhausting. No one sets the world alight when their stomach is twisted into knots.

This anxiety is the cause of the second way in which impostor syndrome holds us back from success. To escape our fears, we tend to adopt avoidant coping strategies – we hide away. When we feel like this, we are less likely to believe that we are able to achieve what we set out to do and vast amounts of research on confidence show that this can have a huge impact on our ability to perform at a high level. As a result, we don't put ourselves out there and we certainly don't fancy taking risks – but no one gets successful by hiding away in the shadows.

Thirdly, even if we do become successful, the success becomes something to be feared – for it is when we are successful that we are at greatest risk of exposure. The more we succeed, the more damaging it will be when we are unmasked. As a result, we follow maladaptive behaviours, unaware that we are self-sabotaging. When we are not self-sabotaging, we set ourselves unrealistically high standards; when we fail (as anyone trying to reach such heights will), our view of ourselves as an impostor is reinforced. This is a vicious circle.

This vicious circle can have a damaging impact on career progression – studies have found that it can impair performance at work and job satisfaction. You do not function as well as you otherwise could. And if you are in a leadership role, self-doubt can prompt you to micromanage your team, making them feel that you don't trust them. You might procrastinate over making decisions – if you don't have the confidence of your convictions, you will fear making the wrong move, and your lack of confidence can be transferred to others. They too can then develop some of the traits and feelings associated with impostor syndrome.

It is hard to manage people if you constantly feel on the back foot or under threat. It is also hard to plan effectively if you assume that you will be fired at some point. Impostor syndrome makes you risk-averse and that means you are less likely to innovate. You will also be less likely to put forward great ideas (because why would anyone listen to a fraud?) and will find it hard to embrace ambiguity – the potential risks can feel overwhelming.

In the longer term, impostor syndrome limits our potential as it makes us less likely to put ourselves up for promotions or new roles. As a result, we don't do as much career-planning and are less likely to volunteer for leadership roles. As well as reducing our wellbeing, feeling like an impostor means that we limit the opportunities we pursue to those that come only when we feel completely ready. We end up missing out on fantastic opportunities that are then taken by others, even those who may be less skilled or qualified than us. The stress that comes with all this can cause insomnia and result in a weaker immune system, leaving us prone to depression, anxiety, stress, exhaustion and burnout.

Harmful head chatter

A further pitfall that can seriously undermine our mastery is in our own heads. Our internal dialogue (known in psychology as 'self-talk') can reverberate around our mind; when we are primed to deal with it, it can create magic, but left untamed it can cause mischief. It has a powerful influence on our behaviour, confidence, motivation, endurance, focus and, ultimately, our success.

The concept of self-talk is widely used in clinical psychology to help people understand how their thoughts can unhelpfully influence their behaviour. In performance psychology, it is used to direct attention towards behaviours that will create changes and actions that can help achieve goals. When used positively, it can be a bit like having your favourite coach or mentor standing alongside you, reminding you how much you have learned, how hard you have worked and what skills you have mastered.

When we are aiming for mastery, the more unhelpful variety of head chatter can undermine all the benefits the mastery itself gives us. Not only do we not believe our own hype, we actively disagree with it. We can end up saying things to ourselves that we wouldn't dream of saying to others. We would never tell a colleague that a work presentation sucked because of one tiny mistake, yet we tell ourselves we should be embarrassed. We would never call out a friend for a spelling mistake or grammatical error on an email, but we're much more willing to berate ourselves. We don't notice a slightly dodgy haircut on anyone else, but on ourselves we imagine the world is laughing. This process, known as 'stinking thinking', often contains unhelpful or negative phrases that we repeat to ourselves, lowering our confidence and leaving us focusing on the things we can't do rather than the things we can. Of course, this also reduces any chance of success.

Perfectionism

Finally, let us move on to consider perfectionism, a trait that can both help and harm us; it can help us to set high goals and to really want to achieve mastery, but it can harm us if we set our goals at an unachievably high level that causes stress. Perfectionism becomes the biggest issue when it is socially prescribed; you consequently feel pressure from around you to prove that you have mastered your subject. As a result, you will no longer work hard for yourself, but just to match others' expectations. Even perfectionism that comes from within can be problematic when motivation is replaced by standards that feel like pressure. When we fail to hit either these internal or external standards – which, of course, we do, because perfection doesn't exist – we beat ourselves up and are more likely to have that negative head chatter rattling around. We may try to focus on things that are measurable, like performance, but this further reduces the benefits of mastery.

Thus we can see that perfectionism creates self-defeating outcomes and encourages unhealthy patterns of behaviour. Instead of seeing mastery as an exciting adventure encouraging us to be the best we can be, we see everything in black and white. The context is lost and our progress stalls. The focus then goes on not screwing up, but when we are trying not to screw up we reject any opportunities for creativity or risk. Proactively focusing on developing a mastery mindset means that we can reduce some of these stresses.

Some people are naturally disposed to follow a mastery mindset, which gives them a great head start. The rest of us need to proactively cultivate that mindset, in order to use the mastery we have developed as a tool to make us successful.

Showing Our Mastery

In some areas of life, our successes will be noticed and doors to more opportunities open as a result; in sport, a male athlete who can run 100 m in under ten seconds will be noticed without needing to tell selectors about his performance. In the business world, a woman who can give an inspirational speech that gets a room buzzing with excitement will be booked again. But in other areas of life, a great many variables contribute to success.

Own your achievements

One important element is confidence. It represents another pillar of success, and one we will examine in detail in Chapter 5. Everyone tends towards confirmation bias, which means that when people receive new information, they tend to accept that information more easily if it matches their prior beliefs. This confirmation bias means that we need to get in early and explain what we can do well. This requires us to suppress our humility, which can feel unnatural. You don't have to go overboard in this process, but you need to make it clear where you have succeeded to ensure people remember you as someone who is competent and trustworthy. You are not looking to be brash and boastful, but rather open and proud of your achievements. If other people don't know where your competencies lie, how will you ever get the opportunities for success that you deserve?

Reframe unhelpful thoughts

If we find it hard to see our own expertise clearly because our negative self-talk has become too loud, we must find a way to replace the unhelpful head chatter with more useful thoughts. Studies have shown that, when we do this, we can persevere for longer, stay focused in the right part of our brain and avoid that feeling of being under threat (we'll investigate exactly what is going on in our brains when we feel under threat in Chapter 6). Understanding the sense of being threatened means that we can control our emotions, even in difficult situations, such as when our nemesis unexpectedly turns up to compete at a tournament or when an urgent request arrives in our inbox at 4 p.m. on a Friday afternoon. This control allows us to show our excellence without being distracted by doubts.

To achieve this we do not lie to ourselves or try to be over-optimistically positive, but rather we switch the focus until unhelpful thoughts become more helpful. We are not trying to suppress unhelpful thoughts – that rarely works, as the more we try to squash them, the more they jump up and down in search of attention. Instead, we are trying to reassign the meaning we give to that thought, so that it becomes more helpful, reframing it into being something that supports our drive to become more successful. This is a particularly helpful technique when the tendency to ruminate leads us to focus on irrational ideas, such as our fear of failure or of being judged.

We can track our unhelpful thoughts in a diary, making a note every time we notice a thought that's holding us back. Identifying themes will provide specific areas to work on. Then, working through each statement, we can consider how we could reframe that thought as something that is more helpful. Again, it is not about making things up – the reframing needs to be realistic and truthful – but if the process is practised over and over again, it eventually becomes a habit.

In order to be effective, every reframing should be personal: 'I'm useless and they're going to fire me once they realize' can turn into, 'I worked really hard on that and if they fire me, well, at least I know I tried my hardest.' A classic example of an unhelpful thought is 'I can't do this' which can be twisted beautifully into 'I can't do this yet, but I'm going to have a go.' It takes some practice and can feel awkward to begin with, but, over time, believing in our mastery can do wonders for our confidence. When we are brave enough to tell ourselves how well we can do something, we might also go on to tell others, which will increase our chance of succeeding in whatever we have set our mind to. This reframing is a skill that needs to be practised regularly, until we can move away from the awkwardness of trying to think more helpfully and make it sufficiently believable that it happens automatically.

Mindfulness training can be used to help us appreciate our expertise and mastery. It is also helpful for identifying what is holding us back: are we having thoughts that suggest we don't have mastery? Are we suffering from impostor syndrome? Noticing what is going on is the first step to confronting the thoughts that hold us back. This self-awareness allows us to live more in the moment, to notice thoughts but not respond to them immediately. Instead of thinking, 'I'm a fraud – they'll soon catch me out', we think, 'I'm thinking that I'm a fraud and I'm worrying that they'll catch me out.' Over time, we can develop even more distance until we get to, 'I notice that I'm thinking I'm a fraud and I worry this means they'll catch me out.' These two stages of separation make a big difference to how much we beat ourselves up.

Define what success means to you

We might also remind ourselves that we have the skills and expertise to achieve mastery. So much in society is focused on winning or losing, right or wrong, promotion or demotion. Such polar opposites don't take in mastery at all, but re-evaluating our perception of success can be a helpful way of embracing a more diverse definition of success around mastery. Finding ways to reward ourselves for different types of success can help us remember its many elements. By noting down all our successes in our work and our personal lives, as well as the skills we used to bring them to fruition, we can remind ourselves of how well we have done. We can objectively view our competence and analyse how much of the success was truly ours, which will help to build a much stronger awareness of our strengths. Capturing these thoughts in one place as evidence can be incredibly powerful when we need to go back and refresh ourselves with a positive reminder of our mastery.

Maxine found an iconic route to establishing that she had reached mastery taking on one of the biggest, most stretching plays of them all: *Hamlet*. 'It was a part I wanted to have a go at. I wanted to push myself into areas that really frighten.' She admits it wasn't easy. 'If you get chosen to play Hamlet, then that sort of signifies you have reached a pinnacle in your career – in the theatre world. It was hard. It was a learning curve. I'm very proud of myself doing it – not only because I was a woman, but a working-class woman and a middle-aged, working-class woman attempting Hamlet. And I think we did a great job of it. It wasn't everyone's cup of tea, but, for me, it is constantly pushing the barriers. When people say "I can't", I have to say, "I can."'

Confront your mistakes

As a complete opposite to recording your successes, you can also do something that may feel very unnatural – creating a shadow CV of all the times you have failed, been rejected or missed an opportunity. Rubbing your own face in all your mistakes like this might sound incredibly counterproductive, but the process of writing the list can help you see the progress you have made, too, including how you bounced back from those setbacks. Things that might have felt huge and career-ending at the time may well turn out to be fairly insignificant when you are able to see the big picture.

Recognize your strengths

We should also be proactive about being aware of what skills we have and where we can use them. Neuroscientists have found that for every negative thought we have about ourselves, we require five positive things if we want to stay in a good place. Just as a shopkeeper will regularly conduct a stocktake to know what they have to sell, we must conduct a stocktake of our strengths to remind ourselves to use them more.

With these strengths in mind, you can foster a climate that emphasizes learning and development, minimize impostor syndrome and develop mastery in the way that best suits your personal style and ambitions.

MASTERY TOOLKIT

Reverse CV

Mastery requires repeated trial and error, and there will be many failures along the way. A reverse CV helps us to acknowledge this. Write below five things you can now do well but you remember being really tricky to learn or that you messed up along the way:

1. _____

2. _____

3. _____

4. _____

5. _____

Getting curious

Developing a 'mastery mindset' is about creating an environment that inspires you to strive for more and to do whatever it takes to be excellent. It changes the metrics we use to measure success and moves us away from outcomes and comparisons towards a focus on being brilliant and collaborating. It turns comparing into curiosity. What one thing have you always been curious about and never got round to investigating?

_____

'If I were brave...'

Impostor syndrome comes when we have mastery but haven't internalized or accepted it. It limits confidence, paralyses us through fear of failure and sees us pick avoidant coping strategies – all of which limit our potential. To help you see what you are missing out on, you can think about the things you would do with your mastery if you felt confident enough to do so. Below, write down three things that you (without your impostor syndrome) would like to be doing:

1. _____

2. _____

3. _____

Circle one that you now plan to attempt.

Strengths audit

One of my favourite techniques with clients when they are struggling is a strengths audit. It helps you see where you are doing well rather than your automatic focus on where you are not. You will be looking to identify ten strengths: two in each area:

Area	Strength 1	Strength 2
Fitness to practise what you do (could be sport, job, caring responsibilities or a hobby)		
Strategies you use which work well (quick to figure out others, compassion, ability to keep calm, ease of seeing opportunities, for example)		
Skills (techniques you have mastered)		
Mindset (approaches or attitudes you bring to challenges)		
Support (people on your side)		

Bag of beads

No one enjoys making mistakes, but, without them, we will be limited in our growth. It is only in figuring out key processes that we become more masterful, and this will involve lots of mistakes - so we need to start celebrating rather than shying away from them. The 'bag of beads' is a way to do this.

You need to get hold of two small bags and 100 beads. Every time you make a mistake when trying to learn a new skill or improve a current one, you remove one bead from the first bag and place it in the other. After 100 mistakes, you will have moved 100 beads and you can feel confident that you have moved significantly closer to mastery.

3

Autonomy

When you feel in control of your environment and are offered choices regarding what you do and a voice to state the way in which you would like to do it, you increase your efforts and have more motivation. Your wellbeing is enhanced and your performance improves as a result.

Early in my career, I ran a large team in a corporate organization. I wasn't very good at it. I wanted the best for all the members of my team, but my positive intentions were thwarted by my poor understanding of how to get the best from people. I had years of specialist experience and knew how to do every job in the team. As a result, I strongly encouraged my team members to do things in the way I did, and that was my downfall. After spending a lot of time reflecting on the situation, I realized that there were many different ways of achieving the desired results. Being fixated on doing things in one particular way meant that I failed to realize that it was more important to achieve the right outcome; finding different ways of doing things would have opened up new opportunities and given the team a sense of achievement for succeeding on their own. I didn't provide what we would call an 'autonomy-supportive environment'. I would have been a far better leader if I had.

I am not alone in being a bad leader of a big team. How often do we see a new initiative being offered at work that doesn't have the desired effect? Those impacted might say, 'I don't want yoga classes and free cupcakes on a Friday – I want to be asked what I want and for my opinions to be heard. I want to choose how I spend my time.' We all want to have choices and to feel that our voice is heard. When we do, our motivation and wellbeing increase and our performance improves.

The previous two chapters covered two fundamental needs that have to be addressed in order for us to feel motivated: we need to feel a sense of belonging and to have the feeling of mastery. This chapter covers the third need: autonomy. When these three elements are in place and we truly love what we do, we find the Holy Grail: an intrinsic, self-determined motivation. However, for each of these pillars that either we don't have or we lose, our motivation changes and we find ourselves driven instead by rewards, threats and punishments. The more externalized our motivation, the lower our persistence and efforts, the less focus we have and the harder it becomes to find success.

In this chapter we meet someone who absolutely embodies autonomy, using it to propel himself around the world: Sean Conway. Sean is a world-record-breaking, ultra-endurance athlete. He was the first person to swim the length of Britain, the fastest person to cycle across Europe and he holds the world record for the longest triathlon. His push towards autonomy came when he was thirty when he working as a school portrait photographer, snapping ten thousand kids a year. He realized that he was working on autopilot. 'I sold my business to my business partner for £1 and walked away. I decided I wouldn't make any big decisions in life based purely on my financial outcome.'

He was set on adventuring. 'For hundreds of years,' he discovered, 'Brits have thought of bonkers ideas to explore the world, and amazing companies and people have backed those ideas to make it happen. The type of adventures I choose are the world's first, furthest or fastest. It is the "three Fs" of endurance. And if I can get a world record in one of those three Fs, that really gets me excited.' It was a world record he was looking for in his first adventure, trying to be the fastest person to cycle round the world, something that would require a huge amount of autonomy as he only had his body and his bike to rely on.

What Is Autonomy?

The formal definition of 'autonomy' suggests that it is the state of being the source of your own behaviour. It means feeling psychologically free and having the ability to control your life. In short, autonomy is all about having a choice and a voice. It fulfils an innate need to feel that we are acting of our own volition, allowing us to fully accept the consequences of our actions.

There are three different aspects to autonomy:

1. The belief that we are in control of our actions.
2. Freedom from being pressured by others to do things.
3. The flexibility to make choices.

When we have a choice over our actions and feel in control of the decision-making processes that will impact us, we possess autonomy.

Autonomy isn't about standing alone and shunning everyone else; as we've seen, we still need a sense of belonging and the ability to develop our mastery with others. However, while the concept of autonomy accepts that we should sometimes be influenced by others, it is about feeling that we are able to make our own choices. We don't ignore other opinions or ideas, but we do get to choose whether or not we listen to them. There is no feeling that we have to conform to expectations or coercion.

Autonomy is about being able to make decisions that are in line with our own values and purpose. Anyone who is wealthy and chooses to use their autonomy to vote for a political party that would increase their taxes is paying more attention to their values than their self-interest. A cheerleader who knows that they are not yet strong enough to perform a signature move and nominates a more competent teammate is showing how much they care about the safety of others. A team leader who hands over high-profile work to a better skilled staff member is putting mastery and quality above their own ego.

When we are able to be autonomous, our behaviours and the choices we make feel more authentic. As a result, we buy into our work and have a stronger sense of self. We can express what we believe in, and our behaviours and activities represent who we feel we are. When our 'choices' are instead driven by guilt, shame or the threat of punishment, they are not autonomous and there is a greater chance that we drop out at the earliest opportunity. When we get to own our choices and pick the route we take to get to our goal, this autonomy allows us to grow, and the benefits are huge.

For Sean it is the fact that he chooses his own challenges that adds to their appeal. 'Making my own decisions to do these records really inspires me to do them better because it is my idea and I'm not being told to do it. Having that autonomy to decide it for myself and be flexible on the way I do it, excites me more really to go off and do these things.'

The sponsors he has brought on board over the years understand his need for autonomy too. 'I was really nervous in the early days that the project wouldn't be mine any more. But I have to say the people who sponsor these ideas and the companies that get behind them, get behind them because of your pitch and your idea, so they let you get on and do your thing, as long you do it well and provide them with a good story and blog posts, photos and videos.' This autonomy allows Sean to maintain his passion. 'It is hard to fake it. It is hard to put yourself through months and months of misery when you are not that excited about it. Because you just won't perform as well.'

In the workplace, higher levels of autonomy tend to result in increased job satisfaction because we feel more responsible for the quality of our work. And with job satisfaction, we are more likely to be loyal to our employers and less likely to want to move elsewhere. We are more engaged, meaning that we are more productive, and we are also more likely to have a better work–life balance. The authenticity that comes with autonomy has another beneficial side effect: instead of having to deal with the tension between our values and those imposed on us by others, which can be stressful and tiring, we can just get on with doing a great job.

Let's take surgeons as an example. There are many legit-imate reasons why autonomy is limited in medical settings: there are restrictions on the hours that medics are allowed to work and, in some countries, regulations require other medics to be present during operations. There are also financial pressures, with growing waiting lists (so trainees are keen not to slow down operations) and the occasional legal case (that may cause fear of litigation from mistakes). And yet, in studies of trainee surgeons carried out to understand the impact of autonomy on learning a procedural skill, autonomy has been shown to increase their speed without sacrificing technical performance. When they are allowed to take control of the procedure (with oversight but not interference) their skills become better honed. Their mastery is increased by autonomy.

Away from the workplace, autonomy means that we enjoy sports and hobbies more and make faster progress, and the increase in motivation reduces drop-out rates. A swimming club in Quebec that worked to give its swimmers far more autonomy, allowing more choices in their activities and soliciting their opinions, saw its drop-out rate fall from 36 to just 5 per cent.

Home life is also better when we have more autonomy, and the feeling has been linked to increased quality of life. In a study on the effect of autonomy within friendships, it was found that when someone offers a friend far more choice over shared activities and prompts them to express more of their views, the experience for both friends led to increased emotional resilience and psychological security.

School life also benefits from autonomy. A study back in 1984 found that students who had autonomy tended to experience more intrinsic motivation and higher levels of creativity, leading them to achieve better grades and make more of the opportunities they were given. While possessing complete autonomy from birth would obviously put us in some tricky situations as young children, growing up in autonomous environments helps us learn when to ask for advice and support from parents, teachers or coaches. Over time, we internalize the advice that suits our personality and we develop our own decision-making skills. Studies of students have found that those in this position have a more defined view of themselves and have greater awareness of their ambitions. It gives them clarity, and Sean agrees. For him, autonomy is getting rid of the noise so you can find out what you are good at and what you enjoy.

'I find there is a lot of noise in the world; whether it is online noise or the little noise in your head saying why you shouldn't do things and why you should do things. For me, it is having an idea that you are passionate about, sticking to it, finding people who will support your idea and, kind of, just going with your gut.'

As Sean suggests here, when we feel like we have a choice and a voice we are able to go with our gut. When we are completely engaged in our work, feel psychologically safe and know that we have good levels of support if we need it, we are happier, more enthusiastic and work harder. We are able to innovate and can work more creatively, taking full ownership of what we do with confidence and optimism. And this all builds a perfect pillar for success.

Autonomy often requires others

With many of the pillars of success, we can focus on setting each of them in place ourselves. We might choose to increase our focus on mastery or on working to deepen and strengthen connections with others. It is an irony that we can't suddenly obtain autonomy and then have the ability to make more choices or have our opinions listened to. If we tried, we might find ourselves fired from work or ostracized from our sporting teammates. Many of the changes we need often have to be driven by others: those leaders, teachers, parents or coaches who can see the value in autonomy-supportive environments. There are a few options to increase our autonomy (such as bluntly requesting it), but, often, as we shall see in the toolkit at the end of this chapter (see page 89), the approach has to be more pragmatic, and we have to assertively find ways to engineer elements of it.

In autonomy-supportive environments, leaders offer as much choice as possible, provide explanations for tasks or rules, ask other people how they feel and acknowledge those feelings. They give opportunities for team members to take the initiative, provide constructive feedback and refrain from taking control, criticizing, punishing or rewarding. They encourage choice and problem-solving, and proactively call for participation in decision-making. In this type of environment, regardless of your level, you are aware that your voice is not only valid but welcomed and that decisions that impact you won't be made without your input.

Autonomy-supportive parents provide accurate information and open communication, but ultimately allow their children to make choices for themselves. Autonomy-supportive coaches focus on the individual needs of athletes and have a real belief in each athlete's capabilities – not just in the sense of performing in the short term, but in making the best decisions for their career. For parents, teachers and coaches, the goal is to build up those in their care so that they are capable of making good choices, rather than controlling them because they assume that they are not able.

But being autonomy-supportive is about more than just giving people a choice and a voice – it is about offering transparent leadership, which means listening and providing focused, supportive feedback. Sean had to do this when he swam the length of Britain. That, he says, was the first real adventure he did where most people said they really had no idea whether it was possible. 'Doing a 900-mile swim up the coast of Britain – no one had a clue. I really had to do my research and become quite self-motivated to do that. On top of that, I also had a crew who were going to give up months and months of their time, free of charge because I had no way of paying them. I had to think outside the box to keep them motivated.'

Sean knew that following a swimmer at 1 mph in the water is very, very boring, so he found things each of the crew members could do on their own, something they could take back with them and feel that they had achieved, on top of being a part of this amazing world first. 'When I felt they were a little bit down I would give them a fishing competition. Or suggest the skipper could create a navigation photobook of the west coast of Scotland. She has now got this amazing database of all the anchorages up the west coast of Scotland.'

In order to create autonomy-supportive environments as Sean did, leaders might use a style called 'transformational leadership'. This revolves around four key behaviours:

1. idealized influence (which is basically using their charisma)
2. inspirational motivation
3. intellectual stimulation
4. individualized consideration (that is, making it personal)

In short, leaders provide a role model for behaviour and help others to generate their own sense of confidence. They offer helpful feedback, give social support, treat people as individuals and share relevant knowledge.

In a study of 360 junior male football players, parents were encouraged to follow a transformational leadership style, setting boundaries but also respecting their sons' points of view and supporting their decision-making. This included open communication, with parents explaining the rationale behind their decisions to encourage the development of critical thinking. When both parents collaborated to create this environment, there was a reduction in burnout among children who were fully brought into the process of setting and achieving goals.

Some have complained that transformational leadership can feel a little manipulative and that it isn't a transparent way of managing people. It can, they say, feel too forced and even a little fake. 'Authentic leadership', by contrast, is an approach that can feel more inclusive and more encouraging of autonomy. Leaders are encouraged to be cognizant of their teams' psychological wellbeing and to assess how their own strengths and weaknesses may impact on others. This self-awareness means that they see their own and others' moral perspectives, processing information in a way that takes in a wider range of views. If employed within an autonomy-supportive environment, authentic leadership enhances feelings of inclusion and confidence in how and why everyone is working towards achieving a shared purpose.

Those leaders who are seen to be authentic are also considered to be more trustworthy; they appear more honest and more personable. We can say that we feel more open towards them and better relationships develop as a result; our sense of belonging is enhanced. People are less likely to feel coerced, instead having the experience of being involved in how things are done.

Developing an autonomy-supportive environment needn't mean opening the doors to anarchy. It is also important that a rationale is given for decisions. Strategies and boundaries can be set, as long as they are accompanied by clear reasoning. We might set tasks or goals to be achieved, explain why they are important but without stating what hours must be worked to achieve them or how it must be done. With a sensible rationale, a task seems meaningful and, when the purpose is clear, studies have found that it is more easily accepted and, as a result, more likely to happen. The beauty of this is that decisions are made in a way that feels like they work on our terms, with the strategies seeming as if they are part of our own thought process and belief systems. We can see this at work in a study on a group of business students who were asked to proofread a number of documents and then assessed on their motivation to help with the task. Some students were told the task came from book publishers who wanted their opinion on the stories, and they reported far higher motivation than those not given the same sense of purpose.

This is the way Sean has chosen his challenges. 'I've always chosen adventures that I've thought up or that I've personally wanted to do. It's a no-brainer for me because, if you think of it and it is your decision to do it, you are going to be far more resilient to carry on when the chips are down. If someone has told you to do something, you are never really as invested in it. When you think of it yourself, then that is when you really go for it.'

It is also important that we take everyone's views into account, even though they can't always be acted upon. This process of asking for thoughts and opinions indicates that everyone involved is important, that all views are valuable and that all needs will be considered. Sean has taken the views of his wife and children into account now they are central to his life. He has changed his focus away from risky challenges towards trickier ones. 'I am going to do things that are even more difficult. And that for me is what excites me. You know, some of these speed records now are getting really, really tough to do, and that excites me, to try to break even bigger and harder world records.'

Finally, in an autonomy-supportive environment, it is essential to incorporate constructive feedback. Positive feedback is far better for our motivation than no feedback at all but, if we are to make better decisions, what we really need is feedback that reinforces desirable behaviours and also suggests ways in which we can improve. This feedback needs to tick five boxes – it must:

1. give reasons for change
2. consider the person's perspective
3. offer choices for resolution
4. avoid using controlling or judgemental language
5. focus on behaviours rather than performance

This last point is important because we are able to change our behaviours, which means that receiving comments about the way we act feels less personal. We are not being personally judged when we get this type of feedback and our self-esteem remains intact.

When we offer feedback, it should be given soon after the activity under consideration has taken place and it should be private, to limit embarrassment. So, rather than waiting for formal appraisals, a quick comment highlighting what went well and what could be improved for next time would suffice. It should also be respectful, allowing the recipient to feel confident that the feedback is being given with the best intentions. These aspects enhance the recipient's sense of psychological safety, ensuring the comment is taken as intended rather than interpreted as a threat.

When you work alone and aim to complete difficult challenges, your feedback is usually in the form of failure. Rather than shying away from this, Sean has embraced it by putting a list of challenges he didn't succeed in on his website. 'I wanted to become this world-renowned travel photographer and I failed at that. I tried to get the world record of cycling around Australia and I failed at that. I failed at the first attempt at cycling across Europe. I failed at the first attempt of trying to run the length of Britain.'

Sean talks about his failures openly because he realizes that this honesty will help others feel emboldened in seeking their own autonomy, rather than being restricted by the fear of failing. He also reminds others that he is just like them. 'I'm biologically no different. I genuinely have been tested. I went to the same lab that Jenson Button got tested in, the Brownlee brothers and Chris Froome. I secretly hoped that there was something in me that would be written about for centuries to come. But they looked at my results and they are like, "Ugh, no, literally, mate, you are Joe Bloggs."'

An experiment in the nineties showed how vital the individual elements of feedback and support can be. Researchers put participants into three groups and asked them to detect a dot of light on a computer screen. The first group received one element of autonomy support: they were offered the choice on whether to take part. The second group were offered the choice and also received a rationale for why they were undertaking the experiment. The third group were offered the choice, a rationale and also acknowledgement that the task might be a bit boring. They found that motivation was increased in the third group which offered more autonomy-supportive behaviours. Other studies have also found that these elements can improve self-esteem, job satisfaction and wellbeing.

When autonomy-supportive leaders – whether coaches, parents, managers or teachers – ask others about their needs, they should use welcoming and informal language and actively invite contributions rather than simply allowing people to participate in the decision-making process. When they do this, people flourish. And when these leaders encourage people to take initiative, give great feedback and follow an individual's development, the benefits really start to roll in. In such environments, teams feel more autonomous and persevere for longer with tricky tasks. Individuals have greater wellbeing, are more engaged and motivated, and tend to perform better. The process also helps to build up other pillars for success; people have a greater sense of belonging and feel more competent, and consequently have greater motivation to be successful.

Studies in big companies have examined how autonomy can benefit performance – when leaders are brave enough to try it. One company, facing a tough period with profits plummeting, decided to train its managers to encourage more autonomy-supportive environments. The managers did this by trying to understand their employees' perspectives, listening to their ideas, asking for their views and trying to put themselves in their shoes. They then tried to encourage more group decision-making and helped employees to make their own choices regarding how they did their jobs. They also worked on how they gave feedback, making it informational, positive and focused on specific behaviours. When negative feedback was given, it revolved around finding solutions and problem-solving.

The change in approach worked. Managers were able to create a more autonomy-supportive environment, which meant that their teams were happier in their jobs and more trusting of management. The cost of implementing the approach was compared to the savings made in terms of mental health support such as counselling services; the return on investment was found to be three to one.

Interestingly, it isn't just staff that are helped by such environmental changes; clients can also benefit. When a psychiatric hospital for young people encouraged its staff to become more autonomous, they not only reported greater job satisfaction and wellbeing at work, but their patients engaged better with their treatment.

Pressure Points

There are times when we feel under pressure, however good our intentions might be. As a result, we often retreat to a place where we feel safe and autonomy goes out of the window. Periods of transition can be particularly stressful.

Our psychological response to endings – whether jobs, sports or relationships – is hugely affected by the extent to which that ending is our own choice. Whether someone leaves a job because they are fired or because they start their own business, the outcome is the same – but their psychological response will be different. An elite athlete may end their sporting career due to an injury or because they have retired on a high, having achieved all they could. A romantic relationship could have ended because the couple grew apart and both realized that they wanted different things or because one had an affair. In each case, the factual outcome is the same; the psychological response is not. The amount of choice we have has a decisive impact on how well we adjust to our new life and our ability to make that transition a smooth one.

When we truly don't have autonomy, we need to choose acceptance instead. We might have a heart problem that prevents us from competing at a high level, or perhaps we're hitting the menopause and realizing that we will never have children. Acceptance protects our wellbeing and mental health. Disengaging ourselves from unattainable goals lowers the amount of the stress hormone cortisol we release, reducing our inflammatory markers and meaning that we are less likely to become ill.

Autonomy was restricted for Sean when, only 4,000 miles into his round-the-world cycle race, he was seriously injured by a speeding, phone-using, car driver and ended up in hospital. 'Once I realized that I couldn't break the world record, I very nearly just came home because I thought, if I can't break the world record, what's the point? But then I remembered thinking, well, actually, there are two ways of climbing a mountain and, for me, the top of the mountain was cycling around the world. So, yes, the world record was gone, but I could still get to the top of the mountain by a different route with different goals, which for me would still be very satisfying.' By changing his perspective and realizing that there were many ways to get the same outcome, he was soon able to get back on his bike.

There are whole areas of life where autonomy is restricted: in prisons, care homes, schools and sports teams. Sports teams are a fascinating area, as demonstrated by the huge media interest in coaches and how they work with their athletes. Coaches can be incredibly powerful. They don't just organize and run training sessions, but have a much more complicated role; they are authority figures, role models, confidants and educators. How coaches behave has a huge impact on the success of an athlete and their wellbeing. The relationship with their coach is one of the most important influences on an athlete's motivation and performance, and the power disparity can be significant. If a coach is seen as successful, athletes will flock to them and overlook any lack of autonomy-supportive behaviours – after all, if they don't seize the opportunity, dozens of other athletes would be only too willing to take their place.

Student athletes in the US are a great group to observe. Once they have signed up with a university for a sports scholarship, their autonomy is greatly reduced. They must follow their coach's directions, fulfil commercial obligations, achieve pre-arranged goals and meet expectations for behaviour, training, studying and socializing. Their scholarships may save them money and help them avoid debt, but the price they have to pay usually comes in the form of surrendering their autonomy. One way they deal with this lack of free will is by subsuming their status as an athlete into their sense of identity, which allows them to reframe non-autonomous activities as being part of their core value system. They take on the values espoused by their coach or team, which allows them to make what they term 'autonomous' choices that are compatible with these new values. By absorbing the team's goals, they feel more autonomous and less controlled. We sometimes see this with certain companies where people feel incredibly proud to work for that company and subsume their own values beneath those of the organization. This isn't an ideal solution as you begin to lose yourself, but it is a coping mechanism that many have felt they needed to use. More effective coping mechanisms can be found in the toolkit at the end of this chapter (see page 89).

However, when a coach does develop an autonomy-supportive approach, their athletes demonstrate higher levels of satisfaction, better commitment, more trust and also feel as if they are more in control of their destiny. A study of 435 team and individual athletes playing within the British university system found that those who enjoyed their sport most and were most committed to it were more likely to have a coach who they felt was authentic. Such coaches genuinely listened and helped their athletes to have a choice and a voice; as a result, they felt more motivated and performed better.

This improved performance in sport that comes with autonomy is something that can be measured. In an experiment prior to the 2012 Paralympic Games in London, a number of coaches for the Korean national team were chosen at random and asked to create an autonomy-supportive environment, while other coaches continued with their usual control-based focus. The results were convincing: the athletes who were coached in an autonomy-supportive environment not only felt better connected to their coaches and teammates, but won significantly more medals.

So, when the case for achieving autonomy is so clear, why does it feel so elusive?

Control

On an individual level, we tend not to help ourselves. Often, our lack of self-confidence or impostor syndrome means that we fail to use our autonomy to its fullest extent. If we don't trust ourselves to make the right choices or don't feel that our voice is worthy of being heard, we are more likely to defer to others and not make the most of opportunities. Confidence is something that benefits everyone and we will examine it later in this book (see Chapter 5).

On a larger scale, the desire for autonomy can be frustrated by those who are able to impose their own control. At a societal level, it could come from a military coup, a democratically elected government changing voting laws or Supreme Court justices restricting rights. At an organizational level, staff may feel that they are part of a machine that relies on following orders, ticking boxes or being micromanaged. The repercussions are also clear at home, where questioning a partner's actions results in receiving the silent treatment, or at sports practice, where missing a shot in training leaves you on the bench for that weekend's match.

We can consider this control to be the opposite of autonomy. We see it in a leader who pressurizes their juniors to think, feel and act in a way that matches their own goals and preferences. And it is the way I behaved with my team, focusing on every tiny detail and expecting them to do things exactly as I would. None of us are immune. Even Sean admits that he struggles with it. But he has managed it by being incredibly clear on where his limitations lie. 'There are some things that I'm aware I know nothing about. So, for example, when I was swimming the length of Britain, if the skipper had said, "Sean, you look really cold, I think you should get out of the water and stop swimming", there is no way I would have stopped swimming. Because how does she know how cold I am? If she had said – and she did say – "Sean, there is really bad weather coming, there are gale-force winds due in the next hour. I think you should get out", then, 100 per cent, I would get out. It is important for me to hand over the autonomy to other people in their field of expertise. I'm an expert in me. My skipper was an expert in tides and weather.'

Most controlling leaders don't set out with the intention to be prescriptive. They may think that they are providing a safety net, a way to guarantee success, but in the process create a restrictive environment that leads to a whole host of negative behaviours: threats, punishments, withdrawn privileges, guilt-inducing criticisms and rewards that manipulate the ego. These are all things that are detrimental to intrinsic motivation and our wellbeing.

A controlled environment might well be successful in the short term, but eventually those who are being controlled will start to fight back. When managers are prescriptive, staff stop making an effort and may well leave to work somewhere where they feel that they can make more of an impact. Those who are left behind in that environment will feel anxious, bored and alienated.

Maybe the controlling and prescriptive approach is a result of measuring the wrong things. We can look again at sport here, because metrics in this area are usually clear. If we measure the success of coaches by how long athletes stay on their team or how they score on wellbeing tests, they would surely welcome the opportunity to offer more autonomy. But these outcomes are not tangible and visible and, instead, we measure how many medals their athletes win – focusing on the outcome rather than the journey. As a coach's personal success is linked to that of their athletes, they generally want them to follow what they believe to be the one proven way of doing things. The more pressure there is to succeed, the more stress coaches feel and the more controlling their behaviour becomes. Their ego and sense of identity are intimately involved in their work. When people become stressed, they fall back on what feels natural and necessary – but such an approach can be self-defeating and counterproductive. It can end up forming a vicious circle, with the coach becoming increasingly controlling and the athlete less and less motivated.

This type of controlling approach results in leaders withdrawing after a poor performance, insisting on strict compliance, arguing against resistance, imposing their own values and acting impatiently. Such leaders might put more pressure on their staff and use stronger, harsher language, which might result in their team feeling intimidated. And for all that stress and effort created along the way, the process doesn't even work. Performance is lower in these environments and staff are more likely to suffer from burnout and resentment. Furthermore, it is not just staff who feel useless and undermined; the leaders also suffer. They might feel like they are doing their job, but their own satisfaction plummets.

It is easy to understand why leaders create controlling environments, for example, in response to staff not putting in effort or displaying disruptive behaviour. Studies in education show that the worse students behave, the more controlling their teachers become. It makes sense; if students can't be trusted with autonomy then teachers retreat, using forceful teaching methods or imposing punishments. Yet long-term studies have found that, even when there is disruption, an autonomy-supportive approach elicits greater engagement and, in most situations, can obtain better results. When students feel heard and understand why they are being asked to do something, most will feel more comfortable in complying. Being yelled at may get things done, but that compliance is accompanied by resentment and defiance.

This controlling approach also comes to the fore when leaders panic. Controlling others helps them feel as if they are being proactive and doing something about the problem. If your own level of autonomy as a leader is being suppressed and you are dealing with new external pressures, it takes a brave person to risk thinking in a way that doesn't fit in with your organization's cultural norm by creating a more autonomy-supportive environment. This all emphasizes the importance of leaders focusing on not becoming controlling. Instead, they should step back from a prescriptive approach and try to build a more autonomy-supportive environment.

Building Autonomy

Developing an autonomy-supportive environment isn't easy, but it is worth it. Even in areas of life where autonomy is restricted, it can still be grown. Medicine is one such area that is gradually creating more autonomy-supportive environments through the ways in which clinicians engage with their patients. A good bedside manner no longer simply means having kind eyes and listening to the patient; in the modern medical environment it covers shared decision-making, facilitating forums of those sharing a diagnosis so they can educate and support each other, and identifying ways of putting patients at the centre of their treatment. All these approaches have been shown to improve medical outcomes and patient satisfaction.

We can encourage this type of approach in all areas of life by focusing on four particular factors: showing appreciation, delegating outcomes, explaining and trusting.

Showing appreciation

This is simple. It means recognizing good effort in a way that matches the motivation of those working with you. You are not looking at how their efforts have made you feel as a manager, but how the person in question has contributed to the bigger picture. Everybody wants to be appreciated for their contribution and, when we feel undervalued, we tend to take it personally. This is true both at work and in our personal lives.

Work is just another social system and, when we don't feel a sense of belonging, we reduce our effort or move to another organization where we might be more valued.

Delegating outcomes

This one is not quite so straightforward. Our capability and knowledge have helped us get to where we are and that makes it hard to delegate, as we can feel our expertise is being wasted. Delegating requires real trust in our team. Giving up control is tricky, particularly if we know exactly how we would like to do something. But effective leadership is all about identifying a goal, setting a strategy, modelling great behaviour and letting others reach the goal in their own way. It is important that we don't delegate actions or processes. When we do, we simply hand over responsibility without giving autonomy. Instead, we should be sure that we are delegating the outcome, giving our team the autonomy to achieve in whatever way they choose.

With a heightened sense of control over the situation, a better performance is more likely. Regular catch-up meetings should not be used as chances to check up and clamp down on others, but to offer support where problems are encountered and to ensure success is celebrated. When we stop micromanaging people, they find their own way to succeed. After all, we should try to remember that people rarely leave companies – they leave bosses, and often because they have been micromanaged. Demotivated employees simply go through the motions, lacking all sense of themselves and feeling unable to shape their activity. Without independence, they feel part of a transaction rather than part of a solution or a purpose.

Explaining

Explaining is imperative. When we tell people why we have set out a goal, this helps them buy into that bigger picture, which also encourages them to commit to it. When everyone is on board, it's not necessary to employ any tactics because everyone is focused on achieving the same outcome. Sean does this through social media – putting out ideas and seeing how much others feel that they can get behind them. 'I call it the "snowball of life". You have this tiny snowflake of an idea and it is just stationary. Then a few people go, "Oh, that's brilliant", and they jump and attach on to your little snowflake. And it starts to move down the mountain, and then a few more people jump on and it becomes a mini-snowball, and then a few more people jump on. And the momentum kind of gathers and then actually the more people who jump on to the snowball and jump on to your idea, the bigger of an idea it gets and the more momentum it gets, which actually makes more people want to jump on board. It is super-important to build this sort of snowball of momentum.'

Trusting

The other element of managing in a way that encourages autonomy is probably the hardest to get right: we have to expect the best of people. We have all been burned – expecting the best only to experience the worst – and our brains are designed in such a way that we remember these moments so that we don't risk them happening again. But, more often than not, the best happens, and being trusting helps us to get far more out of people. However, we have to fully commit to the process. Some people compromise by using 'earned autonomy', which often seems to be granted as a prize for being trustworthy. It is a welcome alternative to continual monitoring, but it still comes with overtones of being controlled. You feel manipulated if you know that autonomy can be taken from you if you get something wrong. For it to work and be effective, trust needs to be automatic and given, rather than earned.

Trust can be enhanced when we come together to create our own rules and jointly agree the consequences of breaking them. This creates an opportunity to discuss the reasoning behind restrictions and ensures buy-in to new arrangements. There will always be some people who take more than they give. Offering these people full autonomy may backfire, but it might also increase their motivation. They can still be held accountable for their performance. There will still be boundaries and they can have as much support as they ask for, but most people will want to do their best and work in their own way. As teams usually feel a sense of group responsibility, the powers that come from a sense of belonging mean that those who aren't working effectively soon know that their behaviour is unacceptable and step up or leave.

Incorporating these four factors – appreciation, delegation, explanation and trust – to shape an autonomy-supportive environment means that we all get to feel more autonomous. We all feel that we have a choice and a voice and, when our motivation increases, securing success is far more likely. If we don't have the power to give autonomy to others, the toolkit below suggests ways in which you can take some of your own.

AUTONOMY TOOLKIT

Model best practice

Autonomy means having a choice and a voice in what we do and how we do it. It is the belief that we are in control of our actions, are free from being pressured by others and have the flexibility to make choices. As we have explored, we can encourage greater autonomy when we are leading within an organization by showing appreciation, delegating outcomes, explaining and expecting the best of people. Even if you are not an official leader, you can still show autonomous behaviours with others which help them feel more comfortable. Ways in which you can model autonomous practice include:

- Showing appreciation for anyone helping you or doing great work. Everyone loves to be praised and recognized – from both those above and below them in a formal hierarchy.

- Being clear about your values and how the work you do helps you meet them.

- Resolving to do what you can to lift others up.

- Completing the control map (see below) and focusing your attention and energy on the areas where you can have impact.

- Knowing why you are doing what you do. Your job may well not be your purpose in life – often it is simply to pay the bills – but even remembering that when you feel micromanaged or underappreciated is helpful to keep things in perspective.

Control map

Autonomy often makes us feel good because we feel like we have control over what we do and how we do it. There will always be some things we cannot control, but having a strong awareness over what we can and can't control means that we can put our efforts and attention into the things we can impact – and this increases our feeling of autonomy.

Think about an area of your life where you would like more autonomy and use the template below to consider first what you have no control over, then what you can influence and finally what you can control. All your focus and effort should then go on the things in the control section. There is an example below to get you started.

No control	Influence	Control
The weather.	*What time I arrive.*	*My attitude.*

Remember your why

Autonomy allows us to make decisions that are in line with our own values and purpose, and is essential in order to feel truly motivated. Knowing (and repeatedly reminding ourselves) why we are taking on a task is incredibly helpful for feeling autonomous. It gives us perspective and, even if others are interfering, we can use a mantra around our why to keep us from getting irritated or angry. You can find some examples in the next chapter.

Every possible solution

Autonomy is a difficult pillar to master because so often it depends upon others giving it to us. Sometimes we may need to get creative. One way to give ourselves more autonomy is to step away from the black-and-white thinking. When we feel under threat or we are told how to do things, we see most options as either Option A or Option B. But there is usually a full range of options which we don't even think to consider. Instead of seeing only these two solutions to an issue, we can take some time to consider all of them – even if some are easily dismissible. We are aiming to get at least five options for every issue we have. Here is an example that someone in my team could have done when I was micromanaging:

Issue	Possible solution
Boss keeps telling me how to do my job	*Do it exactly the way she says and just work to rule.*
	Do it the way she says and put my energy and attention into my side hustles instead.
	Suggest the way I would like to do it, explaining why I think it could be really effective.
	Approach her and say that I am uncomfortable being micromanaged and could I have more autonomy?
	Raise the issue in my next appraisal.
	Do it both my way and hers to prove that my way might have a better outcome.
	Find a new job.

Here we can see seven different approaches which could have been taken and a number of these would have helped the person feel much more in control. Below is an empty table. Take an issue you are currently struggling with where you don't feel you have autonomy and see what possible solutions you might be able to find.

Issue	Possible solution

4

A Powerful Purpose

A powerful purpose gives you a guiding philosophy that can ensure decisions are easier to make and helps you use your passion to accomplish the things that are important to you.

Business schools often ask applicants to write an essay based on the question, 'What matters to you?' It might seem fluffy and out of sync with the cut-throat business world, but it is actually really astute. For when we combine the feelings of belonging, mastery and autonomy that we have already learned about, they give us self-determined motivation – but motivation is only valuable where there is a direction to channel it.

We might think of belonging, mastery and autonomy as representing a car, its fuel and the engine; they work together to take us on a journey. To extend this metaphor, 'purpose' can be regarded as our destination. We won't always know how to get there or what the journey entails, but it is vital that we have an end point to aim for, a place to program into our car's satnav. Without that destination, we might have ideas of places to visit and a navigation mechanism, but we will drive around in circles getting more and more frustrated and lost. We need a destination that we can identify on a map – something we can put into words; something we can articulate.

A purpose isn't the same as a goal. A goal might sound something like, 'I want to visit France, Australia and Mexico.' A purpose, on the other hand, might be something like, 'I want to travel around the world to learn from people of different cultures.' A purpose is bigger than a goal and it keeps us progressing in a way that makes us proud of ourselves and confident that, when our life is over, a part of us will live on.

Let us take the career of one of the world's best ultra-runners as an example. His name is Damian Hall and he has represented Great Britain for ultra-marathon running and set seven records or 'fastest-known times' for iconic Britain routes from 115 km up to 1,000.

One of these was set when Damian's race plan for 2020 went out of the window when the COVID-19 pandemic hit. He got creative and decided to focus on running challenges instead – a long one in particular; the 431-km-long national trail called the Pennine Way that runs along the backbone of England from the Peak District just over the border to Scotland.

'I do love the Pennine Way. It's very British, it's very bleak. There is a record for the Pennine Way which has stood for thirty-one years. I'd thought of it for about four years, but had always been too intimidated and made excuses. But then, when lockdown came along, all the races vanished and, really, I just had no excuses left and it felt like the time was right to give it a go.'

There was some added excitement in that his friend, the ultra-runner John Kelly, was also going for the record, a week earlier. John broke the record. 'This helped me – he made me see that it was breakable, but he didn't knock it out of the park, so it still felt within reach.' He was right. Damian achieved his goal and broke John's record by over three hours.

How did he do it? Well, alongside a huge amount of physical preparation and training, Damian worked on his mental approach – and one element in particular: reminding himself of how setting a new record would help him reach his purpose. When you watch the videos of his attempt, you cannot help but notice 'FFF' written on his arm in permanent marker. 'That stood for "friends" – all the people who were helping me there; "family" – which has always been a motivating factor, thinking of my children, and given me a good sentiment of why; and, thirdly, the final F was for "future" because of my concerns about our ecological and climate emergency. And those three Fs were a visual reminder of my purpose, my "Why?" Why was I doing this? What would success be for me? And that visual reminder was really powerful. It really helped me.'

While the distances Damian runs seem unimaginable to most of us, he believes that if your purpose is strong enough, you too would be able to run that far. He uses the example of a house on fire. 'Say your house was a hundred miles away and it is going to catch fire if you don't get there within a certain time frame, almost everyone would do that. Physically, 99 per cent of us could do that. Yes, it gets uncomfortable, but the stronger your sense of purpose, the stronger your motivation – you are going to do that. We are all capable of doing that.'

Having a purpose doesn't get us out of having to do the more mundane tasks in life. We can't spend all our time running across the country to raise awareness of environmental issues – even Damian has to hoover the living room, earn a living and do the weekly shop. However, our sense of purpose gives us a reason to do these things that all fit within the bigger picture. You buy food so your kids grow strong. You coach other people so you can pay the bills. And you hoover the living room so your family has somewhere pleasant to relax. All these things might feel peripheral, yet they all help life feel more purposeful.

What Is Purpose In Life?

The Japanese have a lovely word for purpose, 'ikigai', which refers to the perception that your life is worth living and causes you to live it with energy and motivation. When you reach old age, you can look back at how you have lived with joy, pride and satisfaction.

We can think of purpose as being made up of three key elements. Firstly, there is the direction in which it sends us. In setting a target that we work towards, we might feel that we have found our calling. As a result, we act with intention and organize our lives around goals that move us in our chosen direction, prioritizing our resources to support those goals. And while the route to achieving these goals might be flexible, the ultimate aim remains the same.

The second element of purpose is wanting to contribute to the wider world. Helping others through your purpose isn't about being a walkover and putting your own needs last; it might, rather, be about the way you teach others, support your children, help other people develop skills or volunteer for something that makes a difference. Your purpose is more than just a goal that you tick off; it represents the way you add value and contribute to the success of others. What lends stability to our purpose is the knowledge that it will leave the world a better place. The knowledge that our life will have a purpose even after our death makes our goals and efforts feel more worthwhile and gives our life more meaning.

Finally, having the stability of purpose allows us to behave with consistency. We won't always behave in exactly the same way – there will always need to be some psychological flexibility to adapt to changing environmental conditions or to deal with obstacles or opportunities – but an overarching purpose means that we have a motivating force to achieve things. Rather

age and lose some of our vitality, we have fewer clearly defined roles and opportunities to enliven our purpose. However, with a purpose, the freedom that retirement brings can give older people more time and energy to devote to the causes that matter to them.

In a meta-analysis of dozens of studies, people who are most purposeful in life have been shown to have above average health, to feel some kind of competence or mastery and to have higher quality relationships. They are also more likely to be married, to be working (even if they are eligible for retirement) and to have higher socio-economic status. It might be that those who are privileged are less dragged down by the stressors of life and find it easier to identify and follow a purpose – they have the money and resources to set and achieve goals. On the other hand, it might be that these people have been able to develop such lives in the first place because they were driven by purpose.

Might these people also possess a personality trait that makes them more purposeful? Some traits are more common in those who are purposeful:

- extroversion
- agreeableness
- conscientiousness
- emotional stability
- openness to experience

Extroversion has been found to be a particularly strong characteristic; a true purpose sees us try to bring about the change we want to see not just for ourselves, but for others, and that requires engagement with people outside of our usual groups and environments.

This doesn't mean, though, that we can't work on finding a purpose if we have different traits – we just might need to focus more carefully to identify it.

How Purpose Helps Performance

Having a purpose in life has been shown to make us happy. It has this effect because of the way in which it influences our wellbeing; it increases our resilience, giving us more energy for the things that matter to us. It also helps us develop coping mechanisms to combat stress and distress, improving our relationships with others (in turn boosting our self-belief) and giving us a sense of achievement when we reach our goals. When our achievements match our values, we experience joy. All these things contribute to greater life satisfaction. We can see this clearly when we look at various people working in the same profession but with different types of intent. A study published in 2014, looking at 'what makes lawyers happy', compared lawyers working in commercial firms with those who specialized in public services. The profit-focused practitioners earned more money, but they also reported lower levels of wellbeing, drank more alcohol and had a greater number of negative feelings.

We might also expect those lawyers whose work had a wider sense of purpose to be more emotionally stable. When researchers have studied people using MRI machines, they have found that those who report greater levels of purpose are better able to regulate their amygdala, the part of our brain that is sensitive to threats. They are consequently able to control their feelings more effectively and make decisions that are rational and sensible rather than made as a response to a perceived threat or fear.

Having a purpose also protects us from psychological threats. Death is not the happiest of subjects, but it is one in which purpose is important. While we know that it is inevitable, fear of death can lead to existential anxiety; if we have a purpose in life, the feeling that we are contributing towards something that will outlive us can be reassuring. It can also help us feel more worthwhile, as we sense our brain and body slowly weakening over time. Purpose acts as a protective buffer against depressive thoughts. It is also physically valuable, as we know that chronic stress and lacking a sense of control leads to reduced immune function. If we reduce stress by adopting a new outlook or take control by having a purpose, our immune function improves.

However, purpose doesn't just cancel out some of the threats – it also helps us to maximize our brain's reward system, making us feel more positive. When we experience something that matches the sense of meaning we have in our lives, our dopamine system is set off and we receive a buzz. The more we live in congruence with our purpose, the more dopamine buzzes we receive. It is much cheaper than gambling, but it gives us the benefits of that same reward system.

Purpose has strong physical health benefits, too – it can literally add years to your life. A study in Japan followed over forty-three thousand adults over seven years and found that those who had a strong sense of purpose had lower levels of mortality, particularly with respect to chronic complaints like cardiovascular disease. Studies of those who volunteer find these volunteers have a mortality rate at least 50 per cent lower than those who don't. The suggestion is that the ability to find meaning and direction in life helps to slow the impact of ageing.

Perhaps these results also show that those with purpose are more open to hearing health messaging and following advice. This might explain why, when the Hawaii Longitudinal Study of Personality and Health (a project which tracked nearly two thousand five hundred people on two Hawaiian islands over a forty-year period) tested the health behaviours of 749 adults, they found that those people with a sense of purpose exercised more, ate more vegetables, flossed their teeth more often and slept better. It certainly works for our Irongran, Eddie Brocklesby, who in her late seventies is still doing more than twenty hours of triathlon training each week.

Our cognitive health also improves when we have a purpose. In the Rush Memory and Aging Project, a study conducted by a Chicago-based health facility, those whose sense of purpose was in the top 10 per cent of the 1,000 older people studied were found to be 2.4 times more likely to stay free of Alzheimer's disease than those in the bottom 10 per cent. A similar link was identified in those people with mild cognitive impairment. It can be suggested that purpose enables us to better manage stressful situations and protects us from the functional decline associated with stress, which also helps our mental health.

Without purpose, we drift – whether from one project to another or from one group of people to another. We are less pro-ductive and more likely to get bored and to struggle to sustain close relationships. Higher levels of psychological distress can lead to higher levels of depression, anxiety, suicidal ideation, antisocial behaviour and the use of harmful substances.

However, there is something even worse than drifting: having purpose forced on you. As we saw in the last chapter, autonomy is an important factor in success – without it, we have to model our lives through the purpose of others. This can be considered to be a kind of socially prescribed perfectionism – our purpose is to live up to the standards and expectations of others in order to meet their approval. We don't just feel miserable, but also increase our chances of burnout and depression. We will look at the risks of all types of perfectionism in Chapter 6 as it can be so detrimental to success, but for now it is important to remember, the longer we follow an incongruent purpose, the worse we feel.

Being healthy gives us a platform for being more successful in life, but having a sense of purpose has specific benefits that feed directly into success. As we learned in the Introduction, we all have our own definition of success and purpose helps us to shape it (see page 3). For most of us, once we have thought about it carefully, success isn't about being powerful, rich or famous. If it was, 99.9 per cent of us would feel like failures. And even those people who have great wealth and fame don't always find fulfilment. Finding purpose first, around which we can lay out our goals, is more likely to lead to our own version of success. And the earlier in life we are able to identify our purpose, the longer we have to work towards it and the more successful we get to feel.

When we are focused on a purpose, we can allocate our resources effectively, helping to overcome those obstacles that prevent us from behaving in ways that are consistent with our aim. We can shift our physical and cognitive resources to where they will be most useful. This means that we will have greater persistence in facing difficult tasks, giving us resilience and emotional stability – something that Damian really needs during his challenges. He did this on the Pennine Way challenge by fully embedding his purpose into the preparation.

'I planned to fuel without any animal products or creating any plastic waste. I had friends kindly cooking for me and I looked into companies that could provide compostable wrappers. We also wanted to pick up litter as we went. I must admit, it was mostly my pacers who very kindly did that. So I had these three climate-related aspects that we did as we went along. That helped with the motivation. I was acting as authentically as possible, living by my values, and I think for me it certainly helped.'

The purpose didn't just push him on when it got tough; it also gave him a further motivation. 'I know that if I do well in a race or if I break a record there will be some attention of sorts and I will get a chance to talk about the things that I care about. It makes it a double win: I get the athletic results, but I can also share my purpose and discuss these values on a wider platform.'

As well as yielding mental and physical benefits that provide the foundation for success, purpose gives a sense of psychological safety. When we have a sense of purpose, we feel more empowered. We don't need to check in with other people, but instead find ways to use our skills to achieve our goals. This builds responsibility and the knowledge that we can question less and move forward with intent. With psychological safety comes psychological flexibility. We can become more adventurous, which gives us the chance to work on things that really excite us. There is less reason to procrastinate and we are motivated to push on through the tough times, confident that the outcome will be worth it.

One of the reasons having a purpose makes us feel safe is because we tend to find a tribe, associating with people who share our aims, feeling stronger together. This feeling of togetherness is a powerful motivator. As we progress and see our goals being achieved, our motivation increases; we have a sense of belonging, we feel mastery and, because we are working of our own volition, we also have autonomy.

When we have a purpose and the motivation to achieve it, we are able to set goals. When we are clear about where we want to be, we can make a solid plan to get there. This clarity means that we stop getting distracted and instead focus our energy to the right place. And we do all this proactively, rather than simply responding to other people's agendas.

With goals in place, it is easier to prioritize what is important and allocate our resources accordingly. We can make strategic choices about how we allocate our time, energy and cognitive space. We fritter away fewer hours on non-purposeful activities, leaving us with more time for the things that matter.

Having a purpose can feel like being granted permission to say no to those things that don't align, freeing up time for the things that do.

A study in the US looked to see if purpose in life helped people with emotional recovery. Participants' eye-blink startle response – a measure sensitive to emotional states – was analysed after they were shown emotionally negative pictures. Those with higher levels of purpose recovered more quickly, suggesting that purpose helps us develop resilience. Increased resilience and persistence help us get better at coping with the tough times. When we can find meaning in life's experiences and see them as part of achieving our purpose, we build resilience. It is particularly helpful when we are dealing with setbacks, helping us reframe stressful situations.

An American man called Darell Hammond shows us the true power of purpose. In 1995, Hammond saw a newspaper story about Iesha and Clendon, a four-year-old girl and her little brother who had died after becoming trapped in an abandoned car they had been playing in. Hammond's response was to create KaBOOM!, a movement designed to give every child somewhere to play safely. He focused on finding partners to sponsor and build children's playgrounds in inner-city neighbourhoods. In the twenty-five years since he founded KaBOOM!, over seventeen thousand play spaces have been built or improved, 1.5 million people have volunteered and 11 million children have benefitted. Hammond successfully used his purpose to amplify the power of communities. It motivated him to find his tribe, show his vulnerability, prioritize what mattered to him and stick with it through the tough times.

From leaders like Hammond, purpose flows to their organizations. When organizations have a sense of purpose, recruitment becomes far simpler; they employ people who align with that purpose and will put in their passion and persistence. This allows organizational values to be promoted both inside the company by staff and externally to customers. In the last chapter, we saw the harm that can be caused in organizations when staff lack autonomy, but when everyone is committed to the same purpose, micromanagement is unnecessary and autonomy abounds.

A poisonous purpose?

Despite all these benefits, there is a downside to the power of purpose: it can make people with bad intentions successful. Dictators, mass murderers, terrorists – all can be driven by something they feel passionate about and their clarity of purpose, evil as it might be, helps them achieve awful things. Having purpose can be effective in making us successful; it isn't always beneficial for society. And, of course, societal values change over time. A lung doctor in the twenties might have seen a purpose in promoting smoking, to improve the health of their patients. They had no way of knowing that they were causing great harm – they did not have the science or evidence. And it also works the other way round. The violence of the suffragettes in the early twentieth century would have been viewed as extremely harmful by many at the time, yet millions of women worldwide are now thankful for their actions.

Identifying Purpose

Our lives can get so busy that we can be distracted from our goals and struggle to see what our central purpose is. For most of us, life is not about making TikTok videos, getting caught up in WhatsApp group chats or engaging with trolls on Twitter – but we spend far too much time being distracted by these things and have less time to do what really matters.

Ideally, we find our purpose as a teenager and during early adulthood, as part of our general identity formation. Purpose stops us drifting through life without any focus. Furthermore, teenagers are already engaged in shaping their identity and understanding who they are, making them well placed to focus on purpose. They are trying to navigate major life changes and, without purpose, decisions may be regretted later. Teens are starting to build the belief systems that will guide their life path and to make choices that will stay with them forever.

If you are a parent or carer trying to help a young person identify their purpose, studies have found that it is best to be trusting and non-judgemental. Even if your child's search for purpose is not aligned with yours, it is essential that you give them space to make their own decision. Otherwise, you risk them following a direction set by you, trying to keep you happy and living a life that will never feel like their own. They might be successful living someone else's life, but resentment will build. As we learned in Chapter 3, autonomy is vital; your children need the freedom to follow their own passions.

Figuring out your core purpose isn't quick. It is unlikely to appear suddenly, in a light-bulb moment – you will need some focus to identify your purpose. It is a slow and deep operation that develops through engaging with others and assessing your responses to difficult situations:

- What values do you follow when you find yourself up against it?

- What sort of injustice raises your hackles?

Only after assessing yourself, often over many months, will your purpose emerge. When there is alignment between what you feel is important and your own values, you have hit the jackpot in identifying a powerful purpose.

We can ask ourselves whether our purpose provides us with a framework to make difficult decisions. And when it passes this test, we must ask if it is social; does it help others? If it doesn't, it may be a goal, but it won't bring with it all the benefits of purpose and will be limited in its impact. A fascinating study followed a group of 416 undergraduates whose ambitions for life were assessed – whether creative, social, financial or involving personal recognition. When the same people were interviewed thirteen years later, those whose purpose was based on helping others reported higher levels of personal growth and integrity. Other studies have shown that the more self-focused your goals are, the lower your life satisfaction levels will be.

Some of us will be able to quickly identify our purpose. It may be a transformative event in life that establishes what matters most to us. It might be helping to fundraise for research after a family member has suffered a rare type of cancer. It could be going from feeling secure in life to losing your job unfairly and campaigning for better redundancy laws. It might be helping others access information that helped you thrive. It is often something dramatic that helps us find purpose.

Another route to purpose comes from social observation – noticing what other people are doing and wanting to emulate them. A study on the motivations of black students in science, technology, engineering and maths (STEM) found that twenty-three out of forty-four of those interviewed wanted to study for a PhD in order to serve as a role model and encourage other black students into STEM subjects. Many of these students had themselves received the encouragement and confidence to apply for a PhD from a mentor – they wanted to pass on their gratitude.

The area we have most control over is that of hunting for our purpose. We might think of it like baking a cake. We need the right ingredients – the right people believing in us (whether they are guiding us, affirming that we are on the right path or helping us cultivate our purpose). Then we need to measure those ingredients, realizing that what we choose has benefits for people other than ourselves. Next, we need to mix everything together, to assess if this is a purpose in which we can excel. And finally, we decorate with a pinch of passion. This is powerful, but we have to be careful not to let it become too powerful – when we become obsessive about achieving something or bringing people around to our way of thinking, we can become boring and lead other people to go out of their way to avoid us. When our purpose feels 100 per cent us, our self-worth can be bound up in it; by contrast, when we have a harmonious purpose, we can find space for other things, other passions – we can hear opposing views and openly consider them.

Bring to life

Two key ways of proactively identifying a purpose are by using visualization and free writing.

With visualization, we have two options. The first of these can involve the delightfully titled 'death reflection', where we put our future life in context and think about what we would like to leave behind when we die. What mark would we like to have left on the world? A new law which protects people, a brilliant piece of artwork which inspires people, a book someone will never forget or simply a few people having better lives because we were there for them? A less gloomy process sees us visualizing our 'best self', in terms of our personal, professional and social lives. Perhaps a good question to ask is, 'If I had all the money and time I needed, what do I see myself doing? Where would my joy, my passion and my satisfaction come from?' We are effectively writing our own ideal Wikipedia page. It gives us the freedom to choose what we would like it to say.

The other option is 'free writing', which might mean answering that business school entrance question, 'What matters to me?' No structure is required and your spelling can be dreadful – no one else will ever read your essay. You can even write in bullet points if that's what you prefer; getting something down on paper is what matters. Then, once you have written something, rewrite it using half the words. And keep doing the same thing, until you are left with a single sentence. Mine began with pages of ideas, scribbles and spider diagrams, and over time reduced and reduced until I was left with: 'Help people to accomplish more than they previously believed they could'; a sentence that feels authentic and intentional.

If you struggle with this approach, write a list of all the things that are important to you. You can include your core beliefs or values, the things that make you you, your favourite characteristics, the things you love in life and your talents. Now comes the tough bit – editing that list down to five words. What do they have in common? How would they combine to describe your purpose? Try turning the words into one sentence.

Whichever route you have taken, what you now have in front of you is your purpose. It will take more shape over time, but it should reflect your core; your heart. It will be the destination towards which you should set your personal satnav.

Establishing Purpose

Without action, a purpose is ultimately pointless – not only do we not achieve anything, we feel worse for having hoped to achieve something, but failing because we didn't even try. We might break our purpose down into a succession of smaller goals that will direct our behaviours, getting us closer to achieving our purpose and long-term success. Once we have done this, we don't just have a will to succeed, but a way to succeed. There is a four-step process to follow:

Step one: 'If I was successful in achieving my purpose what would that look like?'

With this knowledge, you can then work backwards to identify specific goals and put into place the processes to get you there. You may have found your purpose because you realized that you could fulfil a social need and enjoy the process of achieving it. In this case, setting a goal is pretty simple. For example, if you are a singer, struck by how much the residents in your grand-mother's care home enjoy music, your purpose might be to give them back the joy that music brings. Your goal might be to set up a series of singalong concerts. Or, if you are a businessperson, frustrated by the lack of ambition you see on CVs that come to your HR team, your purpose might be helping younger people to strive. Your goal could be to set up a mentoring scheme.

Other purposes can be more complex. The person whose purpose revolves around making the world a safer place for women or creating equitable opportunities for disadvantaged children might have to first come up with a small, local idea. And the person who wants to fix the world's environmental problems will need to focus on the one they are most passionate about or are most able to contribute towards.

The goals we set can be connected to our primary purpose; the singer might want to sing to older people, but she could also fundraise so they can go on a trip to the opera. Each goal should be focused on moving closer to our purpose.

Step two: Once you have identified your goals, write them down – and take your time

Studies have found that we should spend at least fifteen minutes on this process to have the best chance of achieving the goals we come up with.

Step three: Break down the goals into tiny steps through 'if-then' planning

We will learn how to goal-set effectively in Chapter 6, but it is important to remember that purpose drives goals, which in turn drive the processes we develop. These processes provide a way to live our purposeful lives. Using the concept of our purpose as a sounding board – asking ourselves whether our behaviours match it – will help us to live according to that purpose.

A nice way to do this is known as 'if-then' planning. This method uses the goals we have developed and identifies all the potential problems in achieving them. We then consider each obstacle in turn. 'If this happens, then I will...' In sport, this might be: 'If I lose a shoe in cross country, then I will leave it there and run barefoot.' In business, it might look more like: 'If I don't win the big contract, then I will do a deep analysis of the submission prepared, see what is usable for other proposals and consider other similar companies I could pitch to.' This technique helps us see how we will move towards our goals and highlights the purposeful life we will be living.

Step four: Success statements

Here we write one sentence on how we will feel when we achieve each of our goals. This not only provides the motivation to keep working towards the goal in the face of any obstacles, but also keeps goal-relevant behaviours at the front of our minds so we live more in line with our purpose. For an actor, that might be, 'When I receive a standing ovation, I will soak up the audience atmosphere and feel proud that I was able to transfer so much energy.' A teacher who has been teaching a child to read or understand a maths concept might write: 'I will be delighted to see the pride in their face.'

Sustaining Purpose

Once you have a purpose, and goals to help you fulfil it, you might look at what kind of habits help you to sustain this purpose. These will be small behaviours you can build into your life to make your purpose more achievable. You can then audit your habits and behaviours to see what gets in the way of your purpose, then gradually replace unhelpful habits.

You don't have to conduct this process alone – the beauty of purpose with a social element is that you can use social capital to stay on track. That might mean fuelling yourself through positive feedback, asking someone you admire to mentor you or contacting peers who have a similar purpose to help you.

Using purpose to fuel our success requires flexibility. Sometimes we manage to achieve our purpose and we then need to find something else. For example, a group of people who had lost loved ones in car accidents felt their purpose was to campaign for seatbelts to be a legal requirement in the UK. In 1983 they achieved their aim when a law making seatbelts mandatory was introduced. Some campaigners went deeper, lobbying for seatbelts to be required for backseat passengers. Others went wider, starting road safety campaigns or working to encourage car manufacturers to introduce other safety measures, such as airbags.

Have a mantra

To sustain your purpose, particularly in the face of obstacles, an easy but highly effective tool is to use a mantra. When I started out as a sport psychologist, I ran a workshop for a triathlon club that focused on the benefits of self-talk for athletes. We discussed research that affirmed the benefits of having a mantra, but I didn't have any specific examples. One of my attendees stuck up his hand and asked if the thing he told himself in races would count as a mantra. He told us his story.

About five years earlier, he had been very overweight and was leading an incredibly unhealthy lifestyle. His GP had told him to immediately change his eating, fitness and health habits or risk an early death. That GP visit was the encouragement he needed. He started eating more healthily, began to exercise and eventually found triathlon. His first race was a daunting experience – he survived the swim and the bike ride, but was struggling on the 5-km run. Then he saw his dad by the side of the course, cheering him on. As he ran past, he heard his dad say to the spectator next to him, 'That's my son.' The pride in his dad's voice lifted him towards the finish line. In every race after that, whenever he was struggling, he repeated 'That's my son' to himself, to remind him of how his changed lifestyle had made his dad proud. He was living his purpose – and the use of his mantra helped him stick with it. There is no better example of a mantra – it was emotive, short, positive and powerful.

To find your own mantra, you need to identify something personal that resonates deeply. Whenever you come up against an obstacle, repeating the phrase can help you remain focused. If you struggle to come up with one, think about what someone you trust might say to you in that moment. If you can, make it tug on your heartstrings – a phrase that gives you a bit of a lump in your throat is the one that will work best. If you can find something as powerful as the mantra of our friend in his triathlon, that matches your purpose and is full of emotion, you will have a brilliant motivational tool that will help keep you on track.

Damian had just the thing when he set his Pennine Way record. 'I literally sat down and wrote "Why am I doing this race? What is motivating me, what is my purpose?"' The three Fs Damian told us he came up with and wrote on his arm – family, friendship and future – worked beautifully as a reminder of all the reasons he was running. 'They reaffirmed my sense of purpose, especially when it got difficult and I felt really tired and I wanted to lie down or sit down or just go a lot easier. I wouldn't have broken the record if I'd done that.'

It doesn't always have to be a phrase says Damian. 'I've learned it is important to make some sort of visual reminder that, ideally, you can carry with you. My daughter and I both love squirrels and, before a recent challenge, she gave me a little acorn. When I saw the acorn during the record attempt it made me think: "the faster I run this, the sooner I can get back and see her", but also, I wanted to tell her that I did well, that I didn't let her down. That gave me more purpose, made me run better and ultimately it made me feel motivated. I had a strong purpose. It pushed me along.'

Purposeful planning

A nice example of identifying, establishing and sustaining a purpose is a tool called 'life crafting' that was used by the Rotterdam School of Management when they established their mission of being a force for positive change. They created a three-stage programme to help their students develop purpose.

First, they asked the students to write down their values and ambitions and describe both their ideal life and the life they wanted to avoid. They were then asked to develop these notes into specific goals and include plans to achieve them. Finally, they were asked to do a photo shoot, incorporating a statement linked to their goals, starting with 'I will...' Examples included, 'I will... inspire and facilitate sustainable development' and 'I will... lead by example and inspire others to reach their goals.' The 'I will...' phrase ensured they were clear about their goal, and the process helped to create a feeling of accountability. A study to assess the effectiveness of this life-crafting process found that students achieved better academic results than previous cohorts and fewer of them dropped out.

We can follow a similar process to this life crafting to identify and develop our own purpose. It becomes the book that tells the story of our life and helps us to stay on track. Damian uses his purpose in just this way: 'I'll get a bit distracted, but when I remind myself of my purpose, I think it is a lot easier to go "But actually that email isn't important to reply to for now. Do I really need to be on Twitter right now? They don't relate to the purpose I have. These two or three tasks are much more pertinent to my purpose. They are the ones I'll concentrate on" and then at the end of the day you feel more satisfied because you have made some steps towards what matters.'

Now you have heard Damian explaining how his purpose helps him focus, think about your purpose and visualize the Wikipedia page that will be written about you when you become successful and achieve your goals. How will your purpose in life be distilled?

PURPOSE TOOLKIT

Purpose clarity

Our purpose can be defined by its scope (how ubiquitous it is in our life), its strength (how much influence it brings to our decisions) and our awareness of it (how far to the front of our mind it sits). To identify our purpose, we can try visualization or free writing (see page 109). Our goal is to neatly summarize our purpose in one sentence, but the process to get there does take time.

- To begin, fill a page with bullet points of the things that really matter to you; the things which get your tummy flipping with excitement, passion, frustration or anger.

- Next, look for themes. Are there elements which stick out?

- Summarize those themes.

- Condense down and filter out the elements which feel weaker.

- Finally, turn those few bullets into one sentence. Leave for a few days then come back to it. Does it feel a purpose worthy of your time and efforts?

Purpose checking

Purpose offers us three elements: a direction of travel to help us prioritize resources and efforts, a contribution to the wider world and a channel for consistent behaviour. It becomes scaffolding for our decisions. Does your purpose meet all three elements? Without the wider world contribution, it is just a nice goal. Without consistent behaviour, it is inauthentic. Without a clear direction, it is just an area of interest.

Purposeful mantra

When we are clear on our purpose, we need to keep it front of mind. A mantra is incredibly effective for this. There are six rules for creating a great mantra. It must be:

- ☑ positive
- ☑ personal
- ☑ purposeful
- ☑ memorable
- ☑ short
- ☑ a little bit emotional

5

Cultivated Confidence

Confidence is the most critical differentiator between success and failure, but it needs to be the right kind of confidence: the 'I've prepared brilliantly, practised extensively and so, whatever happens, happens' type. This is cultivated confidence.

Emma Wiggs, MBE, double Paralympic gold medallist and nine-time World Champion paracanoeist, says she has never once lined up in a race expecting to win. She doesn't have what we might think of as traditional confidence – that 'I can do anything' forcefulness we expect to see in the world's best athletes. What she has is even better.

'I may not have huge confidence that I can achieve something, but I have absolute 100 per cent confidence that I can give it my very best shot,' she says, 'and I think that is the difference. Did I ever believe that I could win one World Championship title, let alone nine, or two Paralympic titles? Probably not. Did I believe that I would do everything that these incredible staff had asked me? Yes. Did I know I work harder than anyone else? Yes.' That means she can genuinely sit on the start line and think: 'I couldn't have done any more.'

We imagine confidence as a sense of being bullish. We think that it is the state of mental toughness, something experienced by a member of the SAS, a CEO or a gold medallist, ready to smash anything that gets in their way. From this perspective, confidence is muscly and aggressive, but it can tip over into a sense of arrogant overconfidence that leads us to miss things that we should have checked and being unsure that all bases have been covered. Would you rather do a parachute jump with someone who brashly announces that they know what they are doing or with someone who double-checks the equipment and has practised tandem jumping many times previously? Our first instinct might be to go with the confident person, but some reflection might well make us go with the one who is less brazen, but clearly better prepared.

It is the preparation behind building confidence that sustains our success, rather than the confidence itself. We want to develop Emma's cultivated confidence – the knowledge that you have done all you can, that you have listened and learned, put in the work and left no stone unturned. You know that something unexpected might happen and you might not achieve your goal, but you can feel secure in knowing that you truly tried.

When you are confident, you don't fear failure. You can happily apologize if something hasn't gone to plan, or you might take a risk – knowing that, even if it doesn't work, it was worth trying. A confident person will be prepared to ask challenging questions without worrying that others will take offence. They'll also be better able to accept criticism because hearing it won't make them feel attacked. Consequently, they can take comments on board and improve their performance.

Studies have found that we perform at our worst when our confidence is low and our motivation is high. Those pillars of success that we examined in the first four chapters – belonging, mastery, autonomy and purpose – increase our internalized motivation, but that will be wasted if we do not believe that we can achieve the thing we are motivated to do. The good news is that the supply of cultivated confidence isn't limited. And when we understand how we can cultivate it, we can enjoy a much more successful life.

What Is Confidence?

Confidence has been widely studied in sport, professional services and academia, where everything points to it being a key ingredient of success. In sport, confidence levels have been found to be the biggest differentiator between success and failure. In elite sport, where much of the research takes place, 90 per cent of Olympians say they have a very high level of self-confidence and a study pulling together the data from forty-eight studies, covering over three thousand athletes from a wide range of sports, found a clear relationship between confidence and performance.

As a mixture of self-belief and positivity, confidence tells us whether we are likely to achieve the goals we set for ourselves. Studies have found that it boosts resilience and helps us feel more secure; rather than our heads being filled by doubts or nerves, we have the space to focus on specific and helpful targets. They might be physical skills or tactics in sport, the ability to make speeches more passionately and persuasively as a leader or the facility to create more inspiring lessons as a teacher.

Confidence filters into every area of our lives and especially into our work. A study tracking competitiveness and confidence in US universities studied young women in the lab and then followed them through the first few years of their careers. They found that confident women earned more – in fact, they earned the same as their male counterparts, which suggests that it is a lack of confidence often holding women back. This doesn't excuse a system in which competitiveness and confidence are rewarded over hard work or compassion, or where a misogynistic culture reduces women's opportunities to thrive, but it does highlight the power of confidence in the workplace.

When we are confident, we make more positive choices, we set higher goals and we tackle big challenges instead of avoiding them. We are more persistent and able to keep going on a project until we know whether it is viable, rather than giving up when the going gets tough. And when we arrive at the challenge we've set ourselves, we feel calm under pressure, excited to put ourselves to the test. Some nerves might still be there, but the head space that confidence gives us means that we are able to think about what we need to do to be successful, which is much more positive than a default, 'How do I avoid failure?'

Being focused on doing something well, rather than on simply not failing, is not just an issue of semantics; it has a huge psychological impact. When we are confident and able to focus on doing well, we use different and more effective strategies. To use business as an analogy, it means the difference between expanding or simply fighting to stave off a takeover. Or in football, it means shooting to score rather than playing defensively. Perhaps a way to look at confidence is to see it as a pair of filtered glasses that we can put on in order to see everything more positively and in better focus.

Cultivated confidence

As we can see, confidence has a huge impact not only on our performance, but also on our enjoyment of getting to the point of performing. It makes everything feel easier and less stressful. However, some sources of confidence can be fleeting.

Winning a new business contract will feel fabulous on the day, but if you doubt that you are sufficiently skilled or experienced to complete the work, that confidence will be pretty fragile. If you win a tournament, but put your success down to better athletes not turning up, the confidence the win brings will be quickly undermined.

To earn long-term, robust confidence, we need to cultivate it and nurture it, which means being proactive with the way in which we build it. We can then be sure that it is not fragile. We can learn from our successes and grow small shoots of confidence into long-term self-belief, which will hold up even when we are faced with challenges or setbacks. It keeps the serious doubts at bay. This isn't about feeling invincible, but about being sure that, when we have left no stone unturned, success of some kind is inevitable.

It can help if we think of there being two types of confidence. The first is fairly stable and you pretty much either have it or you don't. If you have high levels of extroversion (where you recharge your internal batteries by surrounding yourself with others – as opposed to introverts who prefer to recharge by having time alone) and low levels of neuroticism, you have probably been blessed with natural confidence. But that doesn't mean you can switch off and stop reading the rest of this chapter. Even when we have natural confidence, we can still find ourselves knocked back by a run of poor results or a time when it feels we are battling everything that life can throw at us. We all benefit from the second type of confidence, whether we are an introvert, lower in emotional stability or if our natural confidence has taken a hit – this second type helps us build ourselves up and become more successful. This confidence can be developed and nurtured. It is our cultivated confidence and, when we learn how to grow and maintain it, we will have a secret weapon for success.

For Emma, developing her cultivated confidence became part of who she is as an athlete. 'Knowing I'd done everything I possibly could was calming, but also very, very empowering. It became a real part of the athlete that I am, because it meant that I always searched for more. I always searched for what we could be doing differently. I questioned my staff and my coach endlessly about what we could be doing to be better.' Leaving no stone unturned became Emma's super-strength.

Where Do We Find Confidence?

There is no map to cultivated confidence and there's no algorithm to locate its sources – it's different for everyone. Helpfully, though, there are multiple ways we can gather this cultivated confidence for ourselves. And when we learn the methods to find it for ourselves, we will have a strong resource every time we need a boost. Some sources will be stronger and more effective than others, while others still might work really well, but be fragile and risky.

The two sources we should start with are the ones that we can cultivate the most to give us robust, long-term confidence: mastery and preparation. These remind us that we have reasons to be confident, offering physical and psychological evidence that we are able to do whatever we need to do. Studies in both these areas show that working on them makes us more resilient, focused and adept at keeping distractions or setbacks in perspective.

Mastery

As we learned in Chapter 2, mastery helps us achieve our goals by giving us the skills we need. But, as we also discovered, even when we have mastery, we can suffer from impostor syndrome, meaning that mastery needs to come with confidence to be effective. It's not enough to have high levels of competency in specific skills; we also have to have experience in using those skills.

The first time we do anything it can be scary and stressful because we are outside of our comfort zone. The first performance of a new play, the first match at a new sports ground or the first day in a job all bring bucketloads of stress. Novelty is good when we want to have fun, but terrifying when we want to be in control and don't know how. Yet collecting first-time experiences that we incorporate into our repertoire adds to our mastery. Each time we repeat that once-new activity, it becomes more mundane and less scary, allowing us to focus on what is important and not on what is worrying.

As well as collecting experiences, we also need to collect evidence if we are to be able to use our mastery to give ourselves confidence. For athletes, this might be learning a particular skill, a set piece or attaining a speed they have reached in training. For someone heading into their annual work appraisal, it might be hearing positive client feedback, revisiting deals they have won or adding up the money they have saved their company.

We should flag such achievements because success breeds confidence, confidence breeds success and, in this way, we can establish a positive circle. We can see this in the psychological concept of 'hot hands', when we seem to be on a winning streak. Researchers suggest that the phenomenon comes from the fact that increased confidence cements our improved performance when things start to go well and we go on to continue to do well.

A study in golf tested how success influenced confidence to secure future success. The researchers defined 'success' in a tournament as making what is called 'the cut'. After the first two days of a tournament, only the top seventy players stay on the course to play days three and four. These are the players said to have made 'the cut'. The interesting thing is that it's possible to make the cut and feel successful while only having taken one less shot than someone who didn't make it. While both players will have performed almost identically, the player just one stroke behind will feel as if they completely failed. Studying those golfers who were six strokes either side of the cut, researchers found that a golfer's chance of making the cut in their next competition increases by 3 per cent if they made it in their previous one.

This isn't an unusual phenomenon. In another study of golfers, about half of the participants identified past performance as their biggest reason for confidence, a finding that we can see replicated widely across both sport and life. Our experiences of mastery are incredibly powerful in helping us create initial belief and also a good foundation for other types of confidence. When we know that we have already achieved a skill, we start to build a bank of evidence to fuel our confidence. It becomes self-fulfilling and our confidence continues to grow as we do more things that stretch us beyond our comfort zone and bring us closer to realizing our ambitions.

The real benefit of the confidence that mastery gives us is that, once we have it, we have it for a period of time. If we evaluate events smartly and find positives in each performance – whether a strength we spotted or something to work on – we will appraise our success differently.

Preparation

This is the other element that Emma highlighted at the start of this chapter. The more planning, research and practice we put into our preparation, the more confidence we have when we step into the limelight. Emma is clear that her age (she is forty-two) and disability (the nerve damage in her legs) should limit her speed in a canoe but, nevertheless, she has become a World Champion because she believes that she trains harder than anyone else, studies her sport more than anyone else and lifts more weights in the gym than anyone else. She even jokes that she eats more cottage cheese than anyone else!

A good way to prime for flawless preparation is to get to know your environment. This is why the British Olympic and Paralympic associations spend so much money setting up training camps ahead of big tournaments, sending athletes to test events and even taking non-competing athletes to games to soak up the experience and make it less daunting when it is their turn a few years later. All this gives the athletes insight into the environment they will be competing in and helps get them used to the pressure. It is the same reason that actors do dress rehearsals, schools run mock exams and sales teams practise big pitches. It takes the edge off for when they have to perform for real. The more elements of a situation we are familiar with, the better prepared we feel.

However, there are some things that we cannot control, no matter how hard we try. The cyclist James MacDonald provides a great illustration of this. In 2019, he was aiming to set a new world record for cycling on the track for twenty-four hours, non-stop. He had eight hours to go when he increased his speed and crashed. He watched the video of the event back and saw that he'd been derailed by a few drops of water from a leaky bottle.

He said, 'I could see the bottles we were using were dripping on the racing line. When I was out of the saddle, stretching, my rear wheel slipped out of line on the water. I corrected it and then it slipped again and I went over the top.' How did James regard the failed attempt? He saw it as a test run. He said, 'There's nothing quite like the pressure of spectators and camera crews to make sure it's as real as possible, and we can use those experiences to help my next attempt.'

As James shows us, the more focus we direct on preparing the basics and covering for every eventuality, the more confident we will feel about our ability to achieve success. It is not just about doing the training (if our goal is something physical), the studying (if it is something cognitive) and the development of skills and mental practice – we also need to ensure we cover logistics, coping mechanisms and routine, leaving nothing to chance. We then know that our performance won't be undermined by something annoying like getting lost on the way to a venue or forgetting the USB stick with the presentation.

If we are physically, logistically and mentally prepared, we will be able to ignore distractions and focus on what matters most: our performance. The real joy of this type of confidence is that, if we have done everything possible and covered every base, we'll have no reason to beat ourselves up if something goes wrong – we can still be proud of what we achieved on the way to the finish line.

One of Emma's proudest, most confident moments was the one race she didn't win. She dislocated a bone and ruptured some ligaments in her wrist. It needed surgery, but, as she wasn't able to get it before the World Championships and she couldn't do any more damage to it, she decided to race anyway. The goal became learning and delivering the best performance possible. 'That probably was the first moment when I really felt on the start line that I was confident. I was going to deliver the best I've got. I knew that it was about seven out of ten because of the wrist injury. I did deliver with less stress, less anxiety and more confidence than I ever had. I knew I wasn't going to be at my best, so I allowed myself to think "just confidently deliver what you've got".' Emma (and her broken wrist) did just that – and came second.

Supporting sources of confidence

Cultivating our mastery and preparation will serve us well, but there are also other sources of confidence. They won't all work for everyone, but when they do, they can be very powerful.

Vicarious confidence

Vicarious confidence is particularly prevalent in influencer marketing, communication techniques and promotional campaigns. It is the idea that watching other people who are a little bit similar to us can give us the belief that we can achieve the same as them. We will explore the negative side of comparison in Chapter 6, but vicarious confidence is one of the positives of it. One of the justifications in sport for the money spent on developing elite athletes has long been that seeing their success inspires the public to get fit too. But Sport England research showed the opposite and, as a result, they launched the 'This Girl Can' campaign in January 2015. They had found that, while we all love to watch amazing athletes, they rarely inspire us – their abilities, skills and physiques are too different to our own. The people who inspire us are people who are like us – who have done well and who have overcome barriers similar to those we face. They may have the same body shape, the same health problems or the same childcare issues. It is when we see people like us achieve things we want that we realize what is possible. This was what their campaign showed and it was incredibly powerful.

Verbal persuasion

Using verbal persuasion is another way of obtaining confidence. It can be powerful to hear other people tell us that they have faith in us; school researchers told teachers that specific students were gifted (even when they weren't) and these children were given far more support and encouragement as a result. By the end of the school year, they were ahead of their peers and living up to the 'gifted' label. Other people believing in you can really help you believe in yourself.

You are most likely to be persuaded by people you trust and respect. If you go to a new company to work for a boss who you look up to or if you've successfully auditioned for a theatre production because you want to work with a particular director, their expertise and mastery can rub off on you. It isn't a particularly stable confidence – there's always a risk that they may leave or you may move on – but, as Chapter 1 showed, the power of feeling part of a great team is pretty potent.

Social support

It isn't just leaders who provide confidence; the social support we get from our peers can also provide an effective confidence boost. Whether it's our family, friends, colleagues or team-mates, being aware of the confidence they have in themselves, the team and in us can influence our own psyche. This can be used as a tactic as we go all out to find the cheerleaders in life and align with them.

Emma has been incredibly grateful for her social and professional support. 'Having people around you who you trust, who have confidence in you, is hugely empowering. The people I surround myself with are absolutely crucial to everything that I do, whether it's paddling a boat or just living my daily life. And their belief, their confidence, is really crucial in helping me build my own.'

The risk with this confidence, though, is that sometimes we might unintentionally translate someone else's confidence in us into a sense of pressure or expectation. Research has found that when we expect to do well – having developed mastery and self-belief – we are likely to perform well. But if we have not yet built up our own confidence and know that other people are expecting us to do well, we can actually be pulled down. The fear of failure and the anticipated loss of face that would come with not living up to other people's expectations create pressure that prevents us from functioning effectively. It is essential that we build our own strong foundation of confidence first, to protect ourselves from the expectations of others. We have to have enough robust confidence of our own, and any further confidence that we cultivate will then help rather than hinder.

Innate confidence

We don't have to go to others for additional sources of confidence; we can also look inside ourselves. We might consider innate factors, asking ourselves if we feel that we have a natural ability, such as being able to charm people, being capable of organizing every situation to the nth degree or having a sporting talent. After a while, this rubs off and we establish a reservoir of confidence to draw upon. Similarly, when we see a situation as being favourable or likely to give us an advantage, we gain in confidence.

When Confidence Goes Pear-Shaped

Getting exactly the right level of confidence is tricky: too much and we become arrogant; too little and we show timidity and hold ourselves back. We rarely think about the problems that come from being too confident, yet it is absolutely possible to find ourselves in that situation. Overconfidence can stunt our growth, making us so complacent that we stop trying; instead of putting in place a meticulously planned routine, we wing it. Mastery disappears and instead of constantly trying to improve, trying to learn more or preparing brilliantly, we just assume that we'll be fine. This approach can seriously limit our success; if we fail to prepare, we will always be up against others who have worked harder. In this scenario, a modicum of self-doubt can actually be beneficial, helping to keep up our desire to stay hungry so that we prove ourselves.

At the other end of the scale, a lack of confidence can be a real dream destroyer. What is the use of being brilliant if it is hidden away? And if our lack of confidence means that we hide our mastery away from ourselves and don't believe that we can do what we've trained to do, we avoid challenges rather than grasping opportunities with both hands.

When we lack confidence, self-doubt can set off the threat system in our brain. And once that gets going, there's no room for rational decision-making. Everything becomes emotional and the mental bandwidth we should be using to put our preparation and mastery to good use gets used up in fighting anxiety, nerves and negative thoughts. The only decisions we make are ones that keep us safe. As a result, we end up performing well below our ability and never get close to our potential.

In sport, this would be manifested by struggling to perform as well in competition as we do in training. On the stage, we may perform brilliantly in rehearsal, but lose the magic when it comes to the actual performance. And when we have to present an idea, we may find ourselves glossing over the more creative thoughts and sticking with what feels safe. This is because the ideas that would make us stand out also make us scared of how they will be received; as a result, they stay buried. We need to stand out to be successful – but without confidence we don't feel able to do so.

Some of this can come down to being shy. Shyness can result from high levels of introversion and neuroticism – the traits at the far end of the scale of natural confidence (see page 123). Shyness can come from self-consciousness and a fear of being judged by others. It tends to be a trait that stays with us throughout life and it can impact how we get on with others, increasing our chances of being excluded or walked over. Shy people tend to internalize fears rather than sharing them, and so feel lonely. Shyness stops us joining in, which prevents our contributions being noticed or valued.

Shyness doesn't necessarily restrict our attainment in school because we are usually tested in ways that don't require huge amounts of confidence – our shyness won't impact our ability to go into a hall and take an exam, for example. But when we enter adult life, we are measured over a much wider range of activities. We have to give presentations and updates at meetings and perform at job interviews. These things require us to speak out in order to get ahead, so not being able to do this can present a real barrier to success. We can't completely rid ourselves of shyness, but there are some strategies to help you handle it in the toolkit at the end of this chapter (see page 144).

Faking it

Cultivating good-quality, robust confidence takes a while. But, as a quick fix while we wait for the first shoots to appear, we can utilize that 'fake it till you make it' phrase by learning to act confident when we need to, even if we aren't. Emma uses this tactic regularly, putting on a confident face to her competitors. 'Pulling on your big girl pants and faking it on the morning of a race is a good strategy. Because you can kid yourself. You can go to the start line thinking: "I'm so tired that I'm not going to have the energy to race" or I go to the start line thinking:

"I'm not tired. One night's bad sleep doesn't affect you. I can smash this race." That is a very different place.'

It can help to think about faking confidence as a placebo. Experiments have been carried out in which confidence is manipulated by providing deliberately inaccurate feedback to make people think that they are doing better or worse than they actually are. The results show that people whose confidence is boosted perform better. When this type of experiment was carried out with weightlifters, the athlete's confidence rose after they were misled about how much weight they had lifted; as a result, they were able to lift increasingly heavier weights. In another experiment, a group of weightlifters were told they were being given performance-enhancing drugs. Their confidence rose after taking them and their performance improved. Once they were told that they had simply been taking a placebo, their performance returned to normal levels.

We should note that while this type of confidence boost requires others to manipulate us, we can manipulate ourselves through the way we physically present. If we feel good about our body and what we are wearing, we will feel battle-ready. If you want to use how you look to maximize your confidence, wear red – a colour that is powerful, dominant and physical. When athletes were randomly assigned either a red or a blue uniform in martial arts events in the 2004 Athens Olympics, those who were wearing red won significantly more often.

Emma sees her GB kit as an additional power. 'I find putting on the race kit really empowering. I think it is really important to take a moment to think how lucky we are that we are in a position where we have been selected for our country and we are then able to go and race for our country. And, for me, putting on that race kit is a real moment. It is a reminder to yourself that you have done a huge amount of work – you've earned the right to be there. You just have to go and deliver your best and what will be will be.'

Our body language is another good way to tell others, and ourselves, how strong we are. Using body language in this way has been found to increase our risk tolerance, our testosterone levels and our feelings of power; it can also decrease our levels of the stress hormone cortisol. We call it 'power posing'. If you want to try a power pose, stand up with your legs slightly apart, send your shoulders back with your arms apart and relaxed, hold your head up and breathe deeply.

An analysis of fifty-four studies found that people who use open, expansive power poses like this feel more powerful – and it can influence how your competitors see you. Even at a performance level as high as Emma's. 'I think I'm a real sucker for being influenced by how confident other people look. One of my favourite pastimes has been to sit and say, "Oh, they look good", "Look, they look confident", "They look big", "They look fast" and I can remember my coach saying to me at one point, "They are not even in their boat, how can you possibly say they look fast? They are standing on the edge of the lake!"'

Another way we try to develop this fake confidence is through the use of superstition. Tennis legend Serena Williams apparently ties her shoelaces in a specific way and bounces the ball five times before her first serve and twice before her second. The footballer Cristiano Ronaldo always steps on to the pitch with his right foot. We might think, 'wearing my lucky socks will give me the edge in the pitch' or 'seeing two magpies on the way to my interview means I'll get the job'. Some of these thoughts seem strange, but few of us are immune to them. I have a limited edition necklace that I always wear when I have a tricky day ahead. Superstitions like this give us a sense of security and help us feel everything is under control, making us feel more confident.

The problem with these superstitions comes when they involve a specific object. Colonel Dame Kelly Holmes, who we met in Chapter 1, came close to missing the final of the 1,500 m at the Athens Olympic Games, the race in which she won a gold medal, because she had to use a specific Portaloo first. When I lost my lucky necklace at the gym, I spent a few days frantically searching for a replacement on eBay. Without that necklace, would I suddenly become less competent or poorly prepared? Of course not. But the doubt that can seep into your mind in such situations is very real. One way to get the same level of control and confidence – in a far more effective and less risky way – is to replace the superstition with a routine. This is something Emma has cultivated well over her years in the canoe: 'I find having a routine really calming. I know what my warm-up looks like. I know the timings that I use, I know where I'm going to be, I know what I'm going to do. And being able to have that routine and repeat that is really, really powerful.'

Boosting Confidence

What is so nice about confidence is that it is malleable. We can work on it, manipulate it and grow it. The strategies below all help with that.

Set clear goals

As we have seen with superstitions, our reasons for feeling confident aren't always rational – confidence is closely linked to our emotions and threat systems. That means that, if we are going to use preparation to cultivate our confidence, it is vital that we prepare properly. And to do that, we need to know what we are preparing for. What goal or ambition are we trying to reach? And how far is it within our control?

There are thousands of studies that show the importance of setting clear, specific, realistic and timely goals. When these goals are entirely under our control, aiming for them is even more effective. Having them in place increases our motivation, commitment, concentration and, most importantly, our confidence. They are also fantastic for reducing anxiety, which helps us nail our final performance when it counts. They help us turn our intentions into actions, and completing actions is what gives us that confidence. Having them in place helps us to concentrate on processes rather than outcomes (we'll learn more about this in Chapter 6), so that we have positives to focus on. We then have less need to compare ourselves to others, something that can sap our confidence.

Once you have set the goals (as we will learn to do in the next chapter), the magic comes from the behaviours, actions, strategies and tactics that we employ to get stuff done. They are all things we can control ourselves; by incorporating them into our lives we can see how they will help us achieve our goal and help us feel in control. When we get closer to our goal, we can look back and reflect on the processes we've followed and the activities we've achieved in the build-up, confident that no stone has been left unturned.

If there are specific skills we need to reach our goal, we should practise them. Making a note of the key tactics or techniques we know we need to be successful might act as a useful prompt. Every time we achieve one of these skills, we should add the date it was attained, and we will eventually have a page of irrefutable evidence that we have prepared properly and covered all the key bases.

These processes keep athletes like Emma focused on their targets rather than the trophies – and as a result they are more successful. This was crucial in the Tokyo Paralympic Games which took place in 2021 with strict daily COVID-19 testing. 'It was vital to focus on the controllables and not waste precious energy on things out of our control... easier said than done when you are being tested every day and the results could mean "game over". I stuck to a process of control and felt in a "tunnel" to maintain energy levels and stay calm.'

Control the controllables

Meticulous planning is important. It puts us in the best possible place for a great performance – whether in sport, on the stage or in business – boosting our confidence and calming our nerves. It means that we arrive in plenty of time with everything we need, are well fuelled, have warmed up using techniques that work for us and have incorporated the mental skills that help get us into the right head space. Feeling confident in this will mean that we feel in control of all the controllables; routines can provide this security. They keep our head busy with task-relevant thoughts and actions so that we don't have time to be anxious. They also help us reach the right level of activation, meaning that the task at hand is a challenge rather than a threat.

A routine should match the event you are attempting, your personality traits and the required logistics. The more you are able to practise a routine, the more automatic it becomes and the more helpful it will be in getting your head into the right place. It might last for the day before your event or just ten minutes before you head into action. What makes it effective is that it is matched to your needs and replicable; you can use it again and again. In sport, the routine will often be your warm-up. On the stage, it might be voice preparation like scales or tongue twisters. For a presentation, you might do some deep breathing, visualize your audience nodding along to your points or have a quick read through of the first slide.

Keep a score of your successes and strengths

To feel confident we need some evidence that we can do the thing ahead of us. Keeping evidence is a good way to do this. As our brains have an inbuilt negativity bias we need to be proactive about this. This bias keeps us safe and reminds us to stay out of harm's way, but the side effect is that it downplays the positive, leaving us lacking in confidence. Regular reminders of our efforts and achievements help to counter this negativity.

One way we can develop these reminders is by keeping score of our successes – this is vital if we are to remember the evidence for our confidence. This technique has many different names – we might call it a 'confidence jar', a 'victory log' or a 'file of fabulousness'. Regardless of the name, they are essentially a way of keeping our successes and accomplishments in one place so we have them to reflect upon, reminding ourselves how well we can do. Having these reminders can help keep us rational when self-doubt and frustration creep into our heads. You can find instructions on how to make your own confidence jar in the toolkit at the end of this chapter (see page 144).

Whatever method we use, we are essentially writing notes to ourselves to cover the skills we have, the events or activities at which we have thrived, the times we've faced a barrier but have overcome it and the successes we are proud of. Each point we make is a small reminder that we have the mastery, we have done the preparation and we are sufficiently qualified to attempt our goal. We can think of it as a 'look what I did' list rather than the far more traditional – and stress-inducing – 'to-do' list. When we shift our focus to our achievements, we will be happier and more grateful (a key pillar for success, as we'll see in Chapter 10).

Leaving a confidence jar by the side of your bed or a file of fabulousness on your phone means that, if you find yourself awake in the middle of the night worrying that you won't do well, you have evidence to counter that right next to you, in your own words.

Emma did this in the build-up to the Rio Paralympics in 2016. 'The jar was full of pieces of paper on which I had really religiously, over the whole winter leading up to the games, written positive things that had happened. Or examples of when we had overcome conditions and still delivered. I would write it on a piece of paper, put it in the jar and forget about it.' When she got to Rio she could open the jar and pull out examples of real, tangible things she had done. 'It reminds you, "Yeah, I have done this and if I just do that again it will be fine" – and, for me, that is really empowering. I can see it in my own writing that I've had to acknowledge that these things have gone well because I've done something well. If that doesn't come easily, being able to read it is really, really important.'

It also helps if we keep score of our strengths – the strengths audit in Chapter 2 (see page 62) that helps boost our mastery is useful here as it keeps the things we are good at in the forefront of our mind. When tricky moments come, instead of panicking, we have reminders of the skills or strengths we can use. Capturing our strengths is crucial and, again, it counters our cognitive bias towards negativity (see above).

Use mental imagery

When we haven't had an opportunity to build up evidence of our skills or successes, we can develop them through mental imagery. Although it may sound rather wishy-washy, mental imagery has a strong scientific basis and is used regularly by successful performers to practise tricky moments in advance. The foundation for this lies in the way in which our brain is able to bypass movement and physical activity while being able to simulate sensations, actions and experiences. If an image is strong enough, our neuronal groups fire in defined patterns and structurally modify themselves to become more effective. As a result, we gain a functional equivalence with the same areas of the brain firing, whether a skill or event is performed or just imagined. This gives us familiarity with the specific task we will be doing or the environment we will be in.

Imagery isn't just the equivalent of daydreaming; it is pro-active and purposeful. We can think of it as forming a detailed mental rehearsal that focuses not just on the activity we are working towards, but on the senses we will need to use on the day. All of these bring our mental rehearsal to life and give us more functional equivalency.

We can use imagery to motivate ourselves about what we need to do, imagining how it will feel to ace the exam or get the phone call to say we are being offered a job, or we can use it to practise strategies we might use to achieve our goal. Both types increase our confidence and help us believe that we will be able to hit our target.

Whichever type you prefer, mental imagery seems to be most effective when you write a script covering the part of the event you are most worried about. If you're doing it for a job interview, write your best answer to the questions you are most scared of answering. If it is about a race, include the decisions you will make when the going gets really tough. If it covers a difficult meeting, include how you would like to react when a colleague talks down to you. In your script include all your senses. What can you see? Smell? Feel? Taste? Hear? These details will really bring your scenario to life. Once you are happy with your script, record it on your phone and listen to it as part of your preparation. You are practising performing at your best, which will give your confidence a massive boost.

Emma describes herself as a big fan of imagery. She used it in the build-up to the Tokyo Paralympics. 'We knew there would be no spectators, so I had spent a lot of time visualizing being on the start line and looking up at the large bridge and imagining my family and friends waving from the bridge... I knew they would be proud of me whatever the result and it gave me such confidence to know I just needed to stick to my process and deliver the paddle I had practised so many times and that would be enough, regardless of results. It was amazing to have practised this technique and then actually sit on the start line and feel more relaxed than I ever have. I even said out loud to "the people on the bridge"... "Hey there! Right let's go!"'

Be motivated by others

If you find yourself getting envious of others you might be up against, rather than viewing them as a secret rival, you can use your admiration of what they have achieved to boost your own confidence. What is it that makes you want to emulate them? What do you think you could learn from them? What have they done that you could do yourself? Once you have figured that out, you can go all out in attempting it yourself. You can use the fact that they have achieved it as motivation that you can too.

If this 'vicarious confidence' relates to someone you know personally, you might also turn them into your partner in crime. Just as elite athletes have training partners, why shouldn't you have someone who spurs you on, inspires you and improves your motivation? Rather than a mentor, this is someone who is at your level and doing similar activities. But it should also be someone who can give you some perspective, increase your accountability and help you stick to the goals you set. This type of partnership has been found to improve the sense of work ethic and accountability, as many studies have found that we work harder and perform more effectively when we think that friendly people are watching.

In such a partnership, you might offer each other the verbal persuasion we all need. This might take the form of feedback conversations, practising a certain routine together or working together when you have a big and scary task ahead of you. Knowing that someone else believes in us can give a real boost to our confidence and may provide a timely reminder that we have everything we need to perform well.

Create a confidence card

Finally, combining your preparation with your mastery, you can create a 'confidence card' before daunting events. A few days before the event you have been working towards, draw six boxes on a piece of paper. One box should contain your goal. The next box should contain a technical instruction that you should follow. Box three should be your motivational mantra – the phrase you will repeat when you are nervous to remind yourself of your purpose and passion. The next box is for the three things you have done in preparation that will help you achieve that goal. In the next box, note three strengths you bring to the event that will give you an advantage. Finally, you complete the sentence: 'I perform at my best when...' This helps you identify your ideal environment and consider how to create it. There is a template for you on page 146. Keep the card in your wallet and, every time you feel nervous, get it out and read it to remind yourself of what you have done to achieve your goal. This cultivates your confidence.

CULTIVATED CONFIDENCE TOOLKIT

Power pose

While we work on growing confidence, we can fake it, acting confident and using strong body language to pretend that we deserve to be where we are – even if we don't yet believe it. This helps us feel more powerful, gives us a performance advantage and reduces our stress levels. We can do this through a power pose. To practise yours, stand up and ensure you have:

- your head held high
- your chest forward
- your shoulders back and down, thinking tall and wide
- your feet apart and firmly placed on the ground

You need to practise this regularly until the stance feels natural.

Confidence jar

As our brains are designed to remember negative things much more than positive ones (in their attempt at keeping us safe), to feel successful, we need to build up evidence of our previous performances and skills so we can feel confident in using them. Having a list or a jar full of reminders of these great performances and skills can be a really good way to prompt us towards remembering our strengths, comebacks and previous successes.

Get a jar (anything jam-jar-sized or smaller is great) and twenty-six thin strips of paper. Write on the strips:

- five achievements of which you are really proud
- five setbacks you have overcome
- five compliments from others that made you feel good
- five challenges you have handled well
- five strengths you see in yourself (these could come from the strengths audit on page 62)
- one thing you love about yourself

Add to your jar each time you notice something you do well or you achieve something that you are proud of. And leave it somewhere you will regularly see it so you get to remember why you are on track to succeed.

Role models

Confidence can come from watching others succeeding, receiving verbal persuasion from those we respect and knowing those around you have your interests at heart. When we see those who are like us doing well, we can use them as role models:

1. Someone (who is similar to me) who I admire:

   _____

2. Something they do that I would like to replicate:

   _____

3. An approach they use that I would benefit from:

   _____

Confidence card

The two most robust sources of cultivated confidence are mastery and preparation so cultivated confidence comes from the knowledge that you have done all you can, that you have listened and learned, that you have put in the work and have left no stone unturned. A confidence card collates this information for us. It is best to complete your card a few days before any big challenge to remind yourself why you should be feeling good about what is possible. Any time you feel nervous, you can pull it out and read it through.

Goal for this challenge:	Technical reminder:
Motivational mantra (for when it gets tough):	Three sessions/events which have gone well in the build-up:
Three strengths that will help me perform well:	I perform at my best when...

6

Process-Driven

When you put process ahead of outcome, you can focus on the moment. This reduces stress, increases the number of successful strategies in your repertoire and allows you to perform at your best.

In the early years of the twenty-first century, when triathlon was a fairly new sport, Windsor regularly hosted the British national championships. It involved a 1,500-m swim in the Thames, followed by a 40-km bike ride across the Berkshire countryside and a 10-km run around the town. The culmination of each year's event was the professional race, with prize money and media coverage.

In 2003, seventeen of the nineteen competitors in the pro men's race started the swim strongly. Then leader Stuart Hayes, a phenomenal swimmer, turned around the wrong buoy and almost all the others followed, completing only half the swim course; they only learned of their disqualification after finishing the bike ride and the run. Two other competitors were so far behind in the swim that they didn't realize the others had turned early and swam the correct distance. They weren't disheartened that they were a long way behind – they just got their heads down and kept on going. When they got to the run portion, the fact that they were running laps meant they could easily see how far behind they were. But they ran at their own pace and kept on going to the finish line. Their process-driven approach meant that the eighteenth competitor to cross the line – an unknown Maltese athlete named Dermot Galea – won the race. In ignoring the outcome and focusing on his process, he achieved the biggest win of his career – and in this story there is a lesson for us all.

Processes are the small actions that we all implement to help us achieve our goals. It might seem counter-intuitive to focus on these rather than our big aims – surely it is the latter that inspire us to work harder? But the irony is that when we focus on the outcome rather than the process, our performance can fall apart and we are less likely to achieve our goal.

Studies on successful people in all areas of life have found that, while they generally have an ideal outcome in mind and have set goals for themselves, their day-to-day focus is on process. Having your eyes too firmly fixed on the prize might help you to set your sights high, but it won't help you to win. Fears will crowd your head and prevent you considering what is most important in the moment. We do need an ideal outcome in mind in order to progress in the right direction, but if we get too wrapped up in it, we forget to focus on getting things done. Think of it like climbing a mountain: just staring at the summit won't help you to climb it – you'd get neck-ache. In order to climb a mountain, you take lots of small steps and rest when necessary. Similarly, we have to focus on the processes that we know lead to success, trust that they work and follow them.

We think of the game of poker as being a strange mix of luck and skill. Success at poker seems far too glamorous to be a result of habit and process. Yet in this chapter we will learn all about the habits and processes of the game from a former player, Caspar Berry.

Caspar has had a fascinating and varied career. He started as an actor in Geordie teen soap *Byker Grove*, the show that made Ant and Dec famous. He then went to Cambridge to study economics, but with a side hustle of film directing. 'By twenty-six, I was working for Miramax and Disney and then I felt I wanted to do something different with my life and so I moved to Las Vegas and became a professional poker player – as you do.' He did that for three years before moving back to England. He is now a professional speaker and trainer, speaking about risk-taking and decision-making.

Putting Process First Is a Strategy for Success

Whether we are playing poker or racing a triathlon, the benefit of putting process first is that it helps us set and achieve more effective goals and maintain control over them. Goals set the tone for our day-to-day lives and provide us with structure. They turn our intentions into actions by showing us where to focus our attention, and this can help us be more successful. The purpose we worked on in Chapter 4 can direct us towards the right goals, while the confidence we discussed in Chapter 5 can help us feel like we deserve to reach them; in turn, process can help us approach those goals in the right way.

There are dozens of types of goals, but two examples are outcome goals (looking at how well we do) and process goals (the actions we take). Outcomes are usually trickier to control than actions. The outcome goal for a new runner might be to run 5 km in under thirty minutes, but their process goal might be to run five times a week. Outcome goals might feel more inspirational, but process goals are more actionable – and studies have shown that they are more satisfying. Outcome goals also tend to relate to things that are further in the future; working backwards from them and creating process goals to use in the meantime can help us stay motivated.

When we set process goals, we can plan more and our processing itself is improved. We are also more likely to achieve that elusive feeling of flow because we don't have to tune out the distractions of what other people are doing or the impact of things that we can't control – we just focus on ourselves, which makes it easier to become absorbed in our task. We don't frame our efforts in terms of 'win' or 'lose', but in terms of learning and improvement. This helps us to develop mastery and gives us control over what we are doing; the feeling of autonomy increases our motivation.

Let's consider this scenario. You are set to compete in a local 10-km race and would love to win it. Victory would give you bragging rights in your running club – you've seen previous winning times and think that, with a ton of effort, you could just about do it. You set an outcome goal: to win the race. You train extremely hard and feel incredibly fit and well prepared, but, on the morning of the race, there is a buzz at the start line – Mo Farah is in the area on a training camp and has decided to compete in your race. Unsurprisingly, he blasts his way around and sets a new course record. You are in the form of your life and have come second to an Olympic gold medallist, but you still feel like you've failed. You missed your goal and it feels like all your preparation has been in vain.

However, now imagine that your goal had been to train in a way you are proud of or to improve your personal best. Your second-place finish would have achieved both these goals and left you on a high. You'd have spotted Farah on the start line and instead of thinking, 'That's it – my goal's stuffed', you'd have been excited at the prospect of him dragging you round, improving your time in the process. And you'd also have a great story to tell your friends, of the day you raced an Olympian. The actual outcome would have been exactly the same, but the different goal would provide a very new perspective on the success of your effort and how you enjoyed the journey.

In poker, Caspar found that you can only really have process goals. And pretty boring ones at that. 'You can't force anything in poker,' he says. 'Any goal that you set yourself that had anything to do with any kind of outcome would be overcome by the events of the cards. Sometimes playing poker is very difficult. It is a real slog. So, sometimes, the process goal was just to put the hours in, just to turn up and do it. Obviously, you don't want to do a bad job, but to just keep going when it was tough. Just play well for eight hours when it was maybe the last thing you wanted to do. That would be the goal.'

Another good example of the benefits of process goals comes from a spinal cord unit in Perth, Australia. The recovery process followed by 100 patients was audited as they went through the unit's goal-planning service. They may have also had outcome goals, but their day-to-day goals focused on tiny processes that helped them feel like they were moving forward. The researchers found that the patients had an average of five and a half goal-setting meetings and each worked on eighty-five small and achievable goals that would help their rehabilitation. Patient feedback identified this process as a key component of their ability to adjust to their new situation.

As these patients found, when we focus on the journey and not just on the outcome, we learn as we go along and engage far more with the process. With our heads down and our focus fixed on an outcome goal, we might miss a lot along the way. Outcome goals yield short, sharp feedback – did you fail or succeed? Process goals, by contrast, continually incorporate feedback, leading to greater mastery. Studies have found that the better the feedback is when following a process goal, the better our performance and the more our confidence grows.

A good example of process-driven feedback comes from John Wooden, the legendary basketball coach from UCLA. When researchers studied his verbal behaviours as a coach, they found that at least 65 per cent of the comments he made during practice were specific statements about what players were doing at that moment and how they could improve in the future. Instead of saying, 'You need to practise more', he might say, 'If you spend thirty minutes a day over the next few weeks working on this drill, it will become a real strength.' He showed that by using challenging, process-driven goals and helpful feedback we can focus on the 'how' rather than on the 'what' – the target rather than the trophy.

When we focus on the trophy, we are unlikely to be satisfied for long – there's always another big race, another promotion or another deal. We do require outcomes to show us which course to set, but it is essential that everything then trickles down into our day-to-day processes. We can then find that, by focusing on the process of doing that thing brilliantly, the results tend to deliver themselves. We get a double benefit as lots of these smaller process goals result in regular hits of dopamine, our reward chemical, alongside that diligent progress towards our purpose.

Increasing Emotional Control

It is not just about goals – being process-driven is also fundamental to maintaining emotional control in all areas of life. As a performance psychologist, I see lots of people who feel that they are lacking the emotional control to perform at their best. This doesn't necessarily mean that they are smashing tennis racquets across the court in anger – they might be turning up to events, but not making it to the start line. They might be miserable after every round of golf because the second they miss an easy shot, they lose focus. Or they might even be sabotaging their own dreams because they don't want to risk failure. A lack of emotional control can be hugely disruptive in our lives and can really limit our ability to be successful. However, understanding what is going on in our brain and becoming more process-driven can make a big difference.

Brain zones

There are lots of ways to describe what goes on in our heads when we are trying to regulate our emotions, make good decisions and perform to the best of our ability. I tend to help my clients think about three key areas they need to consider: the habit zone, the logic zone and the threat zone.

Based in the parietal region of our brain (an area keenly focused on helping us integrate the information coming from our senses), the habit zone acts like a storage library, holding all of our habits. With a need to make around thirty-five thousand decisions every day, and many of these tiny ones, we want this area to do most of our day-to-day decision-making, probably around 90 per cent of it, leaving us free to use our cognition on more important things.

These more important things are managed in our brain's prefrontal cortex, which we can think of as our logic zone. It is rational, analytical and, when it wants to make a well-thought-out decision, it searches for facts, context and past experience before logically analysing what we should do. This part of our brain is great at both day-to-day decisions (what we should have for lunch or how many kilometres we should run), through to the really big stuff (whether to accept a job offer or if the person we are dating is the one to marry).

The tricky area is in our limbic region, which is our amygdala, and we can think of this area as our threat zone. It is a little like a parent who has wrapped their child in cotton wool. This highly sensitive area is attuned to threat and vital for our safety, but sometimes it becomes stifling, preventing you from stretching yourself and achieving new things. When you are out alone at night or with someone who doesn't feel trustworthy and hairs stand up on the back of your neck, that's your amygdala suggesting that you should get away quickly. It can be really helpful when we are faced with physical threats, but most threats today are those made to our sense of self, and the amygdala causing chaos at those times is not helpful at all.

Triggers of the threat zone

Fear

There are three types of fear that tend to trigger our amygdala. The first involves losing a key part of our identity, such as our reputation, our friends or our partner. These are all valid fears – these things matter hugely and, without them, we feel like a failure. As a result, we might avoid trying to achieve what we want because of the risk of embarrassment, negative comments or rejection if we fail. The second fear comes from processing the pain or effort it will take to achieve our goal. For instance, we might put off starting a fitness programme or changing our eating habits because we know that we'll have to go through some discomfort in the process. The third type of fear is anticipatory and concerns potential fallout from our desired outcomes; if we say yes to a date with someone we really fancy and it goes wrong, we'll feel distressed. If we go for a promotion and get it, we'll have to work longer hours and will miss being able to read our children a bedtime story. All three types of fear play on our sense of who we are.

Once we sense one of these fears, our amygdala jumps to conclusions and gets paranoid and irrational. It makes emotional and impulsive decisions based not on logic or facts, but on thoughts and feelings. As a result, it tends to hijack the way we would like to behave and pushes us to behave emotionally in order to deal with the perceived threat. It sends chemicals such as adrenaline and cortisol around our body, encouraging us to respond to the threat in one of four ways:

1. fight (getting aggressive)
2. flight (running away)
3. freeze (making ourselves small, out of sight)
4. fawn (pandering and trying to soothe those who might harm us)

These are often unsuitable responses; our rational self doesn't want us to run away or hide from a big opportunity, but our amygdala wants us to get the hell out of there. In response, it sets off chemicals around our body that can make us feel nauseous, increase our heart and breathing rates and tighten our muscles. We might feel as if we have a stomach full of fighting butterflies – the complete opposite of the relaxed and controlled vibe we would like in the face of a tricky situation.

When Caspar first went to Vegas, he knew the theory of poker – he had read thirty books on it – but he quickly realized that theory was not so helpful when in the cut and thrust of the game when it is played at speed. In one of his first matches he knew that he was on for a win. 'Basically, I know I've beaten him so I just do what's called "cap the raises". I just keep on raising. And the blood is pumping through my veins because I can't lose, so I'm so excited I'm almost offended that he's calling me.' But the cards turn over and Caspar has lost. 'He has got four of a kind, basically, he beats me.' Caspar, at that time, had no control over his amygdala. If he had, he may have been able to shrug and move on. Instead, he felt the entire world was against him. 'It was really difficult. I was trying to play poker for the first time for a living and he gets four of a kind. And he was really smug about it, he had a big smile on his face and he was behaving like he had played the hand well, as opposed to just getting lucky.'

He describes how his body felt when he saw this smugness. 'At a physical level, the blood is boiling up in my chest into my shoulders and up into my head. It feels like my whole head is filled with boiling blood. That is what it feels like. And it feels like your senses – which I now understand – are being closed down so that my body can fight or flight, you know, so it can react physically. I get all that now rationally, but in 2000, all I felt was the blood boiling so high and so hot that I can't see or hear straight because my eyes and ears are full of blood. That is how it feels.'

When we start out doing something new, as Caspar was in this case, our confidence has yet to build and we might have fairly low self-esteem. This can make our threat zone our default status and that's when we turn to external factors – such as outcomes – for validation, in order to give ourselves a confidence boost. External validation comes in the form of outcomes that are easily measurable: exam results, goals scored or social media 'likes', which may help us feel better in the short term, but also ignore the importance of the processes that helped us get there. The judgement that comes with these externally measured metrics can trigger our threat zone so we lose our emotional control and don't perform in the way we would like because we are not focusing on the things that are important. If we gain an understanding of what triggers us – if we put some of those things that our amygdala set off into processes and practice – we make life more controllable and less dramatic.

Comparisons

One of the key triggers is comparing ourselves to others. Caspar was clear that, while most film and drama depictions of poker try to make it about conflict between two individuals, he knew that he couldn't afford to compare himself to others. If he did, he was done for. 'You still have this idea that James Bond could possibly produce his straight flush in that key hand in the showdown with his adversary. It is just a nonsense. You don't get to decide when your good hands are in poker. You cannot afford to have a nemesis in poker. You just have to keep focusing on the moment. The idea that you can have a grudge against someone else or, even more destructively, that you can consider that the US\$2,000 that you lost to this person is really yours and you are going to win it back, takes you away from optimal play.'

Comparison can occasionally give us the encouragement we need to see that we are wasting our time; that if we had spent an hour every day learning French rather than scrolling through Twitter, we too would be able to speak it fluently. Or that if we had done twenty minutes of strength and conditioning work after each run, we would be as fast as our peers and not sitting on the physio table. It can also give us a bit of vicarious confidence; the feeling that 'they're like me and they've managed it, so maybe I could too' (see page 129). But most of the time comparison does nothing more than suck the joy out of our situation. We are unique, with different genes, personalities, purpose, stressors, experiences and environments; comparing outcomes is pretty meaningless. When we focus on ourselves and our own processes, rather than enviously looking at what others have achieved, we soon see it is our own satisfaction and pride that matter – and we can achieve that by becoming process-driven.

Expectations

Another big threat zone trigger is expectation, whether actual or perceived. If we learn not to care about outcomes, we can take the pressure off ourselves; focusing on processes is a way of dampening our outcome-related expectations. Parents assume that their child will win their sports matches, teachers expect certain students to pass their exams and bosses have assumptions about who will follow in their footsteps; such expectations are usually intended to be supportive, but we often interpret them as threats – from the threat zone's perspective, where there are expectations there's also the risk of letting people down, and that means it's easier not to try.

Perfectionism

A key trigger we often see in high performers is perfectionism. A double-edged sword, perfectionism motivates us to strive to be the best and to work hard towards achieving ambitious goals, but it is impossible to achieve and consequently we inevitably feel as if we are failing. Perfectionism turns our outcome goals into expectations – we focus on a validated, external outcome and missing that goal will mean failure. Every potential failure risks triggering us and we lose not only our emotional control, but also our perspective about what we have achieved. We end up only seeing the gap between where we are and perfection, rather than between where we were and where we have got to, and this hinders our performance.

In preparation for a big event or performance, perfectionism can be helpful in making us focus on tiny elements of our skills until we find it hard to get them wrong. Such 'perfectionistic strivings' can be beneficial as they prompt us to be conscientious, follow processes and use mastery goals. But the other element of perfectionism is more negative; 'perfectionistic concerns' mean that we focus our attention on mistakes and discrepancies between our expectations and real-life performance. This leads to obsessively avoiding mistakes, greater amounts of self-criticism and more concerns about being judged by others – all incredibly unhelpful elements of a performance environment.

Perfectionism can mean that you feel that you have failed before you have got going. You can't just start again to make sure you get something 'just so' in an art exam, in a new business pitch or during an on-stage performance. Nor can you not react to what is going on in the environment around you, whether that's the fire alarm that goes off during a job interview, the colleague who makes inappropriate comments in a meeting or the streaker who runs on to the pitch during a match. We end up developing self-defeating outcomes and unhealthy patterns of behaviour that prompt us to see everything as black and white, instead of taking in the bigger picture – and we miss acknowledging skills we have learned or progress we have made.

Perfectionism also holds us back from taking risks because it makes mistakes feel like personal flaws. This may keep us safe, but it won't help us progress towards success. However, by remaining process-driven we can reduce the impact of perfectionism and the threat of expectations and of comparison with others, limiting our threat responses. The word to watch out for is 'should'. When we find ourselves regularly suggesting that we 'should' be able to do things, unrealistic and unhelpful expectations have sneaked in. If we focus instead on practising and dealing with pressure, over time those actions start to sit within our habit zone; we are thus able to use the energy we have to make rational decisions and not threat-focused ones. When our logic zone is in control, we are able to interpret the feelings in our tummy more effectively; the butterflies are no longer fighting, but instead are flying in formation. This makes what is ahead of us a great challenge to take on rather than a scary threat to be avoided.

You Never Lose If You Learn

Hundreds of researchers around the world are trying to understand how we acquire new skills and they usually agree that there is a five-step process: watching, copying, following the process until we feel comfortable with it, adapting and personalizing it into a wider environment, and then doing it automatically. The first three stages are process-driven; if we focus on outcome too early, we'll be bypassing the process we need to learn. We learn well in these early stages because we aren't trying to perform – we just want to get better at something. Process enhances our acquisition of skills and makes us feel more positive about being able to use them.

I have been fortunate enough to cycle with and interview Dame Sarah Storey, DBE. She is probably one of the most process-driven people I've ever met and she's also the most decorated. She began her career in professional sport as a swimmer; after winning six World Championships and five Paralympic medals, she switched to cycling. In this second sport, she has been the British able-bodied track champion six times, and paracycling World Champion twenty-three times on the track and sixteen times on the road. She has also won another twelve Paralympic gold medals, making her the most successful female British Paralympian of all time. I will never forget her telling me that, although she likes winning, she learns more when she loses. She has an insatiable hunger to improve and values the races she doesn't win, which give her performances to reflect on and learn from.

This approach is so refreshing and might have contributed to her being at the top of her field for so long. Having this 'you never lose if you learn' approach allows Storey to take something from every interaction in life – for her, everything will either be positive or a way to make progress. In poker, you need that long-term perspective too. You have to be process-driven with a big-picture perspective says Caspar. 'At the simplest level, in order to make a long-term return on investment when you are playing poker, you have to be prepared, emotionally, to lose games in the short term. And that is very difficult, initially. When you are playing poker, you are out of control of your short-term results. Therefore, it is one of the few jobs in the world you can go out and do a great day's work, play out of your skin and lose money. Conversely, you can make a lot of mistakes and make money because fortune favours you that evening. You have to immunize yourself to those swings. That is an incredible learning to take into the rest of your life.'

Maintaining Motivation

Finally, focusing on the journey rather than on the arbitrary staging posts we pass along the way means that we enjoy life more. And when we are happier, we tend to do better. If we love the destination, but not the journey, we will spend a lot of time being miserable. For instance, if we don't enjoy running, but want the experience of running a marathon, we will miserably run between 600 and 700 miles in training and only enjoy the 26.2 miles on the actual day – not a great ratio! If we want to publish a book, but don't love writing, we'll spend a gloomy six months tapping away at a laptop, and if the book doesn't become a bestseller we'll think that it was a waste of time. If we don't love our academic subject and resent the time spent revising topics that don't come up in an exam, we will feel like our effort was for nothing. If we love running, writing or our subject, it won't matter – we'll still feel like we have spent our time valuably.

When we focus our efforts on an outcome, we are extrinsically motivated, contracting with ourselves to be miserable until our effort pays off and we get what we want. In sport, this result might be represented by a trophy or prize money. In a career, it might be a promotion or a pay rise. Instead, imagine contracting yourself to do things that make you happy – that is what we can achieve with process-driven practice, and it comes from intrinsic motivation.

Intrinsic motivation requires three psychological processes that you'll recognize as also making up our first three pillars: a sense of belonging, mastery and autonomy. If we have these three elements in place, we'll find things we love doing and want to do them simply for the joy of it. Outcome won't matter. And, when we are powered by this type of motivation, we persist for longer when the going gets tricky, focusing on the satisfaction we get from the process rather than just the potential rewards.

I once asked a former Premiership footballer how he felt when he was transferred to a lower-league team. He replied that he didn't care – as long as he got to play football, he was happy. He had such an innate love of the game that it was far more important to him than the trophies, the pay packet and the kudos. He had intrinsic motivation.

When we have intrinsic motivation, we can get into what is called a 'flow state' – the feeling that we are doing an activity for the joy of it and not expecting to get anything out of it. In sport that might be the feeling of playing, or when writing we might lose sight of the overall aim, but instead find pleasure in the method of helping the words find their way on to the page. We achieve flow when the demands of an activity match our capability. If we don't have a specific outcome in mind, we can always feel capable.

When there is an outcome ahead, the demands we feel upon us can seem greater than our capabilities; too much extrinsic motivation can be harmful for our love of what we do. When we have to constantly strive for external validation, we lose our internal passion, becoming focused on the outcome and ignoring the processes. As a result, we are unable to develop, and everything feels like harder work. Focusing on process helps us get an intrinsic value from what we do.

If we set the right type of goals, increase the emotional control we exercise over comparing ourselves to others and the ways in which we set expectations, we will benefit from a process-driven life that will result in us learning more and stressing less.

Developing a Process-Driven Approach

Staying process-driven is not easy. Many Western cultures look for winners and losers in the way we express ourselves through day-to-day language and in the media. Even our conversations with friends focus on traditional and outdated versions of success, where outcome is everything. The question 'How did you do?' inevitably greets the golfer returning to the clubhouse after a round, the actress coming off stage or the student finishing their final exams. Each is likely to respond with a score, a judgement or a potential outcome. 'I hit par', 'I got three curtain calls' or 'I screwed it up'. We rarely reply, 'I loved it – and nailed that tricky fourteenth hole', 'I felt the tingle of flow during my soliloquy' or 'I worked through each question slowly and did my best'. Yet, when we focus on the process, we can learn much more and benefit from using the pillars we discussed earlier to help us move towards success.

Focus on the 'how' rather than the 'what'

To keep a focus on the target rather than on the trophy, we need to prioritize the 'how' over the 'what'. Caspar had to take this into account constantly and explains how he had to make continuous calculations. 'You are trying to do the right thing for the long term, but by focusing on the short term. Let's imagine that you have four hearts in your hand. If you have five hearts, you make a flush. You are not definitely going to win if you have a flush, but are pretty likely to. It's a good hand. And you can do a calculation that will tell you that you are 20 per cent likely to hit another heart to make a flush. So that's not very likely, right? It is much more likely that you won't make it. But if the pot is offering you ten to one, so one in five times (20 per cent) you are going to make ten times your money – then you are going to make a profit. And you need to be prepared to call in that situation, knowing that you are going to lose 80 per cent of the time.'

Like Caspar, we focus on the 'how' over the 'what' through purposeful goal-setting. We can have an outcome goal, as that will give us the inspiration to keep going, but we should try to relate it to our purpose in some way, so we know why and what we are working towards. This means that an outcome goal might be based on a competition, event or assessment we want to do well in, not simply for the ego-driven joy of achieving our aim, but because it helps us to move closer towards our purpose. It also gives us some optimism which, as we will learn in Chapter 8, can help us to focus.

We can really reduce the pressure and other negative aspects of an outcome goal by selecting a goal that is not focused on comparisons with others. Instead, we might think about more intrinsic outcome goals concerning the environment (making the world a better place), fulfilment (using our skills to help others) or development (focusing on long-term mastery).

We can work out what kind of performance we have to put on to achieve our outcome goal, whether that comes in the form of a positive appraisal at work, running a particular time in training or attending a certain number of auditions. We all require a target that demonstrates we are making progress. The most important step to then take is to break these performances into process goals: the behaviours, actions, strategies or tactics we will need to use to achieve them. Positive appraisals at work might require us to give at least one presentation a month or to mentor a new member of staff. An improved run time might require two track sessions every week and the addition of a strength and conditioning workout into our schedule. Attending four auditions a month might keep our skills topped up and means we don't get so anxious when the important ones come up. Introducing such processes will put us in control and lower our expectations; if we make the effort and want them enough, we will prioritize and put them in place. In an ideal world, we then forget about outcome goals and give our attention to those process goals, helping us progress while keeping our mind on the 'how'.

This works just as well in the build-up to a race, perform-ance review, audition or exam, as it does in the event itself. As a result, every time we feel the pressure of expectation or fear weighing us down, we have a comeback: 'I'm focusing on my "how" and that's what will make me successful.' These process goals make it easier for us to be passionate about progress rather than perfection. If we wait until a plan is perfect or only take the next step when we've perfected the last, we'll never move forward. Perfection slows down our progress and suppresses our passion. Next time, rather than questioning whether something is perfect, ask yourself, 'Is this progress?' Progress gives us permission to accept what we are doing and take the next step. This will ensure that we benefit from the dopamine buzz that comes through seeking and finding rewards.

Establish a routine

The most demanding ask is that we establish more emotional control over our brain. We need to put as much of our lives into the hands of our brain's habit and logic zones, reducing the likelihood of our threat zone being triggered. Processes fit into our habit zone well – we repeat them over and over until they become part of what we do. Following a routine can help embed these processes and, as we learned in Chapter 5, it also has the benefit of increasing our confidence (see page 138). The warm-up routine we see footballers or rugby players running through ahead of kick-off or the swimmer marching out on to the swim deck with great big headphones, immersed in their performance playlist, creates a sense of control, reminding the athletes that they are following their process.

When the process is task-focused, it doesn't just help you feel in control, but also helps you move towards your purpose. For instance, a basketball player might bounce the ball a certain number of times before play to help them get into the right rhythm. Or a runner might slap their legs before a race to boost their adrenaline and speed up their heart rate, getting them ready to perform. These actions build helpful processes into preparing for events, resulting in a feeling of readiness and an ability to focus on the moment rather than the outcome.

When we know that we have something big or horrible to do, routine keeps us process-focused. In the build-up, we get anticipatory anxiety running around our bodies. A small action to take in response is 'eating the frog'. Eating the frog involves looking through your to-do list and picking the scariest activity on there and doing it first, getting it out of the way. The action, coined by the motivational speaker Brian Tracy, highlights the fact that we don't just have to do daunting tasks, but we must also live with anticipatory anxiety. Getting the fear out of the way early means that the weight of anticipatory stress can be relieved.

Name your inner voice

Another helpful tactic to keep ourselves process-driven and thinking rationally is to remind ourselves that we are not our thoughts. We sometimes try different, fearful thoughts on for size, wondering, 'Do I think this?' or 'Would this work?' – and those thoughts often come from our threat zone; it wants to scare us off trying something new and risking that we might feel embarrassed or fail. If we distance ourselves from those thoughts, we can have a more helpful perspective and become braver.

To do this, it can be helpful to give your amygdala a name. Some people choose a variant of their name or a nickname they dislike, while others use TV characters or famous people they can imagine keeping them from doing what they love. When it has a name, we can assign the difficult thought to them. Mine is 'Jo', a name that I haven't been called since school and really dislike being called. Whenever I have thoughts that are clearly coming from my threat zone, I assign them to Jo and we have a chat. 'I might fail, Jo,' I think, 'but I'm OK with that. It matters more to me that I tried.' Or, 'I know they're late and you think that means they don't care about me, Jo, but it's more likely that they just got stuck in traffic.'

You can take this distancing idea further still; as well as assigning those tricky thoughts to Jo, I can change the way in which I think about them, going from, 'I'm a rubbish runner', to 'Jo thinks I'm a rubbish runner', to 'I'm noticing that Jo thinks I'm a rubbish runner.' When I move the thought several steps away from reality, it loses its sting. Caspar calls it getting perspective: 'Perspective is literally dislocating yourself from the immediacy of the moment when things are huge in the foreground, so they feel much smaller in the background.'

Identify your triggers

We also need to get to know our threat zone. What does it think? What sets it off? Mine is triggered by feeling disrespected (often if someone arrives late) and envy of those who are doing better than I am. These beliefs hardly paint me in a flattering light, but being aware of them means that, whenever I get into one of those situations, I am hyper-alert that Jo is likely to kick up a stink. As a result, I can work on keeping the 'logic' part of my brain in control.

Changing our breathing technique can be very helpful when we fear our threat zone is about to be triggered. We normally breathe about twelve to fifteen times a minute, but, when in the threat zone, that can increase to a panicky twenty gasps. 'Colourful breathing' is my favoured method (instructions are in the toolkit at the end of this chapter – see page 172) and I find it can take me down to about five breaths per minute. Whenever you feel your threat zone triggering, this process can take you away from the scary, threatening outcomes and back to simple actions you can take to stay in control.

As we saw earlier, comparisons are one of the biggest triggers – every time we compare ourselves with someone else, we see what they have and often find some form of threat in it; that we are not as good, clever, attractive, kind, fit, educated or rich, for example. To reduce the effect of the threat we perceive in other people, we can think about who we are comparing ourselves with and educate ourselves about impression management.

Find people you know well on social media and look at what they post online. Do their timelines mention the fight they had with their other half about whose turn it was to put out the bins or the state of their living room with two toddlers rampaging? I'll bet not. Instead, the focus will be on a date night with their partner and their toddlers looking cute in the park. We share the stuff we want other people to think about us, and it's rarely the real stuff. The more we see both sides, the more we can take things online with a pinch of salt and learn to give ourselves a break.

Focus on what you can control

Getting to know your threat zone is helpful because outcome-based goals – whether passing an exam, getting a new job or winning a new customer – have uncontrollable elements that can trigger it. Worrying about outcome-based goals will hinder rather than help you, as there's nothing you can do about them. You waste energy that you could use to revise for the exam, prep for the interview or practise your sales pitch. You need a process to stay focused on the elements you can actually influence. This is called 'control mapping'. You may have completed one in the toolkit for Chapter 2 (page 61)?

Control mapping is a way of identifying all the different things that could impact our performance, before looking through the list and working out what we can and can't change. We can't control what an interviewer thinks of us, but we can control whether we turn up looking professional and enthusiastic. We can't control whether a potential client will choose our business, but we can offer a great service, positive references and a welcoming demeanour. When we understand which areas we can and can't influence, we are then able to focus on the places where we can make a difference. One list we can completely ignore (elements we can't control) and the other we can focus on (those we can).

This type of filtering is essential in poker says Caspar. 'In poker we know what we cannot control. We cannot control the cards. So you play the hand you are dealt, that old cliché. There is nothing we can do to control them. And therefore, we can forget about them. And you forget about the long-term results because there is nothing you can do about them. You can only control what you can control. You must create an almost zen-like indifference to the things that you can't control. Because every moment spent focusing and worrying about them is a moment wasted. And that is about being outcome-focused. I think, in poker, being process-driven is all about focusing on that which you can control.'

Break things down

To help us focus on process over outcome we can break down big things into smaller, more manageable parts that feel less intimidating and more achievable. In a marathon, this would mean thinking about the eight and a half parkruns we will be tackling as we stand on the start line, rather than the far more intimidating 26.2 miles ahead of us. Then we can have a strategy for each 3-mile chunk; maybe a friend will be on the sidelines cheering during one of them, or a particularly good song will come on through our headphones during another. Project managers do this all the time in business – breaking down huge projects into teams, subsections and specific project groups. Writers break books down into chapters and stage directors break plays into scenes. We can use this 'chunking' to become more process-driven and to tackle every activity that has the potential to set off our threat zone.

Analyse your losses

Finally, if we focus on the idea exemplified by Dame Sarah Storey – that we can win or we can learn – we may see a positive in everything we do, even if the outcome doesn't go the way we hoped. We can analyse our performance following any big activity, whether an exam, a competition, a pitch or an interview. There is a 'win or learn' template to help you do this in the toolkit below. It may not put us in line for thousands of dollars in a casino, but by using this type of process in our own world, we'll learn more, get closer to achieving our goal and, slowly but surely, move towards success.

PROCESS-DRIVEN TOOLKIT

Amygdala distancing

Processes such as reminding ourselves that our amygdala offers us thoughts not facts, naming it, observing its messages and actively distancing ourselves from it all help to manage our threat zone better so we maintain emotional control.

- My amygdala is called:
- If I were to imagine it as a character or creature it would be a:
- Three things my amygdala regularly says to me:

    1. _____

    2. _____

    3. _____

- Three messages I could give back to my amygdala to soothe and calm it:

    1. _____

    2. _____

    3. _____

Colourful breathing

Colourful breathing is a great technique to calm yourself down when your amygdala has been triggered and you are having an unhelpful threat response. It is short and easy to do, but also really effective. It means that you get oxygen deeper into your lungs and it refreshes your posture. You can use it any time you feel under stress – exams, a big social event, dealing with an argument – and it is also a great technique to help you fall asleep if you are struggling with insomnia. To do it effectively, you need about one minute.

- First off, pick two colours. They could be your favourite two colours or the colours of your favourite sports team. Here, just as an example, we'll use blue and red.
- Think about your lungs finishing just behind your belly button. You'll want to see your tummy going in and out as you do this activity.
- Breathe in through your nose as you count to four. Imagine that the air that is going into your nose is hot red air.
- Hold the air behind your belly button for a count of two.
- Breathe out cool blue air through your month as you count to six.
- Repeat four or five times, until you feel calmer.

This exercise works because, when you focus on the colours you are imagining breathing in, you stop focusing on the anxious thoughts running around your brain. And the purposeful slow breathing helps to break the cycle of physical anxiety in your body.

Win or learn analysis

Complete this analysis the day after a big challenge or event. (If you do it straight after it will be too full of emotion.) To fill in your top boxes think about:

- how mentally or physically fit you were
- the skills you used
- the tactics you used
- the preparation you did
- how the logistics worked
- any equipment used
- the mental approach taken

What went well?	Would have gone better if...
1.	1.
2.	2.
3.	3.
4.	4.
5.	5.
Will keep doing:	**Will change:**
ACTION PLAN	

If you keep all your win or learn analysis sheets, you can look back over them at the start of each year to spot any patterns, which can help you set your goals for the next year.

Goal-setting

Great goal-setting sees us set one motivating outcome goal that we then break down into performances we will need to achieve along the way and a number of actions and processes that need to be put in place to make the magic happen. Setting goals like this helps us change any behaviours which are currently holding us back and helps us focus on the ways that will improve our performance. There are three layers:

1. The first goal to set is the outcome goal. They often involve doing better than others so are usually very motivating, but not that controllable.

2. Next come the performance goals. These are much more controllable because they just focus on us and what we can achieve. Our performances feed into the outcome goal, so if we achieve our performance goals, we would be likely to achieve our outcome goal too. But even if we don't, we will still have mastered much more of our area than we would have otherwise.

3. The process goals are the key to success. Drawn from our performance goals, they specify the behaviours, actions, strategies and tactics we need to follow and incorporate into our day-to-day lives. Repeating these actions means that eventually they stop being choices and become habits. By using these challenging, process-driven goals and helpful feedback we focus on the 'how' rather than on the 'what'; the target rather than the trophy.

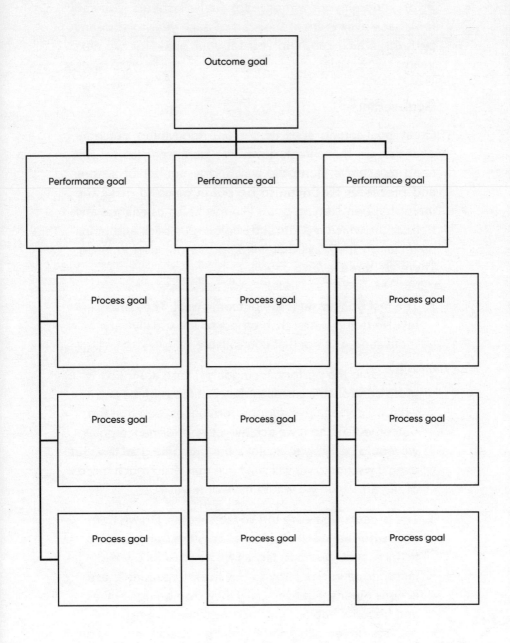

7

Courage

To be successful, you need to leave your comfort zone and act bravely. Understanding your motivations and preparing for obstacles means that you can calibrate a courageous attitude.

In February 2022, as Russia invaded Ukraine, the US offered Ukrainian president, Volodymyr Zelensky, evacuation to safety. He turned down the offer and stayed to fight for his country. As a young activist for human rights, Pakistan-born Malala Yousafzai wrote in her BBC blog that she believed that girls should be allowed to study and in 2012 was shot in the head by a Taliban gunman as a result of her declaration. An unknown protestor stood in front of a column of tanks leaving Tiananmen Square in 1989 as the Chinese military suppressed student protests – what happened to him is not known. In 1955, activist Rosa Parks refused to give up her seat on a bus to a white person, as demanded by the state of Alabama's racial segregation laws, and is now remembered as America's 'first lady of civil rights'.

These are all people we think of when we talk about courage – powerful images of doing what is right, of following purpose and passion, and of going above and beyond what is expected for the good of others. Most of us will never need to stand up to President Putin, a gunman, a tank or enforced segregation, but how would we react if we did? Would we be able to assess our fears and potential repercussions and take that courageous step?

In our own lives, we might need courage to start a new business, to take yet another driving test or to stop trying for children after years of failed IVF attempts. We might need it when we have given our all to a relationship that fails and decide to start dating again. We need courage whenever we want to use our voice, time and effort to strive for something that's important to us.

One of my favourite quotes, from the American author John A. Shedd, reminds me of the importance of courage: 'A ship in harbor is safe, but that is not what ships are built for.' It is a brilliant reminder that we must get out of our comfort zone. Sitting passively in a safe and calm environment does not match my purpose in life or align with my values, and this quote reminds me that, whenever I feel stung by criticism, it is not a mistake to try to do something. As Aristotle is reported to have said, 'Criticism is something you can easily avoid – by saying nothing, doing nothing and being nothing.' We can stay safe, but only if we stand still. And I'm confident that if you were satisfied by the thought of standing still, it is unlikely that you would be reading this book.

We need courage – in fact, it's essential if we are to develop any of the other pillars discussed in this book. We need to feel like we belong with other people and, to do so, we must be brave enough to reveal our vulnerability, approach others and bond with them. To develop mastery, we must first admit to ourselves that we want to become brilliant at something. We sometimes need to assert ourselves to ensure that we are able to make that all-important choice and to know that our voices are heard. If we want to know our purpose in life or to develop confidence and optimism, we require courage. Staying focused, rather than daydreaming, requires courage too. It's hard to focus on gaining internal insight, but when we do so we get beyond our comfort zone; we can then address weaknesses.

Often, we are not talking about huge acts of bravery, the once-in-a-lifetime actions that win awards, an invitation to meet royalty or a newspaper headline. We probably won't be standing up to a gunman, but we might be standing up to a friend who has opinions we disagree with. Most often, we are likely to be facing day-to-day obstacles when, instead of pushing ourselves forward, we hold ourselves back, whether from fear, low self-esteem or a worry that we'll be ostracized. Sometimes holding back might be the right thing to do, but much of the time we regret what we didn't do rather than what we did. When we understand what bravery is, how it grows and what processes we can use to face our fears head-on, we can maximize our chance of success.

As far back as the fourth century BC, philosophers have highlighted how bravery applies not just to big-ticket, heroic activities, but also to the quiet determination that fuels our attempt to live in a way that matches our values and our purpose. As the Confucian philosopher Mencius noted, bravery is not just a physical thing, like climbing a mountain, fighting on a battlefield or facing a tiger in a jungle, but equally applies to feeling able to live a meaningful life that engenders self-respect. Acting bravely is doing what we feel we need to do even though we fear it, and even if the consequences could leave us worse off.

What one person will require courage for will feel easy for another; the distinction comes in what each of us has to lose: our pride, our purpose, our job or our friends. The trigger that causes us to be brave might be a threat to our identity or a value that we feel strongly about. Seeing someone cheat, witnessing discrimination in the workplace or spotting unethical business practices all require us to stand up and do the right thing. We don't require physical courage very often, but we regularly need moral and mental courage. As US president Theodore Roosevelt once suggested, 'Knowing what's right doesn't mean much unless you do what's right.'

One person who just cannot risk getting it wrong is Bobby Holland Hanton. As a former elite gymnast and now stunt performer who can be seen in some of Hollywood's biggest blockbusters, such as *Thor*, *Extraction* and James Bond movies, he has the courage to make moves most of us would never even contemplate. 'Every single stunt that I've ever done where there's any kind of element of danger – I always feel scared. I would be lying if I said that I didn't. I can only speak for myself, but that element of fear is 100 per cent there. I channel that fear into focus and the adrenaline takes over.'

Bobby has found ways to see the fear as a benefit: 'The fear means you care. There is something inside you that you don't want to make a mistake. That's what that fear is – you don't want to fail, you don't want to mess it up – and it is natural to have that fear. It's just that you have to try to channel that the best way you possibly can by just remembering that we have been here before, we know we can do this, we've prepped it, we've rehearsed it.' But the fear, he says, looks after him. 'The day I lose that fear,' he says, 'is the day that I need to quit and retire.'

What Is Courage?

We show courage when we purposefully choose to do something that scares us in order to achieve a greater purpose. We haven't been pushed to act – we have deliberated over the choice and freely make it. We may well be aware that we are taking a risk, but we feel that the potential outcome for wider society is worth it. It is not just about doing what is right, but about doing what is right when under pressure to act differently.

Physical courage means acting in the knowledge that we could get hurt if it goes wrong. That hurt can come in the form of pain, danger or even loss of life. A wonderful story regularly shared on social media tells of a set of twins, one of whom was really ill and in desperate need of a blood transfusion from her brother. When the parents asked him if he would do it to save his sister's life, he thought for a while and agreed. It was only when he was about to have his blood taken and asked his parents when he would die that they realized that he thought he would be giving up his life for his twin. It wasn't the act of giving blood that was courageous, but the fact that he did it thinking his own death would be the outcome.

Whether this story is true or an urban myth, it is popular because we all love to see examples of self-sacrificing courage. Sometimes we need to push our own physical boundaries and become courageous through devotion to an ambition; to see what is possible, like Bobby did in his first movie role, *Quantum of Solace*, where he stunt-doubled for James Bond – Daniel Craig. 'It was a night shoot. It was two in the morning. We were three storeys up in the slums of Panama and it was a balcony jump from one side to the other and it was probably about a 7-m distance. As soon as I heard, "Let's get Bobby ready", I jumped to my feet. I'm like, "OK, this is my chance to put myself on the map, my first ever stunt." I jump from one balcony to the other, land and go through the door. As I go through the door I'm like, "That went well", 'cos I had no safety, no safety mats, no wires, no nothing. When we shot it and when I landed, I heard everyone in the crew give me a round of applause and I was like, "Wow, this is it. This is what I've trained for my whole life."'

Courage isn't always physical, though. Moral courage comes when we act because of values we believe in, values that are suited to a purpose greater than ourselves. The risks relating to moral courage tend to involve social or economic hardship: job loss, poverty, bullying, isolation or ostracism.

Physical and moral courage share two key themes. The first is vulnerability; we must open up about how we feel, not knowing whether it will be reciprocated. The second is the willingness to endure difficulty and to persist. The two types of courage differ in terms of what is at stake. Physical courage is usually short-lived; a burst of action followed by an instant result. Moral courage, however, can live with us for a long time if we are fighting injustice.

It is not the act itself that defines whether or not courage is required, but what we have to lose as a result of doing it or the sense of danger we feel. Individual circumstances make a huge difference. Someone with social anxiety would need vast amounts of courage to walk into an awards ceremony, while someone with bags of confidence would be able to just rock up without a second thought. Someone in the depths of depression would need courage just to get out of bed in the morning but, once recovered, that person would see the same action as a simple habit.

Although courage is an individual matter, it is influenced by our culture. In environments where we are taught to put up and shut up, the risk of speaking out is higher than in those where safety is prioritized over individual embarrassment. Imagine a firefighter knowing that it could be harmful to the Chief Fire Officer's authority to speak out about a safety issue when lives are at risk. Or a nurse who doesn't wish to upset a surgeon during surgery, while being aware that if they don't speak up, the patient will inadvertently be harmed.

This tightrope that we walk requires integrity. Having a strong set of values helps us decide when to be brave and, if we have integrity, we are able to commit to our values through thick and thin, enhancing our courage. We can then design a more courageous lifestyle for ourselves, standing up and taking risks, even when we feel vulnerable. And this approach brings with it a greater chance of success in whatever we want to do.

Bobby has to regularly take this approach: 'There is always that moment where you get that part in your mind telling you that you shouldn't do this: this is dangerous. Where you get that stomach flip. I think to push through that barrier is by having the courage to go for it and commit to it 100 per cent, whatever the outcome may be.' Bobby has found that, thankfully, it usually works out OK. 'It is never as bad as you thought it was going to be.'

The doubts are part of the journey, and each time Bobby has worked to overcome them by looking back at where he has overcome those doubts before. 'Courage is dealing with all of that anxiety and fear and just knowing that everything will be OK. You just draw on rehearsals, you draw on your experience of making it right to get to the point of actually stepping forward and going for it. They give you a sense of confidence to be able to say, "I've done this once – I can do it again."'

Courage is a powerful partner of the other pillars

The pillars in this book have dozens of benefits. Courage may have fewer obvious advantages, but those that do exist are enormous. And most of them involve supporting the other pillars that are crucial to helping us achieve success. One, in particular, is the sense of belonging, as courage helps us develop and sustain relationships, ensuring that we are aware of the importance of a sense of community. Our bravery demonstrates openness; this is required to maintain close relationships, ensuring we remain authentic.

A stunt double's relationship with 'their' actor is key, not just to do a good job but to make the process more enjoyable. Bobby has found this in his work with Chris Hemsworth. So far, they have made thirteen movies together and developed a strong relationship. 'He is one of my closest friends. I want to do the best job I can do for him. I'm employed to be his stunt double, I'm employed to make sure he is safe, I'm employed to make sure he looks the best that he possibly can. So, there is that sense of that loyalty to a friend, and you want to do the best you can for them and make them look the best they can. I'm not just doing it for me, I'm doing it for them as well. We are doing it as a team.'

Another key factor in courage is purpose; when we stand up and fight for our purpose the results can be life-changing. One person who has highlighted this in recent years is Rose McGowan, the Hollywood actress who bravely accused the powerful movie mogul Harvey Weinstein of rape. She knew that speaking out about her abuse would lead to her being ostracized in the industry and ripped to shreds in the media, and yet, in October 2017, she courageously spoke up to protect other women from sexual harassment. By the end of that month, more than eighty other women had amplified her allegations with their own against the same man.

McGowan didn't just go for Weinstein; she was brave enough to call out the actors who had ignored the toxic environment their female colleagues had endured and the studios for their complicity in 'rape culture'. In doing so, she inspired the #RoseArmy and #MeToo campaigns, with women all over the world sharing their stories of sexual assault and abuse in the workplace. Her bravery kicked off a revolution in Hollywood and, when the women's voices became too loud to ignore, Weinstein was arrested, charged, convicted and sentenced to twenty-three years in jail. McGowan knew that speaking out would destroy her career, but she did it anyway. As she hit the headlines, the film critic Scott Weinberg reflected on Twitter: 'Ever seen a movie where one person takes on a corrupt, powerful system all by herself? That's @rosemcgowan & it's not a movie.'

These acts of bravery don't just happen in Hollywood; in January 2019, when abortion was first legalized in Ireland, women were faced with activists picketing their medical facilities. A Twitter hashtag began trending – #SiulLiom, from the Irish for 'I walk with her'. Hundreds of people offered to accompany women to clinics to stop them being intimidated by protestors.

As these examples highlight, our ability to see ourselves and other people being courageous shows that the characteristic has another benefit – it is contagious. The more we stand up for what we believe in and see that the sky hasn't come falling down as a result, the more we feel able to do it again. When we notice other people being brave, we want to behave in a similar manner, standing up to fight for what we believe in.

I love how Bobby uses this infectious quality in his work; to build his own bravery after each take, even after he had to face gruelling surgery for an injury. 'I've had a bad back since I was a gymnast. But this time round was a huge back surgery. I had double disc replacement at L4, L5 level, two titanium discs and six screws and a caging at my lower back. I knew it was going to be a big surgery. And going into the surgery there was that doubt of, "Am I going to be able to do what I did before? Am I going to be able to what I do to the highest level?"'

In his first movie after the surgery, he required extra courage. 'I hit the ground, I rolled across the ground, I stood up and was like, "Wow, I'm actually OK. It wasn't that bad." I busted my arm up a little bit – but a very small amount – but as far as my back was concerned – I was like, "OK, that was

great." And then we did it another six times. And that pro-
pelled my mental state and recovery tenfold. Because once I'd
done something of that scale and tested my back that way, I
knew I was back and I knew I was ready to continue. It really
helped propel my recovery.'

What Gives Us Courage?

Some of the pillars we have already seen in this book take the
form of personality traits that make the lives of those born
with them less stressful and more successful. However, I would
argue that courage is not like this – at least, not true courage.
The personality traits we associate with those we consider
brave might sometimes be better described as recklessness,
overconfidence or anti-authoritarianism. Real courage requires
a purposeful choice of action in the face of potential loss. It is
forethought that separates bravery from rashness. Running
into a burning building without first assessing the risk is fool-
hardy or naïve; it is not brave, because bravery requires
deliberation and calm. Those who have few fears do not need
courage to overcome them because they will act anyway.
Courage comes when the boldness to act aligns with an opportunity to live our values.

A study was carried out on the personality traits of American
soldiers who fought in the Korean War. It found that those who
received accolades for bravery were more mature, intelligent
and emotionally stable. Another study, of bomb disposal opera-
tors, reached similar findings, suggesting that the bravest people
were well adjusted and had high levels of psychological wellbeing. But none of this proves that bravery is a trait – so what
is it that makes us brave? It seems to be a result of balancing the
ability to act with a sense of insulation against whatever may be

thrown at us. These prompts and insulators act together to safeguard us against the mental and physical pain, the punishments or broken societal norms that can come from standing up for ourselves and others.

One of the prompts is autonomy, the pillar we discovered in Chapter 3. It gives us our capacity to choose, allowing us a level of control over what happens. Another element of this control is more internal, coming from our locus of control. This locus of control is a psychological concept that covers how much we each believe that we have control over the outcome of events in our lives. If we have an internal locus of control, we feel that what happens to us is our own responsibility – we control our own destiny. This is especially helpful if we want to get out of our comfort zone and become more courageous. However, if we have an external locus of control, we think that things happen to us and that we don't have the ability to direct events. Do you assume that your successes in life are down to your talents, focus and hard work – or do you assume that you are at the whim of others, unable to control much about your life? The answer will make an impact on how courageous you feel you could be.

As the examples of Rose McGowan and the supporters of women visiting abortion clinics showed, the other key prompt, as we learned in Chapter 4, is purpose. It is easier to have courage when we have a deeply held reason for acting and can see the bigger picture. In fact, some people think that we are only able to live our purpose when we have to stand up and fight for it.

One of the insulators is our own morality, which protects us from the effects of potential condemnation after we have engaged in acts of bravery. We can rest easier when we are comfortable that we did the right thing. Social support is another key insulator that helps us to be more courageous, reminding us that people back us up and making us feel less alone. Receiving respect, validation and positive feedback from others gives us strength.

In support of this idea, studies of armed forces have found that brave behaviours tend to be amplified most by those with strong social traits: positive group interaction encourages courage. Social support creates a sense of duty, which might increase our bravery – we are not just doing something for ourselves, but for others too. We saw this strongly in the first few weeks of the Russian bombing of Ukraine in February 2022 when, instead of leaving while they had the chance, parents stayed behind to fight and protect their country, handing over their children to foreigners; and when the country's president told the US government: 'I need ammunition, not a ride.'

The expectation that bravery will be difficult is another insulator. Studies have found that when we plan to do something and are upfront with ourselves about the problems ahead, we are more likely to follow through. We need to get the balance right: expecting to be able to do something, but knowing that it will be hard is more effective than either thinking it will be a breeze or, the reverse, feeling that we won't be able to do it. Planning for bravery can be helpful. When we are unsure of something, we tend not to act, but when we have a plan to follow, we feel more prepared and better able to do it.

Resilience bolsters both our prompts and our insulators, helping us cope with the continual uncertainty that comes from being brave. It arises when we have made a commitment to something we feel passionate about, when we feel in control and welcome challenge. A nice way of describing resilience, coined by *Harvard Business Review* journalist Diane Coutu, is that those without resilience 'snap', while those with resilience 'snap back'.

We can't teach bravery because it is defined not by any one act in itself, but the context and our personal fears regarding the challenge that faces us. But we should remember that courage is contagious and we can highlight the exemplars who stand up for what they believe in – whether we read about them in books, watch them protest on the news or follow their actions on social media. Research has found that the stories we are told don't even need to be true – they just need to be full of emotional content, pique our imagination and concern morally courageous role models. Leaders who ignore convention and do what they believe is right, despite potentially negative repercussions, inspire us all to take our own stand. Observing the good deeds of others can drive us to transform ourselves.

Steps Towards Courage

When a situation arises in which we might need to show courage, we can follow a four-step process towards action – we have to:

1. Become aware of what is going on.

2. Recognize that we may need to act.

3. Consider our role in the situation.

4. Run an internal cost–benefit analysis on being involved.

Only then do we take courageous action. With so much thought and reflection required before engaging, it is not surprising that we don't behave as bravely as we would like to and often end up with missed opportunities and regrets.

We may simply not be looking for the right opportunity or we may have to spend so much effort on day-to-day survival that anything else is just too much. Perhaps rather than weakness or cowardice stopping us from being brave, it is more often stress (the feeling that we have too many stressors and do not have the capability or capacity to handle them) that stumps us. To protect ourselves from this stress, we try to find comfort.

When we feel comfortable, it is because we have built habits and routines into our lives that provide psychological security; these are wonderful for our sense of control, brilliant at protecting us from stressful or anxious situations and necessary to prevent burnout. However, if we get too comfortable, our world narrows. Without looking at opportunities for expanding our engagement with the world, our comfort zone tends to shrink until we start to repeat the same situations and become more conservative in our thoughts. We end up taking a performance-avoidant approach; instead of trying to achieve something bigger or more aligned with our purpose, we choose a goal based on avoiding failure. We might make the most of our strengths, but, in doing so, we will fail to address our weaknesses.

When we notice that action is required, we assess what is necessary. Most of the time we prefer to keep our head down and avoid getting involved, but if taking part could create a beneficial outcome, we might be tempted. It is at this point that we should decide if we are the best person for the job. If the answer is 'Yes', we subconsciously run a cost–benefit analysis.

We can usually see the benefits of bravery fairly easily, but the costs depend on what the wider repercussions of our actions might be. If we think that it's too risky, we will not act. We may feel worse – if we don't try – knowing that we have a purpose, but we are not able to put it into action.

The repercussions of bravery might be amazing. You might achieve your goal, feel you are authentically living your values or moving closer towards meeting your purpose. But you may try really hard and still fail, and that can be a very harsh place. It is also possible that you might achieve your goal and still experience side effects. Studies of whistle-blowers in business found that they often suffered from depression, anxiety, isolation, powerlessness, cynicism, financial hardship and relationship breakdowns. Despite this, a 1999 study found that 90 per cent would blow the whistle again in the future if required – their sense of purpose and moral fortitude was greater than their fear of potential harm.

Whether you succeed or fail in your goal, the process will feel daunting. The physiological impact of anxiety we learned about in Chapter 6 (see page 153) will hijack your body, even though it is highly inconvenient.

Bobby experiences that feeling before every tricky scene. 'It is just an element you have to accept. It is your mind saying to you, "Not sure you should do this." But as long as it is safe, you have put all the precautions in place, you have to have the element of belief that again you cannot fail unless you try. The only time you fail is when you don't try. To just tell yourself that "I'm just going to give it a go and see what happens." Whatever does happen, I'm definitely going to learn something from it.'

If, like Bobby, we feel the impetus to get involved and decide that any repercussions are worth the risk, we will act. We have found the strength to be brave, knowing that we may suffer harm. In this way, bravery is not fearlessness, but about being fearful and acting anyway. Fortunately, there are lots of ways to reduce those fears, expectations and stressors.

Becoming Braver

The dramatic scenes that we typically think of as embodying bravery are usually one-offs – we may experience just a couple in our lifetime; saving a child about to be run over, giving up a role because we believe someone else deserves it more or stepping into a street fight to protect someone smaller. Much of our day-to-day bravery comes from preparation and practice. Let's take being a stunt performer as an example. From the outside, it looks like a very dangerous job. It does involve an element of risk, but this is mitigated by physical fitness and a great deal of technical preparation. The expertise of stunt performers ensures their bravery becomes a habit. The HGV driver who is delivering toxic materials will have qualifications, experience and all the protective gear. The doorman having to stand up to drunk revellers has been trained, licensed and knows they have support on call if needed. Preparation protects.

We can't be brave all the time – we need time to retreat into our comfort zone and recover. So how do we know when we need to strike out and when we need to retreat? Your purpose and your values are the best indicators – the keys to letting you know when it is your time to be brave.

This is particularly important if we need to use moral courage to stand up against others for something we believe in, whether calling out racism or sexism in friends, family or colleagues, or reporting a poorly performing professional to their regulator. On these occasions, the best way to sustain bravery is to get support. When addicts join twelve-step support groups to help them stay sober, studies have found that what keeps them attending is the support from other members – finding peers to guide them gives them courage to change their life. Standing up to others (or to our own addiction) can be daunting, but with even just one other person behind us we can feel stronger.

Consider ethical boundaries

When we have strong ethical boundaries and see them being breached, at first it may seem likely that we will whistle-blow. But when we actually have to pull the trigger, the boundaries become fuzzier. Will we lose our job, be ostracized or be found to have been inadvertently involved in the unethical behaviour ourselves? Anthony Menendez was in this situation when he worked at the American multinational fossil-fuel corporation Halliburton. He reported on questionable accounting practices at the company and lost his job as a result. He was only vindicated after a decade of campaigning – an incredibly difficult period. Someone watching from the outside with a family to feed and a mortgage to pay might well wonder why he would choose to put himself through that. The courage to stand up in such a situation has to come from your own values. What matters most to you? Sometimes, you can struggle even when your values align with your actions. What if you were in Menendez's position and had his integrity, but knew that turning whistle-blower would lose your family's sole source of income and their health insurance? What choice would you make?

Doctors and nurses working in Warsaw's Jewish ghetto during World War II were faced with a horrific choice. The account of Marek Edelman, a leader of the Jewish uprising who survived the war and died in 2009, includes notes of sick patients being brought from hospital to a holding area close to the city's train station, from where they were to be deported to death camps. Lacking the energy to move, they lay in their own excrement and waited to die, either from illness or at the camp. The doctors and nurses faced a battle between their compassion and their integrity; should they send them to an awful death at the camp or offer a quiet and peaceful death through cyanide and morphine? Going against their professional boundaries, Edelman describes how they took the compassionate route, helping them die in relative comfort rather than in the horror of a death camp.

We can learn from these people how to consider our own values and the possible courses of action we might take. Studies have found that being educated about ethics can have a strong effect on moral courage. Teaching and the use of role models gives students clarity about when they could be brave. When MBA students have studied ethics in business and focused on the benefits of ethically strong organizations, they have been shown to take more moral courage into the workplace.

Develop a brave list

Some of the techniques and pillars we have worked on in this book will help in strengthening our day-to-day courage: knowing our purpose, having mastery of our subject and feeling like we have a choice and a voice. When we know why we are doing something, that we are doing it of our own volition and have a decent chance of success, we can push past some of our barriers.

When I started working in sport psychology, feeling like I was risking it all by starting in an entirely new profession after fifteen years in communications, I read an article that changed my way of thinking about how to become successful. The article by Kim Liao was titled: 'Why You Should Aim for 100 Rejections a Year'. It blew my mind. Here I was, teaching athletes that they needed to set positive, realistic goals and work towards them, but this piece was telling me that I should forget all that and aim to fail. Liao explained that traditional goal-setting can keep us in our comfort zone. As a writer, she might be happy to have three articles accepted in a year, but instead aimed to get 100 rejections and sent her work out far more widely. She needed those rejections to help her hit her goal, so she got braver about who she contacted. She didn't succeed in her goal, getting only forty-three rejections, but she also got five brilliant acceptances, in new and better publications, and six rejections asking her to submit more work. Aiming for rejection had boosted her bravery and her level of success.

I took Liao's approach and developed a 'brave list', with the goal of getting rejected at least once a fortnight. Every time I had an idea about how I might develop my business in some way, I logged it on the spreadsheet and went for it; a contract application, a partnership, a new client opportunity, a research project. As a result, I found myself on stage in front of an audience of 1,200 marathon runners, speaking about superstition in sport on the BBC, working with organizations I admired and getting my first book deal. Over the year, I logged twenty-nine activities and thirteen of them came off – 45 per cent of the goals I had previously been too scared to go for became reality. When we aim to collect as many rejections as we can, we are likely to pick up more wonderful yeses along the way. There are instructions for completing your own brave list in the toolbox at the end of this chapter (see page 205).

Take baby steps

As we discovered in Chapter 6, our fear of failure often turns into our default mode. To begin the process of developing courage, we might ask ourselves the question, 'What would I do if I could not fail?' The resulting daydreaming begins to shape our goals and gives us a reason to be more courageous. It helps us to stretch our comfort zone and we then attack our barriers. What we think will make us fail dictates where we need to become brave. Our bravery doesn't have to occur at a crucial moment; it is just as valid to have many small moments of courage to overcome things we thought we couldn't and knock down the barriers in our way. In fact, it is better that way – exploding out of our comfort zone would be scary and overwhelming, but little bits at a time feels achievable. It might feel like baby steps, but we should see that as a positive; after all, babies don't have fears because they have yet to have context or meaning for their actions. They take their first steps because they want to get somewhere faster, without worrying about the risk that they will fall over.

We can practise baby steps to learn how to cope with adversity, facing risk one bit at a time. This helps us to develop our mental skills and builds up our emotional control, and as a result we can be more courageous. In gradually exposing ourselves to that fear, we can grow stronger and more courageous and slowly expand our comfort zone.

Bobby takes us through how he uses baby steps (maybe better to call them bravery steps in this instance!) in creating a show-stopping stunt. 'There is a stunt I did on *Extraction*. Chris's character is having a fight with a bad guy on a balcony. They have a bit of a tussle backward and forward. They both go over the balcony, they land on an awning. Off the awning on to a truck. From the truck, hit the road, stand up and they have a bit of a fight and then I get hit by a car.'

Before filming he had already spent a week practising on the mats. He has programmed his body in what to do. 'At the call "Action", my body almost takes over. My mind is, like, "It is now" and then I go for it. I know how my body is landing now, I know where to come out of this, I know where I need to hit here, I know where to hit the ground and how to cushion my landing and roll out of it. You are quite dazed and there was a bit of a fight and then the car hits you at 22 mph. Just takes you out from the side.' Bobby wasn't allowed to look out for the car. While his natural body reaction was to react, to protect himself, he couldn't. 'I just had to let it hit me, take the hit and hit the ground. We did the car hit probably eight times, we did the balcony fall about six or seven times. So, they were hard-hitting.'

Breaking down and then taking these steps may feel uncomfortable, but in doing so we learn that we can take action without coming to harm. The audience didn't laugh at us on stage, we didn't embarrass ourselves on the football pitch and we didn't screw up in the presentation to a potential new client.

These small achievements help us move from presenting in front of colleagues to presenting to clients, from doing a read-through in rehearsal to performing on stage, or from doing the run-up and jump in practice to competing in an athletics meet.

Use 'what-if' planning

The key lies in building slow development towards excellent preparation. When firefighters are asked why they have the bravery to run into burning buildings, they say they are just doing what they have trained to do for years and what they have practised time and time again. This sense of normalization breaks down the fear; their preparation gives them a backbone instead of a wishbone, making things that they would be afraid of feel perfectly doable.

One of the best ways to prepare is by using 'what-if' planning. This helps us see what we are afraid of, teaches us to deal with what we fear before we have a chance to go wrong and helps us to put in place a plan to deal with problems if they do occur.

The first element of this kind of planning is probably the hardest to do: reflecting on and admitting what it is we are afraid of. We might call this a 'brain drain', as we are trying to drain our brain of all our worries and fears. If we write down as many things as we can that are worrying us on a piece of paper, when they are in front of us, they feel less scary. This also frees up space in our brain so we can focus on more helpful things and proactively try to prepare for other eventualities.

The brain-drain strategy has been the subject of study: before a maths exam, half the students were asked to spend ten minutes writing up their anxieties, while the others just sat and waited. The second group scored 12 per cent lower than expected; those who completed the brain drain improved their anticipated score by 5 per cent.

The second element of what-if planning involves preventing those fears from becoming reality. This involves breaking down every worry and looking at what we can do to make sure it doesn't come to pass. In sport, our fear might be that we would be poorly on the day of a major competition; preparation would involve good hygiene, avoiding socializing and eating low-risk food. If we are preparing for an on-stage performance, we might fear forgetting our monologue; we could prevent this by practising until we cannot get it wrong. The process helps us feel in far more control. Bravery feels doable rather than risky.

The 'if... then' process comes last. You now plan for what you would do if your fear came to fruition: 'If I did get sick on the day of a competition and my GP said it wasn't infectious, I would take some medication and see if I felt well enough for the competition an hour before the start' or 'If I was on stage and I forgot my lines, I would improvise – knowing the audience doesn't know what's in the script.' Making plans in this way is vital. When we are under pressure, doing something that we fear, our amygdala is on high alert – as soon as one of those threats becomes real, our brain can be hijacked by our threat zone (see page 154). We no longer think rationally and instead react emotionally, and that doesn't usually result in a great outcome. If we have a prepared plan in place, we can use it to keep our emotional responses at bay. We can relax and follow our intentions, with fewer fears of repercussions. You can complete your own 'what-if' plan in the toolbox at the end of this chapter (see page 205).

A wonderful example of this way of thinking was provided by Els Visser, a Dutch doctor who in 2014 went on a four-day boat trip from the Indonesian island of Lombok to Komodo with twenty-four other people. On the second day, the weather became bad and the waves made many of them seasick. As they were trying to sleep that night, the motor stopped and water began to flood in through a hole in the small boat. The passengers tried to raise the alarm, but their phones were out of reception and the boat had no GPS equipment or flares. Visser had two things going for her. The first was that her medical training had taught her not to panic in an emergency. The second was that by confronting her biggest fear – her parents not knowing what had happened to her – she found the courage to try to make it to safety. The doctor knew that she might not survive, but grabbed her passport and the memory card from her camera – ensuring her body could be identified for her family if the worst happened – drank a bottle of water to prevent dehydration and waited.

A wave sent the passengers into the ocean. Visser made it into a lifeboat with five others and they floated until morning. When the sun rose, she spotted an island in the distance and decided to swim for it. She says, 'I felt I would rather die fighting for my life than die not trying.' Hours later, she and one other made it to the island, which had no food or shelter, very little water and – as if that were not enough – was home to an erupting volcano. They had no idea how long they would last, but fortunately they were rescued the next day.

I would never suggest testing how brave you are by putting yourself in a similarly extreme situation. However, we can do something on a smaller scale by creating minor moments of adversity, giving us the opportunity to practise our responses. We can use what-if planning to pick a situation to work through, or we can work backwards from our goal to see what is holding us back until we find the level at which we should start. We might do exam practice in the middle of the family room to get used to focusing despite distractions. Or we could prepare for a difficult cycling challenge by training in the dark or on a very boring loop. Stunt performers do this as a matter of course, as Bobby explains: 'The first time we prep and rehearse something our main aim is to protect ourselves. Once you've done that once in the prep, you then do it again and you think less about having to save yourself because you have done it once and it is prepped and it is repeatable. You do it over and over again, then you can actually start to act the stunt because you are not worried about having to protect yourself. Once I've done the first one, then I start to relax a little bit. It is like a muscle memory. Your brain is a muscle, and you remember how you did it before.'

Develop a courageous alter ego

Bobby has learned that, through preparing for the worst and practising to be the best, he can be purposeful with his courage – and it works. Maybe he is helped by the fact that he is playing a role, a character, in a movie. We can do the same. If we don't feel like we'll ever have the courage we need, we can try acting like the brave person we would like to be. We do this by developing an alter ego, a persona who has the courage that we don't. When you get into character, you are able to achieve things you would normally feel too intimidated to do. Just as you put on a sports kit to compete or your best suit for a job interview, try putting on your alter ego to give you that courage.

We regularly see successful people do this. Tiger Woods is one example. He was born Eldrick Woods, but his father allegedly named him 'Tiger' when he was three to highlight how he should be when playing golf. When Dwayne Johnson moved from American football into wrestling, he needed to hide his shy and humble personality so became 'The Rock'. As his example shows, alter egos are particularly effective when we need to be assertive but it is not in our personality. They mean that, whenever you have to step outside of your comfort zone but feel uncomfortable being the 'authentic' you, you can put on your alter ego and get what you need.

Developing an alter ego can be fun – you can name it, pick the mental skills it may use, an outfit, strengths it might have and, most importantly, its mindset. With all this decided, it just comes down to practising using your alter ego until you feel brave. The more you practise, the braver you become. So put your head down, assess your purpose, face your fears and build your protection. With all this in place, you can hunt down your goals and courageously hurdle over any barriers you find blocking your path.

COURAGE TOOLKIT

Value identification

Courage comes when we feel the fear, deliberate under pressure and then take purposeful action because something truly matters to us. Courage isn't the action, but our vulnerability around the potential personal loss. It is a way to live a life that matches our values and our purpose. To achieve this, we need to be incredibly clear on our values and what matters to us.

Here are 100 commonly cited values. I would like you to pick the three which most resonate; the ones which feel like they are at the core of who you are. The three words you pick will be those which are incredibly important to the way you want to live your life. To help you hone down the list, cross out all the words that are not you. Then get tough and cross out more and more until just three remain. These will be values to try to live by and the ones which would facilitate your courage.

Sustainability

Productivity

Community

Process

Acceptance

Dignity

Discipline

Equality

Cooperation

Comfort

Respect

Belonging

Security

Charity

Connection

Altruism

Harmony

Empathy

Compassion

Spirituality

Teamwork

Gratitude

Wealth

Generosity

Fearless

Humanity

Honesty

Strength

Kindness

Courage

Humility

Integrity

Ambition

Ferocious

Loyalty

Recognition

Ethical

Family

Sincerity

Decisiveness

Conviction

Passionate

Vigour

Consistency

Purpose

Drive

Inspiring

Conscientious

Challenge

Determination

Truth

Dedication

Creativity
Professionalism
Diligence
Capability
Transparency
Accomplishment
Efficiency
Intelligence
Adaptable
Mastery
Understanding
Patience
Effectiveness
Insight
Clarity
Logic
Learning
Persistence
Excellence
Enthusiasm
Quality
Thoughtfulness
Potential
Growth
Optimism
Energetic
Achievement
Spontaneity
Boldness
Joy
Innovative
Success
Adventurous
Health
Certainty
Autonomy
Power
Balance
Confidence
Agency
Independence
Fairness
Grace
Curiosity
Control
Empowerment
Risk-taking
Contentment

Comfort zone stretching

Comfort zones come when we have built habits and routines into our lives to help us feel more psychologically secure. These give a sense of control and protection, but stop us attempting risky but worthwhile challenges.

In the circle below write down the things that sit within your comfort zone; the elements in your life where there is no stress or fear. Outside of the circle, start jotting down the things you would love to be brave enough to do, but have not yet found the courage to try. The scarier they feel, the further away they should sit from the circle. When you have finished, highlight just one thing outside of the circle and resolve that it will be your next challenge.

Brave list

Aiming for rejection can force us outside of our comfort zone and free us up to be braver and more successful. You can create a brave list on paper or a spreadsheet using the following steps:

1. For a specific period, say three months, note down every idea you have that could push you forward and closer to your vision of success.

2. Take one step towards achieving it. It could be researching something, sending an email, following a company or person on socials, making a plan, setting some goals or even just telling someone why you want to achieve that thing.

3. Head back to your list every couple of weeks to check in with yourself over whether you still want that idea to come true.

4. Follow up on the ideas that you still love. Chase up those emails, add to the research or put the plan into action.

5. Jot down the outcomes – what percentage came to life because of your bravery?

What-if planning

Facing a challenge can be daunting. Other people, a difficult or unknown environment, too many logistical worries or outcomes you feel may be out of reach... they all take their toll. Burying our heads in the sand feels very tempting, but research has found that having an acceptance of what is worrying us and having a plan to prevent it is a much more helpful approach.

A 'what-if' plan lets you write down all of your fears about a challenge, think about what you could do in advance to ensure each fear doesn't happen and then, if it does happen, how you would like to respond. Being prepared for all eventualities like this takes away lots of the nerves and means that, if the worst happens, you are already prepared.

Fear or concern	To prevent it happening I will...	If it happens I will...

8

Pragmatic Optimism

Pragmatic optimism is the pillar that helps you reflect on what has already happened in a way that expands your future opportunities by helping you approach them with a presumption of success.

There are thousands of different personality tests. Many of us in the corporate world have been put through personality profiles like the Myers-Briggs Type Indicator or Insights Discovery, and even more of us have downloaded internet quizzes that promise to tell us all about ourselves. Sometimes these tests seem inspired in the insight they give us; other times we scoff and move on. But we don't always need dozens of questions and analysis to assess our personality. And when it comes to one of our pillars of success, we only need to ask one simple question: are we a Tigger or an Eeyore?

Tigger, the toy tiger in the *Winnie the Pooh* stories, is boisterous, exuberant and optimistic. He bounces around the Hundred Acre Wood looking on the bright side. Eeyore the donkey, on the other hand, is a complete pessimist. Perpetually gloomy and sad, he expects only the worst and always feels down. Tigger may occasionally annoy his friends with his incessant positivity, but he is happy in his bubble and thinks he will succeed.

Tigger's assumptions that he will succeed mean that it is more likely that he will. More and more studies are finding that optimism has a significant impact on our success. Sometimes that optimism is misplaced – you might think that you can do something when you can't – but you'll still be closer than if you hadn't tried, and you can also be proud of yourself for trying in the first place. Better to try and fail than to passively sit back and think, 'If only...'

It was Winston Churchill who pointed out that while a pessimist sees the difficulty in every opportunity, an optimist sees the opportunity in every difficulty. The Lebanese-American poet Kahlil Gibran put it more vividly: 'The optimist sees the rose and not its thorns; the pessimist stares at the thorns, oblivious to the rose.' And American author McLandburgh Wilson summarized the issue in terms of cake:

Twixt the optimist and pessimist
The difference is droll:
The optimist sees the doughnut
But the pessimist sees the hole.

As this suggests, when we behave like Tigger and look for the good, we are able to see it. We get more opportunities, we see more beauty and we get more cake. Optimism makes life so much better and gives us a far higher chance of success.

It won't be a surprise to hear that Drew McOnie, our success story in this chapter, is nicknamed 'Tigger'. Drew is an Olivier-award-winning director and choreographer working in film and television. He has created major productions for both Broadway and the West End, including *King Kong*, *Strictly Ballroom the Musical*, *Jesus Christ Superstar*, *On The Town* and *Chicago*. 'Over the years of working in the theatre industry,' he says, 'I've picked up this nickname of "Tigger" from various different artistic directors and collaborators. I think it is down to the fact that I seem to have boundless energy, talk way too fast and my history in being a dancer means that I jump up and down quite a lot when I get excited.'

Optimism is so persuasive that it can even override rationality. Family lawyers know better than anyone that a third of marriages end in divorce, yet they still tie the knot, assuming they will not find themselves within that statistic. We may know that approximately one in two of us will develop some form of cancer in our lifetime and yet only if we suffer from health anxiety do we expect it to be us; we tend to be optimistic. If we are a glass-half-full sort of person, we anticipate good rather than predicting bad, and in doing so follow behavioural patterns and respond to difficulties in ways that make success more likely. As a result, optimists have better physical and mental health, live longer, recover more quickly from disappointments and handle adversity more effectively than pessimists.

This doesn't mean that we should aim to experience unlimited, unrestrained optimism. When we are unrealistic in what we aim for, we can fail spectacularly. The Serenity Prayer, adopted and popularized by Alcoholics Anonymous and similar twelve-step programmes, has the balance about right; it asks for the courage to change the things we can change, the serenity to accept the things we cannot and the wisdom to know the difference. When we use optimism effectively and pragmatically in this way, we can see and reach for the good, but focus only on those areas that are within our control.

What Is Optimism?

Optimism is the belief that good things will happen, both now and in the future. Pessimists prepare for the worst, while optimists expect the best. When optimists come up against difficulties, they see them as temporary challenges that they can use as stepping stones on their path towards their next success. So how does Drew know that he is an optimist? He says it is because 'I look for opportunity and believe that that opportunity will lead to something positive.'

Some people, like Drew, are natural Tiggers. They have dispositional optimism, a personality trait that has a positive influence on how they see themselves and others. It both impacts how we process information and shapes how we act on it, giving us positive expectations about our future. We see ourselves more positively and approach challenges enthusiastically. This is not optimism about current events, but relates to what we expect from our future. As things go wrong or become more difficult, our dispositional optimism levels rise and fall to match how well resourced we feel to handle what is ahead. Generally, we are able to stay positive in different kinds of situations, contexts and life stages.

We might also regard optimism as an explanation of events we encounter and our responses to difficult situations. Our style of explanation will see us variously attribute problems to temporary or persistent aspects, internal or external factors and specific or general causes. We all go through tricky times, but optimists interpret those negative experiences as specific and external to the event itself, and may well think that they have been caused by someone else. That approach enables optimists to explain situations they have experienced in a positive way.

This optimistic explanatory style stops us feeling vulnerable or helpless because optimists give themselves credit when things go well and assume that this positive feeling will impact other parts of their life. If we have a pessimistic explanatory style and fail an exam, we might feel that we are not clever enough and that we will always fail. An optimist will attribute the failure to something beyond their control – they might say the exam was harder than usual or they were poorly so unable to study. Next time, they say, they will be able to focus differently and pass. This may not always be true – but at least they don't beat themselves up and feel negative about an outcome that they have no power to change.

This last approach helps us progress; by viewing past events optimistically we can influence our expectations for the future and we enter a positive cycle. However, we do need to be realistic; relentless optimists take optimism too far and expect a positive outcome even where there are problems that are beyond their control. They may develop an optimism bias, where they believe that their personal risks are lower than other people's (see page 223). They might smoke, but not worry about lung cancer, or gamble, but believe that they'll be the one person who beats the house. Such behaviour is harmful rather than helpful.

Drew's pragmatic optimism comes 'when you are both in control as a realistic, safe and clear leader, but also a dreamer and somebody who can actually use that stability to push people into areas they've never been before. It has led me to being able to make practical choices in imaginative situations.'

Drew explains how his pragmatic optimism got him through one of the toughest challenges of his professional career when he headed over to Broadway to work on a show everyone had flagged as doomed. 'The belief system around this show was really negative. I found myself in social situations with people laughing at the show, thinking it was a joke. I had to reframe it and use my optimism to focus on what was the best possible version.' Drew had to make a proactive decision, when faced with what was perceived to be a failure, to see the opportunity. He ignored the naysayers and focused on creating a piece of work they could all be proud of. 'I came out of it with some great relationships. You look at it and say, "Wow, that was quite possibly one of the hardest moments in my career and yet I've survived." And that does make you more optimistic, 'cos it makes you go, "Well, actually maybe that wasn't as painful as I thought it was."'

It is the pragmatic optimist who is most successful. Whether they expect things to go well in the future or are able to explain away the failures of the past in a way that means those setbacks can't be repeated, their approach allows them to vary their beliefs, based on whether they can control a situation. If a situation is within their control, they can be optimistic about it because they know that they can affect the outcome. If the situation is genuinely hopeless, they can treat it as such and accept the outcome while looking for other opportunities. Pragmatic optimism is about accepting reality while still being able to feel positive about the future. Our goal-focused behaviours when we are optimistic allow us to achieve greatness; this is the behaviour we should seek to nurture.

Everywhere we look we can find examples of optimistic people who refuse to give up. Sir James Dyson made 5,127 prototypes of his Dual Cyclone bagless vacuum cleaner before he arrived at a version he was happy with. Thomas Edison found 10,000 ways a light bulb didn't work before he discovered the way it did. Diana Nyad became the first person to swim from Cuba to Florida without a shark cage on her fifth attempt. When other people would have seen evidence that what they were trying to do was impossible, these individuals kept going until they succeeded.

Some research suggests that optimism has a genetic element. A Swedish study of more than five hundred twins estimated that the heritability of optimism and pessimism was at a level of about 25 per cent. However, an analysis of some eight-nine thousand people in twenty-two countries found that about 80 per cent of us are quite optimistic – regardless of age, gender, race, educational level or socio-economic status. A similar study covering 150,000 people in 142 countries looked even wider and found that the majority of us are optimistic and that the benefits are seen in a huge variety of environments.

A Shortcut to Success

Improved health is one benefit of optimism. The media enjoy relaying the stories of people who defy medical expectations, and we love to hear them because they give us hope. A meta-analysis of eighty-three studies found optimism to be a significant predictor of physical and psychological health outcomes.

Specific studies have found that optimism minimizes hospitalizations for asthma sufferers, reduces the distress of a breast cancer diagnosis and of failed IVF treatments, makes you three times less likely to develop hypertension, reduces the risk of viral infections and results in lower levels of pain in diseases as varied as rheumatoid arthritis, cancer and sickle cell disease. Studies of those with cardiovascular disease have found that optimists generally show lower levels of distress before heart surgery, are less likely to suffer a heart attack in theatre and are half as likely to require rehospitalization afterwards. They also tend to recover more quickly and lead a higher quality life.

In one study in the early sixties, 839 patients had their optimism levels measured and were revisited thirty years later. The results showed that for every ten-point increase in pessimism, mortality rose by 19 per cent. It has been suggested that this might be a result of the link between pessimism and depression; however, other studies of cancer and heart disease have shown similar results. Another study looked at the personality traits of students at the University of North Carolina in the sixties and then again forty years later; the death rate was 42 per cent higher in the most pessimistic people than those who were most optimistic. A Dutch study found that optimists were 55 per cent less likely to die of cardiovascular disease than pessimists.

It seems that optimists follow better health practices, eat a healthier diet, do more exercise and have vaccines and wellbeing checks. If they do suffer from an illness, optimism helps undermine the negative effects, and they feel better able to respond to medical advice. Optimists do not breeze through life assuming that difficult things like divorce, bereavement, redundancy or critical illness will never happen to them, but they are making it less likely that these things will happen.

Optimism has an impact on our mental health as well. Studies show that optimistic people have more positive moods, greater life satisfaction, better sleep, fewer periods of loneliness, more resilience in difficult situations, lower levels of anxiety and a lower risk of depression. In fact, one study of women in Sweden found that their levels of optimism when they were teenagers were a great predictor of their life satisfaction in middle age. Some of these benefits may come from the positive filter that optimists put on life, but it might also be because optimism gives our threat zone a rest. When we don't feel that we have to constantly be on guard, life is far more enjoyable. The hormone cortisol is released when we are under stress and experiencing anxiety, and its levels in our bodies reveal how stressed we are. A 2008 study of almost three thousand otherwise healthy people found that optimists tended to have far less cortisol in their bloodstream.

Another major benefit of optimism is that it improves our relationships, giving us a stronger sense of belonging. Optimists tend to be better liked – they see things in a positive light, solve problems to keep relationships strong and can be more fun to be around. As a result, they cope better in environments that require social networks, such as school and workplaces. It definitely helps in politics – in fact, it's been proven that optimists have a far higher chance of being elected. In eighteen of the twenty-two American presidential elections between 1900 and 1984, it was the candidate with the most optimistic campaign speeches who won.

Optimism has a very significant impact on our careers; it means that we are more likely to get promotions and feel engaged in our work, and less likely to burn out. When we look at people whose jobs involve selling, the difference is outstanding: optimistic salespeople sell 56 per cent more than their pessimistic colleagues and tend to work for their company for longer. When an insurance company screened for optimism in their recruitment, they found that its presence improved levels of staff retention.

The persistence of an optimist means that they perform better in school and so are more likely to have successful careers. Olympic champions are more likely to be optimists – this makes sense, given the huge number of setbacks and obstacles they must overcome to reach the pinnacle of high-level competition. Drew is clear that his optimism has sped up his success. 'The people who are doing what I'm doing, at the same level as me, are mostly kind of ten to fifteen years older than me, so I think that my optimism and my kind of pursuit of positive opportunity has accelerated my career pretty clearly.'

What is so interesting about Drew's perspective, though, is that his optimism is mainly based on future imaginings. 'My daydreaming and positive thoughts are all about the future – where I want to be a long time away – and this takes away the desperation of it having to be achieved tomorrow. It makes opportunities feel less of an emotional decision so there is a calmness because it is not something you are being rushed into a decision about.' He says this optimistic approach has ensured he can future-proof his career.

Optimists are thought to set high standards, which they believe they can reach, and turn those standards into goals. With this in mind, it is not surprising that optimism can make us wealthier. Researchers measured the optimism levels of law students and followed up ten years into their careers; for each point on their optimism score, they made an extra US$32,667 a year. Optimists also save more – a study of 2,000 Americans found that 90 per cent of optimists put money aside for big purchases, compared to only 70 per cent of pessimists.

These benefits of being optimistic make it self-reinforcing; when you behave optimistically and improve your health, wellbeing, career prospects, economic situation and sense of belonging, you also become more successful. This, in turn, reminds you what is possible, so you remain optimistic about the future and continue with that success.

A Source of Success

As well as improving our mental, physical and financial health, optimism reduces our chance of failure by giving us more effective approaches to cope with difficulties. Positive, goal-focused behaviours allow us to develop better coping mechanisms and cognitive approaches, and gain more perspective on the bigger picture.

Optimists and pessimists cope very differently when confronted with adversity. A pessimist will regard a problem as a roadblock that prevents them from moving forward, while an optimist will see it as an opportunity to try a new approach. A pessimist will regard a failed attempt as evidence that they should not have tried, while an optimist will see it as an opportunity to learn. Much of this difference is down to automatic coping mechanisms: optimists tend to have more effective coping mechanisms to deal with tricky situations, which lead to more success in their endeavours. Optimists use two distinct coping strategies, both of which help them tackle problems head-on.

One strategy used by optimists is 'approach coping', which involves fixing problems through better planning, by asking for support or by looking for potential benefits, such as an opportunity to learn. Most problem fixes are situation-specific, but in general will involve reducing the negative impact of the stressor and taking constructive steps to solve the problem. Let's take a cardiac patient as an example. An optimist would seek out information on what they should be doing to aid their recovery and might also improve their diet, enrol in a rehab programme, reduce their weight and increase their exercise levels. All these proactive solutions are controllable by the patient. A second coping strategy comes into play when the situation is beyond their control: the emotion-focused technique. This might positively reframe the situation or use acceptance or humour to deal with the sensations, so as not to waste time trying to solve unsolvable problems.

Pessimists tend to use less effective coping strategies, ones that focus on avoidance; they deny what is happening, distance themselves from the problems, blame themselves for setbacks or disengage from their goals. Our cardiac patient, if they were a pessimist, might avoid visiting the GP in the first place, then ignore warnings given and, if they had the treatment, might be overly cautious about getting back on their feet. The denial process is in stark contrast to the acceptance of optimists. When we are in denial, we refuse to accept the reality of a situation; in acceptance, we restructure our perception and, while we realize that we cannot change where we are, we set different goals. We don't give up.

A study of couples who had been through a failed cycle of IVF highlights the differences. The pessimistic patients used distancing to deal with the disappointment, but this led to them experiencing greater distress. By contrast, the optimistic patients saw positives in the process, learning from it and feeling closer to their partners as a result. Both sets of patients were in identical situations, but they came away with very different feelings.

Ed Jackson is a terrific example of the value of optimistic coping mechanisms. A professional rugby player, he suffered a terrible injury in 2017 off the pitch, while swimming with his dad and some friends. He dived into a pool that was shallower than he was expecting and hit the bottom, fracturing two vertebrae. His heart stopped a number of times on the way to hospital; he survived, but was left a quadriplegic, and was warned that he would probably never walk again. As a pragmatic optimist, Ed knew that his rugby career was over, but refused to believe that he wouldn't be able to move again and was determined to restore his independence. This drive gave him his purpose, and he worked incredibly hard for the tiniest results, using each positive to make him optimistic that he could reach the next one. Bit by bit, he regained some movement; tiny movements (like a small wiggle of a toe), but ones that inspired him to keep on trying and maxing out his determination. By using acceptance, problem-solving coping mechanisms and goal-setting, he gradually gained more movement still. Four months after the accident, he took a few steps without crutches. A year later, he climbed Snowdon.

While optimists like Jackson use their coping mechanisms to overcome difficulties, they also have helpful day-to-day behaviours to ensure they meet their goals. They have positive expectations and can take proactive behaviours to ensure they occur.

The first thing optimists do is set goals and put resources in place to achieve them. They ensure their goals are controllable to guarantee the greatest impact. At the first sign of a setback, they consider the best way to get back on track. The pragmatic optimist is realistic about their resources and knows how to give themselves the best possible chance of reaching their goals. A pessimist, on the other hand, may feel that their goals aren't attainable and, as a result, will lack the motivation to chase them.

Drew has a brilliant example of how to use optimism to overcome a major setback when he was first given the opportunity to create a full-length work for his own company at the Old Vic theatre. He created and wrote a production of *Jekyll & Hyde*. 'I was really, really proud of it. The dancers were incredible. But we woke up after press night and we got very mixed reviews.' He didn't want to get out of bed. He felt sorry for himself. He felt embarrassed. But, as the director, he realized that the actors would feel bad too. 'One of the hardest moments of my career was getting up, getting in the shower, going on the Tube, getting to work and standing in front of the company and smiling at them and telling them that I love them and that I am proud of the work that we've done together.' He knew that was the moment to become a leader.

'We didn't do warm-up on that day. We sat down in a circle and talked about the show and what we thought about it and what we believed about it. And they went out on that matinee and gave their best performance. It was absolutely electric; the audience were mad for it. By the time we got to the end of the week, we were getting five-star reviews saying that the production was career-defining. If I had sat and wallowed in the kind of negative feeling, I wouldn't have turned up that day, the dancers would have lost faith in the production and we would have remained in a place of negativity for the entire run.'

An optimist, like Drew, will collect the resources they need to bring their goal to life – whether skills, knowledge, supporters, performances or processes – and, with these resources, feel optimistic that their goal will be achieved. If negative information or complications get in the way, studies have found that optimists will focus only on the parts of it that are relevant to their goals. Even when there are difficulties, they can reframe the situation in a more positive way.

Let's consider the example of an athlete who has been feeling fatigued and is suffering from a lack of 'bounce' in training sessions. The optimistic athlete will head to a doctor and get blood tests to discover what is going on. They get a diagnosis of anaemia and will immediately start taking iron tablets and change their diet, relieved that the setback was fixable. They are grateful to their doctor and happy to take tablets and eat iron-rich foods; within several months they will be back performing at a high level. They approached the setback as a challenge and tackled it effectively. A pessimistic athlete might initially think that they had lost their ability and might be better off not competing. If they got as far as having a blood test, they would perceive the anaemia negatively, as yet another thing that was wrong with them.

A story that combines these different elements of optimism is that of Nik Robinson, a Briton living in Australia. In 2018, the advertising and marketing creative was talking to his sons Harry and Archie about the environment. They were eight and six at the time and had been learning about the abundance of single-use plastic bottles. The three of them developed a plan to create a business that could help clean up the planet, using those bottles.

Nik, Harry and Archie realized that a pair of sunglasses weighs about the same as a 600-ml single-use plastic bottle, and

Nik's advertising brain came up with the powerful idea of 'one bottle makes one pair'. A great deal of optimism was required to develop the product. Nik not only made 2,500 failed attempts, but even had to replace the suspension on his car because of the weight of the steel machine parts he was taking to welders to manufacture his recycled sunglasses. But two years later his optimism paid off and his company, Good Citizens, now sells sunglasses made entirely from plastic bottles.

When they set up a Kickstarter crowdfunding campaign to raise AUS$60,000, they achieved their target in just six minutes. Robinson and his kids had a mission, a passion and a shedload of optimism, which brought them success.

These thoughts are mirrored by Drew. He has developed a 'win or learn' approach in his career (see page 171). This means that, for him, failure is not a wasted attempt, but instead a brilliant opportunity to learn. 'I've always learned far more from the negative reviews that I've received than I ever have from the positive. The positive reviews or the accolades or the awards just tell you that you did something that people resonated with. And that's great, but when you are on a path that people aren't resonating with, it gives you a much deeper well, a much greater wealth of opportunity of learning and self-knowledge than any pat on the back ever could.'

Drew is highly aware that in the theatre you have to be able to cope with criticism. 'My relationship with that has changed over the years. I think that where I am at now is that failure is only truly failure if you choose to go down the same path and believe it's going to lead you somewhere different.' For this reason, Drew doesn't stop in rehearsals if something goes wrong – a dancer trips or there is a musical mishap, for example. 'The reason I do that is because that could absolutely go wrong on stage. Every opportunity for learning in the studio should be grabbed. Any opportunity for it to go wrong in a safe environment provides you with the chance to learn how to deal with it when you are on stage.' Drew is actively trying to create an environment where failure is seen as a positive.

When all these optimistic elements – positive thinking, goal-setting, motivation, persistence, learning from failure and adaptive behaviours – come together, we can work positively towards achieving our goals. Pessimists might have similar dreams, but they anticipate a negative outcome and, as a result, they will reduce or drop their efforts. The behaviour of an optimist is more likely to result in success, but they definitely need to employ a pragmatic approach; if they go in with too much optimism, they set their goals too high and persist past the point of value. They can become so motivated that they ignore all reason. They need optimism up to a point, but should then realize that any more will lead to a reduction in performance.

The risks of relentless optimism

There are a few specific areas in which excessive optimism can cause us serious trouble and one of these is entrepreneurship. To give up a job and start your own business requires bucketloads of optimism, and yet the majority of start-ups fail. Studies have found that the more optimistic an entrepreneur, the lower their performance. In fact, one study found that optimistic entrepreneurs have earnings that can be as much as 30 per cent lower than those of pessimistic colleagues. It has been suggested that optimism negatively impacts decision-making and judgement, and reduces processing capacity, meaning that optimists make decisions based on fewer inputs and take bigger risks. It may also be that the over-optimistic entrepreneur gets too excited about the opportunities in front of them or has unrealistic expectations about what is possible, exaggerating the ways in which their skill can improve their organization's performance.

The financial crisis in 2008 was a disaster that struck as a result of people becoming too optimistic and expecting the markets to keep on rising, ignoring evidence that growth was unsustainable. If we are optimistic, we scan information for the facts and figures that support what we already believe and discount the negative information, an idea known as 'confirmation bias' (see page 57). We can add to this the idea of 'optimism bias', which arises when we overestimate the possibility of positive outcomes and downplay the likelihood of negative ones. Together, these are a dangerous combination.

Gambling is another area in which relentless optimism can have a negative impact; if we expect the best of things that are outside of our control, being persistent and not making good decisions can quickly bankrupt us. If you see each loss as likely, you will quickly stop gambling, but if optimism bias makes you reinterpret having lost as a near win, you will keep going – usually heading towards financial difficulty.

Optimism towards situations beyond our control, in which our actions will have no influence, is helpful at keeping us positive. But it is unrealistic to expect everything to go well, especially when we have no way of ensuring that we won't encounter problems. It is also unrealistic to assume that we can change how others think about us. Many of my clients fear the judgement of others. We could be optimistic that they will think kindly of us, but with no control over that, the better and more adaptive approach in this situation is to accept the reality of where we are and try to build our own confidence so we care less.

Pessimism may not have many benefits, but it does provide protection. We can use it to manage our expectations, making us less disappointed if we do badly at something. Shifting our expectations downwards can protect us from the sadness that results from not doing as well as we had hoped – that feeling of falling to Earth with a bump when there's a mismatch between our hopes and reality. We call this 'defensive pessimism' and it can be an adaptive approach that we may use when we fear that we haven't done well. The ideal balance to strike seems to be employing about 90 per cent optimism, with a reality check every now and then to help us stay on track, and a dash of defensive pessimism when we wait for big results to come in.

Growing Our Own Optimism

While some of us are lucky to be born with the spirit of Tigger, there are also environmental influences at play which affect our levels of optimism. They can help us see the world as being on our side, and to utilize them we need to start early – ideally in childhood.

Start young

If we want our children to have the benefits of the pillar of optimism, we can help by giving them the resources they require. Some might be beyond our control, such as a healthy financial situation; however, emotional warmth and familial approval are more controllable and have a similarly beneficial effect on children. When adults add to this by modelling optimistic behaviours and using beneficial coping mechanisms, they can help make a child's optimistic mindset become a habit.

We can also learn to practise optimistic attribution styles. Our explanation for past events influences our expectations for future events, and we can learn how to make them more positive. If our explanations for failure are pessimistic – appearing stable, internal and general – we can make them feel more unstable, external and specific. This means that a single failure seems less personal or less likely to reoccur. If we use adaptive or emotional coping skills and offer optimistic explanations, we increase our children's chances of behaving optimistically and having all the benefits that go with it.

Imagine your best possible self

One manipulation that can help us become more optimistic is an imagery technique called 'best possible self'. It helps raise our expectations of what will happen in the future. As well as bringing the benefits of optimism, it also makes happy outcomes more likely. You can try your own version in the toolkit at the end of this chapter (see page 231). Firstly, when we expect something, we are more likely to spend time and effort making it happen, which means being prepared, obtaining all the resources we need and working through the potential barriers.

Secondly, as we learned in Chapter 5, imagery can give us confidence, helping us believe that we have already achieved our goals. The scripts we learn to write can help us in the future. An optimistic script, if practised enough, can provide an optimistic outlook. Drew learned this as a child when he remembers never wanting to go to sleep at night. His parents used to give him things to design in his head; to imagine the best possible garden or most wonderful dress or to make up a story to tell them in the morning over breakfast. 'That has had a massive impact on me from a very young age because my parents encouraged me, trained me on a nightly basis, to sit and meditate what the best possible outcome for something could be and then apply that to different circumstances.'

He has adopted this 'best possible self' technique in every show he creates. 'I always make the cast stand in silence and close their eyes and start breathing together. I make them imagine that there is a light in the centre of their chest which spreads all throughout their body, warming up their muscles. I'll ask them to imagine there is just one section of the show that they find hard and I make them imagine themselves watching themselves do it and then I make them imagine themselves doing it, and it being the clearest, the finest diction, the finest performance, the most on balance, in the air for the longest, turn that many times. And I make them imagine it over and over again.' That 'best possible self' has become a technique used all the time in sport psychology: visualization.

'Visualization is a massive part of my career now. I think it's what I do professionally as I visualize trying to communicate something to somebody. And then I use my technique to implement it, to get that information and that vision over to an audience. So, I think it is something that I do all day, every day – have done since I was a child and, hopefully, will still have the mischief and imagination to do as an old man.'

A Dutch study into pain asked volunteers to use this type of visualization. Participants completed a 'best possible self' manipulation and felt more optimistic and less pain. Another study asked respondents to spend five minutes every day over two weeks imagining themselves as a future self for whom everything had turned out optimally. Of course, these participants increased their levels of optimism.

Write it down

If visualization doesn't feel like your thing, perhaps writing might. A study in 2007 found that writing about negative thoughts puts them in perspective and increases our positive expectations. It is a form of the 'brain drain' we learned about in the previous chapter (page 197); it doesn't need to be related to any specific issue, but is a chance to get those feelings down on paper. Writing about your ideal outcome shifts expectations from negative to positive, from pessimistic to optimistic.

Monitor your circadian rhythm

Another idea may feel a little left-field, but it can be helpful in understanding the rhythms of your body. We all have circadian rhythms that determine when we will sleep, feel hungry, thirsty, tired or alert. Each cycle lasts around ninety minutes, in which time we will have one peak and one dip. If we understand when these peaks and dips come, we can be aware of the moments when we will feel pessimistic and optimistic. When you feel pessimistic, you can use this knowledge to judge if you are being rational or if the sense is simply part of your natural rhythm. When you know that a dip is approaching, you can assign any pessimistic thoughts that arrive at the same time to your biology. If you know that you are about to hit a high and find yourself being relentlessly optimistic, you might delay a decision by thirty minutes or so until you are more pragmatic.

Learning your circadian rhythms needn't be technical; you can just cut down on the caffeine and spot when you yawn. If you note down every yawn, you'll start to spot a ninety-minute pattern. The yawns highlight your dips; peaks will follow forty-five minutes later. You can find a yawn tracker in the toolkit at the end of this chapter (see page 232).

Harness the power of your smile

Smiling is another highly effective way of increasing optimism. It may feel odd and unscientific, but there is research to suggest that we feel more positive when we smile. Studies have shown that smiling during a competition can reduce an athlete's perception of effort and increase their positive thoughts. A study on runners who deliberately smiled when they were struggling found that their running economy improved. In another study, cyclists rode while watching screens in a lab. The researchers flashed up pictures of faces, too quickly for the cyclists to identify – some were of smiling faces and others were of frowns. The cyclists who got the smiles rode 12 per cent longer than those who got the grumpy faces – and reported needing to make less effort. Next time you are pushing yourself, get grinning and see if it makes any difference.

Take another perspective

The vicarious confidence that we considered in Chapter 5 is also useful for developing more optimistic behaviours (see page 129). We can do this through watching the ways a mentor behaves and copying elements of their behaviour. The key here is to find a mentor who isn't relentlessly optimistic and has that crucial nugget of pragmatism – someone who doesn't seem gung-ho, but has enough Tigger in their blood to bounce through life. You might usefully choose someone who has faced a significant setback in their life – severe illness, redundancy, bereavement, divorce or failure in business – and has remained positive throughout. Find out how they managed to translate the tough stuff that happened to them into helpful lessons. And how did they still expect good stuff to happen when they'd recently had such horrible experiences? If you take that perspective and try it the next time you have an issue, it may feel fake to begin with, but with practice it will become a habit.

Reframe your thoughts

Succeeding in generating optimism will require you to use the right kind of language, not only in speech, but also in your head. For example, the way we use language provided a light-bulb moment that took me from communications into sport psychology. I was competing in an Ironman race in Melbourne, Australia. I had to do a 2.4-mile swim, a 112-mile bike ride and a full marathon. I felt confident about the bike ride and the run, but I'd only learned to swim as an adult and had never felt particularly comfortable in the water. Furthermore, most of my swimming experience had been gained in a calm, 20-m pool in central London. As we stood on Frankston Beach, looking out at waves so rough that even the locals looked nervous, the guy on the PA system said something striking: 'You can't control the waves – you can only control how you feel about them.'

That was it: I had the choice either to be pessimistic about my ability to swim or to see it as a challenge. The self-talk in my head changed from, 'I can't do this' to, 'I'm going to have a go', giving me the courage to get in the water. The swim was not enjoyable, but I survived it and recorded my fastest ever Ironman. It made me realize that our own thoughts have the power to move us closer to our goal and our purpose. A few simple words can make so much difference.

Sometimes it only takes an extra word to switch our thoughts from pessimism to optimism. When 'I can't' becomes 'I can't yet', we can see a glimmer of possibility. When 'That's scary' becomes 'That's scary, but...', we can see that things might get better. If we use our language carefully, we can let possibility flood in. The addition of a single word doesn't always just mean a slight reframe. If you are holding back on sending a manuscript to a publisher because you tell yourself, 'They might reject it', you can substitute 'accept' for 'reject' and the thought takes on a far more optimistic shape – hopefully one that gives you the momentum to press the send button.

Drew has a very specific reframe that he uses in his company: 'In the world of theatre and, even more specifically, the world of improvisation, there is a phrase used very often which is, "Yes, and..." What that means is that, when you are given information or somebody presents you with their feelings, you find a way of responding to it with, "Yes, and..."' He suggests what you are doing is finding a way of recalibrating or reframing a situation without dismissing or denying that person's experience. This might be in a workplace, such as 'That project has worn me out... and I am proud we completed it.' Or in a hobby: 'I am gutted we lost that match... and chuffed at the goal we scored.' 'It means that, rather than disagreeing or dismissing, it's building upon and just slightly changing the direction the car is driving in, but still keeping the people in the car with you. If you can add to their experience rather than take away, I find that leads to a quicker form of success, a better form of collaboration, creativity and a sense of teamwork.'

Here we see that instead of trying to suppress thoughts, which makes them louder, we can twist them into something more helpful and optimistic. If we fear loss, we can reframe our language to highlight what we might gain. If we fear the difficulty of something, we might consider how much easier life will be once it is complete. To see the beauty of this reframing, we can think of Lieutenant General Lewis 'Chesty' Puller. In the Korean War, his regiment of marines was surrounded by Chinese soldiers. A pessimistic response would have been to raise a white flag. His optimistic response was to encourage his team: 'They are in front of us, behind us, and we are flanked on both sides by an enemy that outnumbers us! They can't get away from us now!' Use the table on page 234 to note down how you could reframe your unhelpful thoughts.

PRAGMATIC OPTIMISM TOOLKIT

'Best possible self' imagery

To build optimism, we can use a technique called 'best possible self' and match it with a visualization process so we raise our expectations and likelihood of success. 'Best possible self' imagery is not daydreaming. It is positive, proactive and used with a specific purpose in mind. It is a mental rehearsal where you help your brain learn what to do, rather than what not to do. To make it really effective, we use all our senses, as the more vivid and realistic the images are, the more likely our brain is to interpret them as similar to the actual event.

The best way to do this is to write a script. Go full-on Hollywood and make it as convincing as possible so you create rich and realistic images. To ensure you cover seven key areas in your script, note down here:

1. The situation your best possible self will be in:

   _____

2. What you will be able to see:

   _____

3. What you will be able to hear:

   _____

4. What you will be able to feel in your hands or on your skin:

   _____

5. What you will be able to taste:

_____

6. What you will be able to smell:

_____

7. How you will feel when you have achieved it:

_____

Then mix it all together until it feels like you have a realistic script. The finished script should take no longer than two minutes to read out. If you can record it on your phone and listen to it regularly, your brain starts to feel like you already have experience in behaving in this way – so it becomes less scary and feels more doable. Once you get good at it you no longer need a script and can do the imagery anywhere, visualizing successful performances.

Yawn tracker

A yawn tracker helps us figure out our circadian rhythm. The most common times to yawn are after lunch and early evening.

Each time you yawn, jot down the time. Over a few days you'll start to see a pattern and there should be around ninety minutes between each set of yawns. This pattern will show you when your sixteen dips will be each day. Add forty-five minutes to these and you have your peaks.

Date	Yawn 1	Yawn 2	Yawn 3	Yawn 4

My morning dips (a good time to do easier activities):

My evening dips (a good time to go to bed):

My morning peaks (a good time to focus hard on difficult things):

My afternoon peaks (a good time to focus hard or do a technical-type exercise):

Reframing

Pragmatic optimism is the belief that good things will happen. It helps you reflect on what has already happened and expands your future opportunities by helping you approach them with a presumption of success. To develop more of this, we can get into the habit of reframing. With a pessimistic outlook, we tend to use stinking thinking (where we focus on what we can't do). An optimistic outlook will move us towards behaviours that will create positive changes and actions.

Unhelpful thought	Replacement thought

9

Internal Insight

Internal insight helps you design a life that suits your core being, your social preferences, your emotional outlook, your motivations and your competencies. This self-awareness gives you the strongest possible foundation for success.

The ancient Chinese philosopher Lao Tzu is believed to have said: 'He who gains a victory over other men is strong, but he who gains a victory over himself is all powerful.' This idea still stands strong today. The clearer our self-awareness, the more effectively we can choose the skills to match our strengths, weaknesses, personality traits, environmental constraints and life experiences. In doing so, we may find that we don't actually need to change anything – but if we understand ourselves better, we can use the right tool at the right time.

When we lack internal insight, we fail to recognize things about ourselves. By contrast, when we are aware of our own competencies – or know which we lack – we can be more honest about what we observe in ourselves and how we respond to it. It is our past experiences that give us the biggest insight. They force us to prioritize, to get perspective and to understand the driving forces in our lives. These experiences redirect the ways we go on to think about ourselves. Internal insight helps us develop awareness of our mastery of our abilities, behaviours and emotions.

Someone who is used to getting us all to question our abilities, behaviours and emotions, usually through highlighting their ridiculousness, is comedian and author Sara Pascoe.[*] She not only helps us become more self-aware, but she makes herself vulnerable, using her own internal insight to create her content. 'As a confessional comic, I do use my own life, thoughts and opinions or my own research at times. It does mean that nothing is off limits. You are trawling absolutely everything to find stuff.'

Sara realizes that this need to be self-aware can bring issues: 'It can be quite difficult sometimes to be present in your life, especially if you are writing a new show. It means you have a constant to and fro of a very insular life by yourself, planning, and then you give a performance and the audience tell you how funny it is. It is a constant assessment.'

What Is Internal Insight?

Internal insight is the ability to notice and respond to behaviours, habits, motivations and emotions – not just monitoring them, but accurately assessing and reflecting on them. It gives us a more impartial attitude about ourselves and how we feel in different situations.

Some of us naturally reflect on our psychological processes and how they relate to other people; we can consider this to be an expression of self-consciousness, whether public – when

* Note: Sara's comments in this chapter have been abridged from a recorded interview with the author.

we develop an understanding of how others see us – or private, when we reflect on our internal states. Together, they give us an idea of how we see ourselves and how others perceive us.

When we possess such insight, it can be a tool for growth and ultimately success. If we have the mental processes to develop this insight, it can become automatic. We compare our actions to our own standards; in this way, the development of self-awareness never ends. We continue to reflect on our experience and assess our behaviours and responses. As our internal insight grows, we notice more about ourselves.

We are born with some self-awareness: as babies, we naturally cry when we are hungry, tired, hot, cold, bored or lonely. Between the ages of twelve and eighteen months, we start to become more aware and are able to recognize ourselves. As we grow, we tend to focus on what is socially desirable rather than what we are able to do. It is at around the age of eight when we begin to develop a more advanced level of self-awareness, distinguishing between negative and positive attributes.

Our self-awareness develops further in our teenage years; our ability to appraise our own performance improves, but we might still struggle to appraise emotions. This makes it a helpful time to focus on self-awareness; it is a period when we undergo environmental, physiological, cognitive and neurobiological change, in addition to experiencing the stressors of teenage life: academic testing, peer relationships, physical changes and cravings for independence. Teen brains are more reactive to these stressors, which arrive at a time when we are not just more aware of who we are, but also of how others see us.

Types of internal insight

Becoming an authority on ourselves helps us become more aware of our preferences and fears, so we can design our environment to maximize our potential and avoid those things that reduce our success. We need to be aware of our resources and limiters. There are thousands of these; if we were listing them, we would need to include all our traits, behaviours, values, sensations, desires, strengths, abilities, motivations, emotions, goals, beliefs and competencies. We would also need to include the pillars of success discussed in this book: how much we feel we belong, our levels of mastery, whether we have autonomy, our purpose, our confidence levels, whether we feel courageous, have optimism, are able to put process before outcome and how thankful we are. A full checklist would be endless, but we can think about it in five areas:

1. our core self
2. our social sense
3. our key emotions
4. our motivations
5. our competencies

When we understand who we are and how we respond in each of these areas, we can use them to better shape our behaviours.

Our core self

This seems to have the most impact on our performance. When we are aware of our personality and how it influences our behaviour and emotions, we can be clearer about how we work. When we are sure of our purpose and understand our values, we can direct our life in a way that suits us, making choices that feel congruent with our core being.

Understanding how our personality influences us can avoid years of stress and lead to a far happier life. Our personality shouldn't stop us doing anything, but it can help mitigate the stresses that come from doing something that takes us out of our comfort zone.

One of the 'big five' personality traits to consider will be either extroversion or introversion. Many people think of extroverts as loud and boisterous and introverts as shy and quiet, but this isn't quite right; the difference comes from where we get our energy. If an extrovert is tired and stressed, they need to be around other people to reinvigorate; by contrast, an introvert will top up their energy levels by having some time alone. When we recognize this quality in ourselves, we can more effectively schedule how we recover after difficult situations. Similarly, when we are aware of our purpose and values, we have a clear measure by which to make choices. We don't need to think through every decision; we just consider whether it aligns with our goals, values and purpose, and make decisions based on that measure.

Our social sense

A key element of our social being is the way in which we compare ourselves. When we see how we behave alongside others, we can evaluate our performance and we can use the skills in this book around mastery, confidence and process to adapt if we are falling behind. We can also consider how we engage with others: do we prefer to have a few people in our life who we are close to or a wide network of contacts? When we are struggling, do we shut down or open up? Do we prefer to work alone or with other people?

Our key emotions

Having an understanding of our emotional being is also import-ant; recognizing the emotions we have in different situations helps us prepare for them. The ability to read our body can act like an early warning system, revealing hidden emotions. We can understand where our energy goes and remember the things that drain us. This ensures that we carry out activities only when we feel mentally able.

How we respond to stress is a crucial element of our emotional being. The response can take over both our head and our body, as happens when we are confronted with a situation we don't have the capacity or capability to handle. If we want to carry out good-quality decision-making without feeling uncomfortable or triggering our threat zone, we need to anticipate stress and put in place coping mechanisms. When we identify what causes our stress levels to rise, we can look out and maintain the head space to consider the issue differently and arrive at a more positive outcome.

We are then able to approach challenges with excitement rather than see them as threatening situations to fear. Studies have found that people with this mindset performed better on a maths task, and also enjoyed it more, than those who viewed the same task as a threat. We can be more adept at handling stressful situations if we have internal insight into how we experience stress, the skills we have to handle it and the knowledge that we view events with either a challenge mindset or a threat mindset.

Our motivations

This refers to the insight we have about our goals, showing us the direction to take and allowing us to assess every choice. When we understand what motivates us and interpret the elements of motivation effectively (feeling that sense of belonging, mastery and autonomy), we can build those elements into our life and increase our success. When we understand that either we control events or their outcome depends on others, we can adapt our approach accordingly.

Our competencies

Finally, our behaviours and abilities make up our competent being. Our internal insight helps us to understand how we focus best and maintain our attentional control, allowing us to block out distractions. It mediates the ways in which we react to setbacks and how we would prefer to respond. It also powers the coping mechanisms we use every day to function better.

Internal Insight Supports Our Success

When we have developed the five elements of internal insight, there are numerous ways in which we can use them to become more successful.

One of the biggest benefits of this insight is that it increases our emotional intelligence – our ability to monitor our own emotions, recognize them in others and develop management strategies. Possessing emotional intelligence means being able to perceive how we and others feel, assimilate that knowledge into the bigger picture and build a deeper understanding of situations. High emotional intelligence has been found to improve performance among leaders. And being self-aware improves our emotional intelligence and grounds us in reality. If we are ambitious and bold, we may use it to give us a reality check that discourages arrogance at one end of the scale and stops us from holding ourselves back at the other. An emotional map is included in the toolkit at the end of this chapter so you can start to grow your emotional literacy (see page 261).

Day-to-day, internal insight gives us a solid foundation for our decisions and makes us more effective in how we carry them out. As a result, developing self-awareness is actively encouraged in a number of professions. In an American study, seventy-five student nurses participated in a simulation to assess their abilities at delivering high-quality end-of-life care; the higher their self-awareness, the better their care. And when the Royal Navy introduced a course on self-awareness for junior officers, they found that those who participated learned more effectively and performed better.

Internal insight can also improve our communication. When we understand why we think as we do, we can be clearer in our intentions and better articulate our purpose. It is not surprising that studies have found that improved communication in the workplace influences employee engagement and leads to improved performance and better managerial effectiveness. In team sports, communication between players, or players and managers, can make the difference between success and failure.

Sara changed her entire approach to communication because of her self-awareness around how she made people feel, not just on stage, but also in life. She figured out that you should never start a gig with a negative. 'If you are coming on stage to one person and it is a dungeon that's very smoky and you think it is maybe a firetrap and unsafe, the worst thing you can do when you go on stage is go, "Ugh, there is only one of you here, and this is an awful room." You can turn it into a positive so you go, "Thank God, there is only ever one person who gets my jokes and we've got rid of the others, there is just you here tonight." You've already made it kind of funny and flippant, and you've made it OK.'

With greater self-awareness we can learn how to sustain a specific physiological or psychological state, which makes us better at self-regulation. It means that we can avoid distractions and shift our focus when we feel that things are slipping. It also helps us set and stick to goals. When we know where we are in our development and are honest about our strengths and weaknesses, we can be more effective at setting and following goals. It also improves our decision-making. In a high-performance environment, our brain is presented with huge amounts of information; those of us with internal insight are able to sort through and understand the implications of each piece of information.

Sara figured out this self-regulation approach early on to change her approach to performance. She twisted her thoughts to pretend that things didn't matter so much. 'I find taking all of the stakes away makes me much freer, safer, braver, more creative than going, "Come on, Sara, you've got to go out there and show them." People in stand-up use very aggressive words like "Smash it" and I know that comes from business as well. It never got me into a good place because I don't want to feel like I'm in a war. I don't want to feel like I'm in a battle. I want to feel like I'm in a safe space communicating with, you know, open hearts and loving people, so I kind of have to put myself into that state.'

Internal insight can also strengthen our identity – the way we see ourselves and want others to see us. It becomes a filter for the way in which we interpret new information; with every action we take, we are making a statement about who we are. The more time we spend reacting to our identity, the stronger that statement becomes. But there is a balance to be found. If we have too narrow a sense of identity, we may miss out on other experiences, feel lonely or lost when we retire and have little of interest to share with others. If we have many frag-mented identities and lots of different interests, we will never have enough time or focus to do anything deeply and will fail to do well in any of the areas we care about.

When we are aware of and secure in our identity, we can seek to align more of what we do with our purpose, to know who we should spend time with and what we can be masterful at. This means that our other pillars of success are strengthened and we become more motivated. 'Motivational intensity' theory suggests that, when we assume that something is possible and worthwhile, we allocate the necessary resources to it. The more self-aware we become, the more effectively we can assess whether or not we have the skills to achieve our goal.

For people working in high-performance environments or wanting to perform at a high level, knowledge of the conditions they perform best in can be invaluable. Being aware of what happens when they are under pressure and how they act when they are feeling confident is vital to facilitate good performance. In any role where they need to perform above a specific level, whether they are a therapist, a surgeon, an actor or an athlete, for example, they need to be clear what influences their performance and how; internal insight is a crucial component.

Internal insight is a key part of our development as performers. When we accurately self-monitor, are open to feedback and know how we learn best, we can exploit our cognitive abilities to help us learn more. When we realize that we don't know something, we can seek out that knowledge or skill. Ongoing professional development is essential to all careers and self-awareness is invaluable. It highlights where we need to improve or what we need to learn. Without it, we risk resting on our laurels, becoming stale in our thinking or using outdated skills and knowledge, to the detriment of our clients and our career.

In comedy, Sara is acutely aware that self-awareness and feedback can be pretty immediate. 'I often fail and that is something that is very much part of the comedian's life and it is actually one of the most useful lessons in creativity. I have written hundreds and hundreds of jokes that I really thought,

"These are so brilliant", and said them to an audience and they were incredibly unimpressed. You can't be dulled by the fact that people are bored by you. You have to feel it and then drop those things. Nothing is ever good straight away.'

Once you have mastered that internal insight and developed the art of failing and learning from it, Sara reminds us that it can become a strength, because it makes you realize how much you don't know so you have a guide on where to go next. Sara spends time reflecting on each performance to learn from it. 'It is an interesting journey into working out why. Is it because you felt that you could do better? Is it because I wasn't brave enough? Say that I went there to try new material and then the room looked a bit scary and I did old material, at the end of the gig I will feel like, "Why did you come out tonight? You didn't do what you set out to do. You were too afraid."'

While internal insight feels like a pillar that relates most to the individual, what we learn when we are more self-aware can improve how we work alongside others. A study of over two thousand five hundred people in 515 teams found that the higher individual self-awareness, the more effectively the team functioned as a unit. Insight can give us a realistic impression of what we are like to work with – whether we hold back projects, rub people up the wrong way, positively support others or make sure none of the details are missed.

Most problems within teams are a result of conflict, whether it is between personalities or between different ways of doing things. Teams are made up of individuals who all bring their own knowledge, skills, attitudes, personalities and behavioural preferences, and all this has an influence on how the team works. When individuals are unaware of the impact their individual preferences have on themselves and others, there is more conflict and less cohesion. By contrast, when they recognize their own preferences and see how those of others may affect them, it becomes easier to spot potential conflict and to take avoiding action at an early stage.

Possessing internal insight can have a positive financial impact. The consultancy firm Korn Ferry analysed almost seven thousand people working in 486 organizations to find 'blind spots' – those characteristics identified by an individual as one of their strengths, but regarded by their colleagues as a weakness. What an individual may think of as assertiveness, their colleagues may see as aggression. Another person might think of themselves as kind, but be regarded by their colleagues as a walkover. The more blind spots a person has, the lower their internal insight. In organizations that are underperforming, employees had 20 per cent more blind spots than more successful counterparts. When there are fewer blind spots, because of increased self-awareness, a company's performance improves. It takes a courageous person to go and hunt for their blind spots though – you have to proactively ask others for feedback and compare their thoughts to your own.

Insightful Leaders

There has been a great deal of research into the impact of self-awareness in leadership. Where insight is taken seriously in organizations – which can include 360-degree feedback and mentoring programmes that incorporate personality traits, problem-solving and managerial styles – internal insight can be utilized to improve performance.

Although Sara works mainly alone, she has seen how the insight gathered as a comedian could benefit all of us in organizations. 'I find that, if I'm trying to be funny in a group scenario, the worst thing I can do is sit there listening to my own comments, thinking in my own head, "Was that good enough? Did I join in enough there?"' She suggests the way to get comfortable and perform well here is not to focus on yourself, but on others. 'Being aware of other people and then what they need from you takes you out of yourself. Asking other people questions and assuring them that what they said is really useful to you will make them like you so much that you then feel very warm and safe and "I can take a risk on this thing" or, "OK, you've been vulnerable, I'm going to be vulnerable." And you can actually become quite a powerful person without dominating a group.'

Internal insight can help leaders see how they are regarded by others and, as a result, they can better understand how their behaviour affects their colleagues and customers. Leaders are often asked to rate themselves against specific competencies. When their team does the same for their boss, the gap between the two values will give an insight into the leader's self-awareness. Where the gap is small and the leaders have accurately assessed their abilities, they can be said to have high levels of self-awareness, are better able to use those abilities and can bring other people on board to help them with their weaker areas.

Those leaders with high levels of self-awareness tend to be viewed as more successful by their teams; they seem more committed, better at mentoring and more able to influence those they work with, and they have the ability to regulate their behaviour when necessary. This helps them become more inspirational and more authentic leaders, clear on their values and purpose and aware of how to work in line with them. By contrast, where the gap between a leader's self-belief and their team's perception is large, it tends to be because the leader has overestimated their own abilities; they will likely have lower levels of success and less enthusiastic followers.

The business schools at Harvard and Stanford universities state explicitly that their programmes develop students' self-awareness, which they believe is an essential quality in successful leaders. Some leadership experts have suggested that being aware of how we behave, learn and react has a bigger impact on the quality of our work than our IQ, qualifications or technical skills. This seems more relevant than ever before as the world of work changes beyond all recognition. In 2017, a report by the technology company Dell suggested that 85 per cent of the jobs that will exist in 2030 have yet to be invented. Knowledge about a specific area of any industry will become less valuable and knowing your own strengths, weaknesses and preferences will become invaluable.

The challenge is that developing insight is not easy and there are a number of barriers.

When We Lack Insight

There is no single, universal truth about the way we are perceived; other people inevitably see us differently from the way we see ourselves. A small amount of difference might be fine, but when our self-awareness is completely incompatible with other people's reality, there is a huge risk that our day-to-day performance and long-term success will be thwarted. The fact is that most of us suffer from some lack of self-awareness. An analysis of twenty-two studies found that many people have low or moderate insight into their own performance. If we fail to properly use self-examination or to seek feedback from others, we will suffer from blind spots and be unable to accurately assess our own capabilities.

A healthy level of self-esteem is an important aspect of self-awareness because it indicates that we are evaluating our abilities and regard ourselves as successful, giving us protection against negative feedback. This boost to our self-esteem will make us feel good, but if we block out what we don't want to hear, our self-awareness is lowered, as is our ability to work on our weaknesses. This constant internal tension – between feeling good and being truthful with ourselves – is hard to police, and accurate insight can often be a casualty.

The Dunning-Kruger effect that we learned about in Chapter 2 (see page 51) is a cognitive bias that shows how it is harmful for us to overestimate our ability. It highlights that, when we begin to study any new subject, we are both incompetent and ignorant and realize this, but as we gain a small amount of competence, our brains are inclined to suppose that we are more capable than we actually are, as we don't have the knowledge to recognize our own incompetence. This is important as studies have found that when we are unable to accurately rate our performance, we tend to perform poorly. When we are not skilled at something, there is a double effect: not only are we rubbish, but because we think that we're great, we don't listen to the feedback that could help us improve. It is only when we are good at something that we can see the ways to improve and realize how far there is to go before we know what we're doing. It means that those of us who should be confident aren't, and those who shouldn't be, are. We are all susceptible to this effect, but being aware of it can help us stay a little more rooted in reality.

It is not just Dunning-Kruger that restricts our ability to become more self-aware. In an ideal world, we would think deeply, ask other people how we seem to them and make an effort to notice what we do and don't like. Using our brains to think about what our brains are doing (something known as metacognition) is not easy, but becoming more aware of our own self is an essential part in the process of analysing our own effectiveness. At the same time, we must remember that we don't exist in a vacuum. Most things we do affect other people, and their opinions matter. I might see myself as chatty and friendly, but others may see me as annoying and loud. Such perceptions should impact on how we evaluate ourselves.

The balanced development of our internal insight can be hampered by a negative self-appraisal bias that is sometimes known as 'depressive realism'. We may lack confidence in the way we look at ourselves and fail to meet our potential or build relationships with people who like us. This is a common occurrence among people who have depression or social anxiety. If your perception of your abilities is lower than that expressed by others, you might need to work with a counsellor or psychologist who can help you understand what is undermining your insight. But there are also things you can do, day to day, that will give you a more realistic picture of how you are doing and help you to focus on thriving rather than just surviving. These activities require you to be unrelenting in your exploration of opportunities to increase your internal insight.

Building Internal Insight

The most important element of our internal insight is the awareness of what's important to us. We looked at this in Chapter 4 when we discussed purpose, but there's more we can do.

Know your values

We focus on values – what they are and how we align them with everything we do – to feel authentic and achieve our purpose. We all have values, and you hopefully identified yours in the toolkit for Chapter 7 to help you develop your courage (see page 201).

These values keep us close to our ethical framework, ensuring we feel comfortable with what we will and won't do. Knowing our values means that, whatever else happens, we can always act in accordance with what we believe is right. We won't always be able to match up to them, but we can feel as if we are moving in the right direction, getting closer to them. This will boost our optimism and effort levels.

You can use your values to consider how you would behave in various scenarios. If you are playing a game of tennis and your opponent starts to make dodgy line calls, your automatic response might be to lose your temper and yell at them to stop cheating. However, if you have worked on your values and know how they manifest, you can direct your behaviour far more effectively. If fairness is one of your most important values, you might issue a warning each time you spot a cheat, in order to crack down on it early. If achievement is one of your most important values, maybe you will use the cheating as a prompt to beat your opponent convincingly.

Sara has just one value and it is a powerful one: 'I don't want to make the world worse.' She has learned to use this value as a barometer as to whether she is doing her job well. It came up strongly when she did a university freshers' gig and used a joke about anorexics. 'Their eating disorder society wrote to me afterwards and essentially said, "We like you and we like what you do and what you represent, so imagine how hard it was for us to hear you being flippant about something that kills people."' Her first reaction was defensive – that she was one of the good guys and it was just a joke. But slowly she realized that, when something affects you so much, it doesn't feel flippant. 'If you have lost a friend to an eating disorder or you are suffering very badly yourself, someone who treats it like a joke or a choice or vanity, which was what the routine was kind of doing, I realized I was really wrong. It was ignorant and insensitive, and I ended up feeling so grateful to those people. I dropped the routine because I can't bear the thought that someone comes out to comedy and goes home feeling sad.'

As Sara did, we measure what matters to us. With our values unearthed, we use them to identify when we are acting authentically and building our long-term insight.

Practise mindfulness

Mindfulness can be one route to achieving some self-awareness. It does have a poor reputation – you may have sat through a corporate workshop and rolled your eyes when told to eat a single raisin slowly and mindfully. But when mindfulness is taught properly it can be useful in helping us become more self-aware – both in the long term and in helping us to notice what's worrying us right now. Like many of us, Sara is clear that formal meditation is not for her. 'I find it excruciatingly boring and I've never had the experience of my brain quietening. I have the experience of my brain shouting more and more and more.' Instead, she does yoga. That is where she is better at settling her mind.

As Sara highlights here, at its heart, mindfulness is not about sitting still and trying not to think – or even sitting munching raisins. It is about focusing on the present moment, noticing what we are thinking, but without judgement. Not trying to change the content of our thoughts, get rid of them or even control them, but trying to change our relationship with them and distance ourselves from them. In paying attention to the things that are bothering us but not actually engaging with them, we reserve space in our heads for the things that we can do something about, rather than the things we can't. This helps us respond better to our thoughts, leaving us in control of our behaviours. As a result, we don't just have more internal insight, but are better able to use what we notice.

Studies in the world of sport have found that using a mindful approach can lead to increased performance. When the US's BMX team participated in mindfulness training, they improved their self-awareness, were able to feel sensations more acutely, were more present in competition and, when their brains were scanned, they were found to respond differently to stress. Their coach reported that they were able to get out of the gates faster in competitions.

When our emotions are high – often because our threat zone has been triggered – our cognition is low. Practising mindfulness drains some of the emotion, increasing our distance from our thoughts and leaving us better placed to use rational cognition in our decision-making. Think of the financial trader who has to make incredibly quick responses, relating to millions or even billions of pounds, in a high-pressure environment. They will do better when they respond to the rational side of their brain rather than the emotional side, which is focused on protecting them. Or consider the teacher with a disruptive child in their class. Our instant response might be to throw that student out of the room but, with distance, we remember that the child has a difficult home life and only craves attention because they've never had any from their parents. Excluding the child will only increase the rejection they feel and worsen their behaviour. With distance, we respond differently, and the outcome is often far more positive.

Mindfulness can be done with a teacher, on your own or by listening to guided mindfulness on apps like Headspace or Calm or my audiobook *Power Down to Power Up* (Audible) that will talk you through some of the techniques. If you go it alone, you will start by learning to breathe deeply and noticing different body sensations. You don't need to do these exercises for more than ten to fifteen minutes, so it shouldn't feel too restrictive. If the thought of mindfulness fills you with horror, then consider other activities in which you completely lose yourself, like colouring, building Lego or doing jigsaws. These can also help you get some head space to think freely.

Over time, you might try to notice the thoughts that sneak into your mind while you're breathing or engaged in another absorbing activity. You don't need to answer or respond to them in any way – just notice them. Maybe, after a while, you could visualize yourself putting those thoughts on a cloud and watching them drift off to the edge of your vision. When it feels comfortable, you can return to those thoughts after your mindfulness session.

You might think that you have an unmanageable number of difficult thoughts, but when they are organized you will probably realize that they follow a theme. Could this theme be labelled? Common labels are around relationships, housing, work, sport, money or the future.

If you are nervous about labelling thoughts, fearing that putting negative feelings into words will intensify those feelings, you should be reassured by research that has shown that writing down what you are feeling, labelling your thoughts, can reduce the intensity of emotion you feel. Scientists have used neuroimaging studies to show that, when we label a thought, the response diminishes in our amygdala and the thought's impact reduces.

If the worries sneaking into your head during your mindfulness practice are ones you could usefully be aware of – niggling reminders of things that you have been procrastinating about tackling – this practice might be the prompt you need to get working. If the worries relate to things that are beyond your control or big-picture issues, such as the environment or politics, then notice and continue to label them – but put them to one side. Over time, it might be that these thoughts reoccur and cause you to realize how important they are to you. They might help drive your purpose and you can do something with them. But to begin with, just noticing them from a safe distance is enough.

You may struggle with wanting to respond to your labelled thoughts; perhaps you fight back when you find you are telling yourself you're not good enough or start searching for solutions to the issues raised by the thoughts you have labelled. Begin by stating what you are noticing – something like, 'I'm thinking that I'm a rubbish parent.' Then take another step away: 'I'm noticing that I'm thinking that I'm a rubbish parent.' This stops you feeling like you are a rubbish parent and reminds you that it is your thoughts speaking – and not you.

Think aloud

This is a different technique that we can use to develop internal insight. It is widely used in sport, but can cover any area about which you would like to understand more. You need a sound recorder of some kind (most smartphones have a suitable app); as you are carrying out an activity, say out loud everything that is running through your head. Explicitly describing where your attention goes and what you are focused on helps to highlight negative or distracting thoughts that may be affecting your performance.

The technique can improve your reflections and protect you from the biases that we often have once we know the outcome of a performance. If we were trying this 'think aloud' process while working on a piece of academic coursework, we would gain real insight into both our thought processes and our assessment of how we had done. Using the 'think aloud' process can also benefit our performance itself. In a study, cyclists were asked to describe what they were thinking during a 10-mile time trial and found that, not only were they more focused on their performance, they performed better.

Many of the thoughts that might present themselves during a 'think aloud' activity will be stressors or hassles, whether we have more than we can comfortably deal with or just one big stressor that we do not have the capacity to manage. Coping mechanisms make us feel as if we have the capacity to deal with the negatives that come our way. Building awareness of the stressors we don't know how to cope with and anticipating when they are likely to strike is a good way to prepare ourselves and to develop strategies to deal with them. If you are more aware of them, you can analyse how they are preventing you from performing at your best.

Recognize your stressors

You can find a list of the stressors that we encounter in day-to-day life, and those we also expect to see in high-performing life, in the toolkit at the end of this chapter (see pages 263 and 265). Once you have a list of all the things you need to be more aware of, you can start to tackle them, reduce your stress levels and put yourself in a better place to succeed.

Sara has actively thought about what stressors she is up against. Her biggest ones come from the fear that her audience won't enjoy themselves.

'Any dissent from that can feel affronting, but I've always found that my insecurity always expected much worse of people than the truth.' She gives an example of a woman standing up, twenty minutes into her show, grabbing her bag and coat and noisily walking out. 'There was this huge crash of the doors when she left. I interpreted it as anger, as an aggressive show of dissent from what I was performing.' She got through the show, but was really upset that someone had thought her show was so bad. 'When I got home, I got an email through my website. It was a woman and she said, "I was at your show in Edinburgh today. I'm so sorry I had to leave. I had to vomit." She said, "I saw you looking at me and I couldn't even meet your eye 'cos I thought I was going to be sick. I had to run to the toilets. I loved the show. I came back, I was too embarrassed to come in, so I sat on the steps down by the door and listened to the last forty minutes.'"

What Sara has assumed was anger was actually illness. Sara's fear, her trigger, was that she wasn't good enough. We all have our own triggers. Some will be unique to you and will take the form of things that you only notice once you are looking out for them. It might be someone talking loudly on their phone on the train, your children abandoning half-eaten pieces of fruit around the house or your partner leaving tissues in their trouser pockets when they put them in the washing machine. Accepting that these things annoy you and making a plan to avoid them is a less stressful way to live than passive-aggressively sighing and threatening not to buy any more train tickets, fruit or tissues.

Identify your emotions

Every situation has an emotion attached to it and higher levels of emotional literacy are helpful to ensure that we retain insight, whatever is happening. This means that we need to have the vocabulary to understand and explain how we are feeling. Researchers have identified six basic emotions: fear, anger, sadness, disgust, surprise and joy. You can make these far more specific, breaking them down into at least 100 further emotions. You might say you were 'angry' in basic emotional language, but if you were more literate you could describe yourself as 'furious', 'hostile' or 'betrayed'. Being aware of your exact emotion helps you communicate better and decide how to deal with the feeling more effectively. The emotional map you need to do this is in the toolkit at the end of this chapter (see page 261).

We will sometimes feel a number of emotions that might seem to be in conflict with each other. If I was to go rock climbing, I would feel apprehension, but also excitement. The important thing is to recognize the emotions and work out how to cope with them. Doing this exercise with children can be incredibly valuable. Teaching them emotional literacy means that they can better describe their feelings, and studies have found that this can protect them from a number of mental health issues. If you have children in your life, you might try to build it into story time. Ask them what the characters they're reading about might be feeling and why.

It is also helpful to be aware of what is going on in our own body. We can use a technique called 'biofeedback' to do this. It is used in sport and health to help us 'see' inside our body. If you can read a specific heart rate on a monitor, you can learn to replicate the physical feeling that matches the heart rate. I use a tool, made by BioDot, with athletes who become too anxious during competition. You put a small sticker on your hand that changes colour depending on your level of stress. You then practise different breathing techniques to see which ones help you break the cycle of anxiety and change the colour of the dot.

This technique has an impact on performance. A study followed five Olympic-level athletes preparing to compete for Canada in the 2012 Olympic Games. It found that when they took part in a biofeedback programme designed to improve their internal insight, they became more self-aware, could regulate their physiological and psychological states more effectively and had improved levels of personal control.

The technique also functions as an early warning system, helping us to become aware of what we are feeling before our brain is conscious of it. In this way, we can use biofeedback to notice where in our body we feel our emotions. When we learn to 'read' our body, we actively feel our emotions – the heart-swelling moment when we see someone we love, the rush of cortisol when we have to face a fear, the pump of adrenaline when we are about to do something new, the lump we feel in our throat when the heroine dies in a film. We can use this knowledge to our advantage by learning how our body feels about things. Once we have worked it out, it acts like a red flag, allowing us to deal with difficult emotions before our brain has actively noticed that there is a problem.

Sara has learned how to keep her brain soothed. 'I discovered that if I did a yoga class or a swim right before a gig, they are the two things that control your breathing and really put you back inside your body. I found that was so calming that I would go to the gigs and then I wouldn't quite be able to get nervous any more. Like, I would just feel like, "OK, I hope this gig goes well." And it would just feel like a psychological experience rather than a physiological one where my body was scared.'

Find time for reflection

A less intense way to develop self-awareness is to regularly put aside time for reflection. You don't have to sit in a quiet room with a mug of tea, but just be in a place where your brain can relax. My best time for reflection is on a run, but other people might find that same space when drawing, driving or cooking. During this purposeful reflection, you might make a mental agenda of what you would like to consider. We need to be honest with ourselves, to own our strengths and weaknesses, and to consider how we could have acted differently in situations. One way to do this, Sara suggests, is to put ourselves into the mindset of a comedian and write a five-minute stand-up routine introducing yourself.

'Think: how would I introduce myself to a group of strangers in a way that doesn't take myself seriously but also defines me? And then I have to choose something to have an emotional reaction to because that is what comedy is. Even if people didn't want to perform it and even if they thought their jokes were rubbish, they might find it interesting how they externalized what their clown was.'

It is natural to want to escape our internal insight and hide from difficult feelings but, when we are open to insight, we perform better, have more chance of success and can live our life in line with our values and purpose.

INTERNAL INSIGHT TOOLKIT

Insight assessment

Developing the ability to notice, assess, reflect and respond to the five internal insight elements (our core, social, emotional and motivational beings and our competency and knowledge) allows us to spot strengths and weaknesses so we can use the strengths more and work on our weaknesses.

Writing down your insights here so you can note those strengths and weaknesses means that you can use your internal insight for good.

1. A personality trait which helps me move towards success:

   _____

2. A personality trait which hinders success:

   _____

3. A way I use comparisons with others to help me do better:

   _____

4. A way I use comparisons with others unhelpfully:

_____

5. A helpful way I respond when I feel threatened or stressed:

_____

6. An unhelpful way I respond to threats or stress:

_____

7. A helpful way to boost my motivation:

_____

8. An unhelpful behaviour I have when I feel unmotivated:

_____

9. One behaviour that I feel proud of:

_____

10. A behaviour I would like to change:

_____

Emotional map

We tend to become really lazy with the words that we use to describe how we are feeling. The ten words in the middle of each cluster are the words I see clients saying most often. They are our go-to words and we often have just one coping mechanism for dealing with that feeling. If we increase our emotional literacy and start using more of the 'outside' words, we can design coping mechanisms that are much more specific and effective.

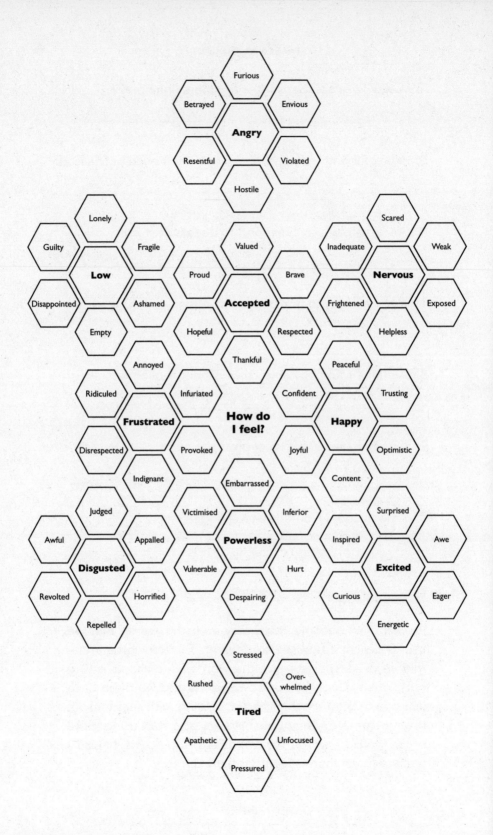

Hassles and stressors in day-to-day life

When we are more highly aware of the hassles and stressors we are up against, we can be more proactive in protecting ourselves from the potential stress they could bring and we can create coping mechanisms that will help us handle them. This list contains seventy-five common stressors or hassles that we might have to handle at any one time.

- Look through the list and put a tick against anything which you are facing at the moment.

- Don't worry about the number of boxes you have ticked – the number isn't too important; it's whether you feel like you have a) the capacity and b) the capability to handle them. When we don't, that is when we can feel stressed.

- Go back through the list and circle those that you don't feel you have the capability or capacity to handle. These will be the ones to pull apart, investigate and make a plan for how to handle them better.

Misplacing or losing things   [ ]
Fear of confrontation   [ ]
Troublesome neighbours   [ ]
Not enough money for daily needs   [ ]
Not enough money to enjoy yourself   [ ]
Not enough money for future needs   [ ]
Social obligations   [ ]
Feeling lonely or isolated   [ ]
Concerns about accidents or injuries   [ ]
Troubling thoughts about the future   [ ]
Thoughts about death   [ ]
Health of a family member   [ ]
Too much time on your hands   [ ]
Unhelpful expectations from others   [ ]
Too many interruptions   [ ]

Concerns about owing money   [ ]
Being owed money   [ ]
Dislike those who you work with or for   [ ]
Financial responsibility for others   [ ]
Caring responsibilities for children or partner   [ ]
Caring responsibilities for other family members   [ ]
Dislike work duties   [ ]
Not having a job   [ ]
Needing to reduce costs and bills   [ ]
Concerns about retirement   [ ]
Unhealthy habits (smoking, drinking, drugs)   [ ]
Caring responsibilities for pets   [ ]
Concerns about job security   [ ]
Housekeeping responsibilities   [ ]
Too many responsibilities   [ ]
Trouble making decisions   [ ]
Concerns about whether to have children   [ ]
Physical appearance (weight, height, looks)   [ ]
Meal planning or preparation   [ ]
Difficulties getting pregnant   [ ]
Concerns about physical health or medical issues   [ ]
Concerns about mental health or wellbeing   [ ]
Trouble relaxing   [ ]
Worries around car, traffic or travel options   [ ]
Fear of rejection   [ ]
Worries around neighbourhood   [ ]
Sexual problems or worries   [ ]
Declining physical abilities   [ ]
Not getting enough rest   [ ]
Procrastinating or wasting time   [ ]
Too much life admin   [ ]
Difficulties with romantic partner   [ ]
Difficulties with ex-partners   [ ]
Difficulties with sight or hearing   [ ]
Inequality or unfairness at work   [ ]
Inequality, unfairness or discrimination in life   [ ]

Feeling exploited   [ ]
Lack of sleep   [ ]
Too many meetings/calls on your time   [ ]
Problems with children   [ ]
Worries about gossip   [ ]
Unchallenging work   [ ]
Concerns about meeting high standards   [ ]
Feeling conflicted about choices or decisions   [ ]
Trouble with reading, writing or maths   [ ]
Regrets over past decisions   [ ]
Menstrual problems   [ ]
Legal problems   [ ]
The weather   [ ]
Lacking in energy   [ ]
Difficulties with friends   [ ]
Feeling unable to express yourself clearly   [ ]
Overload of family responsibilities   [ ]
Lack of financial security   [ ]
Not enough time for family   [ ]
Worries about crime   [ ]
Pollution and environmental worries   [ ]
Not enough time for recreation   [ ]
Ability to maintain high-quality accommodation   [ ]
Noise pollution   [ ]

High-performance stressors and hassles

Below are an additional fifty stressors that you might be subject to if you are aiming to perform at a high level. Go through the same processes as above to highlight which ones you might need to spend some time considering.

Selection (into a team or role)   [ ]
Poor communication around role requirements   [ ]
Issues around sponsorship or funding   [ ]
Rivalries with others   [ ]

Other behaviours or fears creating difficult
    atmosphere [ ]
Lack of support from leaders [ ]
Feeling expectation or pressure from others [ ]
Poor time management (self or others) [ ]
Missing equipment needed to perform [ ]
Poor organization (self or others) [ ]
Poor or unsafe training or event facilities [ ]
Outsiders interfering or disrupting [ ]
Disruptive weather/economic conditions [ ]
Officials behaving unfairly [ ]
Unexpected changes in format/structure [ ]
Needing to compete/perform too often [ ]
Performance equipment different to practice
    equipment [ ]
Unable to fuel performances effectively (self or others) [ ]
Difficult relationship with team [ ]
Difficult relationship with bosses/leadership/funders [ ]
Unhelpful coaching/leadership style [ ]
Organizational tactics/approach feeling outdated [ ]
Lack of technical information needed [ ]
Not feeling like you belong in the team [ ]
Lack of technical or mental preparation [ ]
Confusion/poor communication around rules [ ]
Dealing with an illness or injury [ ]
Fear of illness or injury [ ]
Wanting to live up to previous standards [ ]
Feeling 'should' be able to do well [ ]
High expectations of self and abilities [ ]
High expectations from others [ ]
Feeling you need to win [ ]
Others wanting to beat you or your team [ ]
Worried about being dropped from team or sponsors [ ]
Worries around ranking/status/reputation [ ]
Seeing media coverage [ ]
Giving media interviews [ ]

Others discussing you or your performance   [ ]
Social media trolling   [ ]
Worry about letting leader down   [ ]
Worry about letting teammates down   [ ]
Worry about letting friends or family down   [ ]
Competing against those who are considered better [ ]
Competing against those who are considered worse   [ ]
Poor behaviours from competitors   [ ]
Poor preparation for challenges   [ ]
Overtrained/burned out   [ ]
Overambitious goals   [ ]
General fear of failure   [ ]

10

Gratitude

Gratitude is the glue that holds together all the other pillars of success. Developing a grateful mindset requires only a few minutes a day, but gives benefits which last a lifetime.

It might seem hard to imagine that Persil washing powder, an ancient Roman writer and Oprah Winfrey have much in common, yet they are all connected by our final pillar of success – gratitude. This final pillar pulls together all the others and allows us to appreciate the success that comes, in a way that works for us.

The pillars we have considered in the previous nine chapters put us in a place where success is within our grasp, but without gratitude we won't realize that we have developed them or be sufficiently aware to make the most of them. And gratitude doesn't just make us realize what we have developed; it brings a multitude of other benefits. It improves our wellbeing, our life satisfaction and our physical and mental health, and helps us connect better, both with ourselves and other people.

The benefits of gratitude have long been known; it is espoused as a virtue in many religions, including Buddhism, Christianity, Judaism and Islam. It was cited by the writer Cicero over two thousand years ago when he called it 'not only the greatest of virtues, but the parent of all others'. In more recent times, Oprah Winfrey has put this belief into practice, becoming known for her dedication to highlighting the power of gratitude. She has kept gratitude journals for decades and has talked about how gratitude has helped both her opportunities and her relationships. But it isn't all about keeping a journal. Saying grace before a meal, learning the importance of saying thank you at an early age and giving someone a box of chocolates to thank them for their kindness are all traditions that have developed as ways in which we can show our gratitude.

Once we have developed a grateful mindset, we can see talent as a gift rather than a pressure; upcoming work as an investment, not a sacrifice; and competition as an opportunity rather than a threat. We can move from the attitude of 'I have to' to one of 'I get to', and from 'I must' to 'I can'. Thinking in this way moves us from the threat mindset we discussed in Chapter 6 (see page 154), where our focus is on not screwing up, to a challenge mindset, where our focus is on doing brilliantly.

Let's meet someone who has done brilliantly in two careers so far – and is still in her thirties. Her name is Lucy Gossage and she is not only an oncologist, but has also won fourteen Ironman races. These consist of a 2.4-mile swim, a 112-mile bike ride and then running a marathon. She also co-founded a wonderful charity called '5K Your Way, Move against Cancer'.

Lucy uses gratitude to excel in all that she does; even on the darkest days of her triathlon career. And it wasn't a career to be sniffed at – not only did she win those fourteen races, but she regularly qualified in the Ironman World Championships in Kona, Hawaii; the pinnacle of any long-distance triathlete's career. Lucy took a sabbatical from work to train full-time for two years. The sabbatical was coming to its end and two weeks after Kona she was back to work. 'This was to be the last defining race of my career. And eight weeks before it I fell off my bike and broke my collarbone. The standard advice for a collarbone is not to lift anything heavier than a cup of tea for twelve weeks.'

After surgery to plate it, Lucy went through a dark time – unable to see any positives – but once she was able to move her arm a little she picked up. 'I was then able to focus on the little things that I was achieving rather than what I hadn't, and I actually got to the stage where I was telling myself things like "you were overtrained before you broke your collarbone. It's actually really good that you have had this enforced two-week rest. That's a positive. Your body will have recovered."' Over that time, Lucy would just focus on what she could do and not what she couldn't.

'I did go on and race the World Championships eight weeks later and I finished ninth, which was actually a position higher than the year before, despite the injury. Looking back, that experience, no matter how hard it was at the time, changed my career. It allowed me to find my limits. And I think as an athlete all I ever wanted to do was find my limits. It also helped me realize that, whatever happens in life, there is always a silver lining; you might not know it at the time, but there will always be one.'

What Is Gratitude?

Gratitude comes when we appreciate what we have; it is the quality of being thankful and acknowledging the good in our life. But it is actually a little more complex than that, because there are three different types of gratitude. The first is the most obvious type – the emotion we feel when someone has done something nice for us that makes us appreciate other people. The second is a personality trait; this prompts us to actively seek out the positives in life, making us a grateful person. The third type of gratitude is a mindset that we can develop and practise in order to secure the benefits that gratitude offers in our pursuit of success.

When we are thankful, it is usually a brief but intense emotion. When we receive something that was not earned or expected due to the good intentions of another, it promotes a beneficial trade. In recognizing the generosity and showing our gratitude, we create a reciprocal exchange, a 'tit for tat'. In acknowledging that we have benefitted from the actions of another, we and they feel good, and a cycle of kindness develops. The swapping of a generous act for a thank you enables positive relationship building, which develops social capital.

When we are in this state of gratitude, we are thankful for the actions of another, whether they have paid for our coffee when we forgot our wallet, ensured we were given the credit for a piece of work or helped us learn a new skill. It is not necessarily the action itself that we are grateful for, but our interpretation of what motivated it. If we think that they have gone out of their way to help us, we will be grateful. In that moment, flooded with adrenaline, we will feel fortunate, and our gratitude becomes a valuable emotion. However, gratitude is more than just our appreciation for the support of other people.

Some of us are born with a personality trait that makes us more grateful. If we have a naturally thankful outlook and an orientation towards appreciating the positive things in life, we will experience gratitude more intensely and frequently. Those of us with this sort of personality are thankful for small acts of kindness and more likely to feel grateful for simple pleasures. We are less likely to show envy towards others or to openly express annoyance at the 'good luck' which happens to our peers.

Those with this trait are more likely to be extroverted, agreeable, open and conscientious – all qualities that help us become successful. They might also possess traits that are connected to positive social functioning – things like empathy, forgiveness, warmth, gregariousness, trust and altruism. These adaptive personality traits are all things that help us develop positive relationships.

Possessing the trait of gratitude gives us a mental structure that directs our attention towards kindness and benevolence, and, as a result, we are constantly aware of the good in life. With a schema like this in place, we will tend to appraise situations in a positive light, interpreting actions as helpful and well intentioned. Even if we later realize that this is not the case, positivity is where we go first. A team member with a grateful outlook will be happy when their boss steps in to help on a project because it will save them time and effort. By contrast, someone with a different schema may choose to interpret the boss as interfering or mistrustful, or be suspicious that they might be trying to take the credit for themselves.

Lucy realizes that she has an inbuilt tendency to see the best in situations, but that she has also learned to use it to her advantage in difficult situations. 'During lockdown I realized how I could consciously shift my mentality by using gratitude. So there were times where we were all as a nation, as a world, we were all scared. Pretty much one day every single week I would wake up and feel really low, and I used a lot of the psychological strategies I'd learned from sport, including gratitude, to shift that feeling. Now I think it's almost automatic that, when I am fed up, I look for the good things around me that are happening – even if it is just a nice cup of coffee in the middle of clinic.'

Even if we don't have a naturally grateful mindset like Lucy, with the right activities and lots of practice we can cultivate one, making gratitude a habit. It means reorganizing our mental focus so we are looking for kindness and able to see the good and the helpful, moving away from jealous comparisons. Stimulating gratitude inhibits those negative feelings, reducing the noise and negativity in our heads, and giving us the head space to focus on what really matters. A grateful mindset means that we think about what we have rather than being jealous of what we don't have, and we appreciate the simple pleasures in life and notice the contributions of others.

How Gratitude Supports Our Success

When we practise gratitude, we appreciate what we have and focus on what we enjoy. If we have spent time mastering skills, gratitude helps us appreciate what we have learned and, as a result, we go on to use those skills more. For those of us on a journey to put each of our pillars in place, gratitude helps because, as well as bringing its own benefits, it also boosts the other pillars.

The pillar that gratitude supports most is our sense of belonging, which we explored in Chapter 1. When we are thankful for the people around us, our sense of belonging intensifies – the feeling literally pulls us closer to the people we spend time with. Gratitude is a key element in creating and sustaining great social relations, in part because it helps us spot when other people have done things for our benefit. It also motivates us to do more for others and reinforces the idea that looking out for other people has a positive effect on our relationships. We note the kindness that has been offered and store it away, returning positive behaviours in the future.

However, gratitude is more than just tit for tat. It doesn't only help the connection with the individual who helped you – we tend to reciprocate upwards, passing on benefits to others and creating a spiral of support. This idea of 'upstream reciprocity' was exemplified by a study at the University of California where a group were asked to keep a gratitude journal every day for three weeks. Not only did they become better connected with their friends, they also became more socially engaged, getting involved in volunteering or donating their time to others. So we can see that gratitude helps us socialize, build connections and make new friends, and enhances the friendships we already have. A study examining levels of gratitude in 243 people found that those who were 10 per cent more grateful than the average person had 17.5 per cent more social capital. We can think of it as adding meaningfulness to our relationships, whether with other people, groups, nature or religion.

Gratitude also increases our sense of belonging because, when we have a grateful disposition, we notice more kindness and lean towards reciprocating, even when we hadn't intended to. 'Interpersonal complementarity' is when we naturally follow the social cues of others, and is highlighted in a fascinating story about a Stanford psychologist who used this knowledge to his advantage when he realized that he was about to be mugged late one night. Instead of being either aggressive or defensive, the psychologist pretended that he knew his attacker and was friendly towards him. The mugger was completely confused and backed off, giving the psychologist a chance to escape. We can use interpersonal complementarity in day-to-day life; if we are kind and grateful, that is what we will often get back.

Gratitude is also incredibly beneficial in our closest relationships. The most common reason given for divorce is not feeling loved and appreciated. We can fix this in long-term relationships by showing reciprocal gratitude towards each other – when we appreciate what our partner does for us and express gratitude, it is more likely that they will appreciate what we do for them. As a result, we then act in a way that we know will benefit our partner. We can test how supportive we are of our partner with the Losada ratio, which divides the number of positive gestures in each interaction – such as support, encouragement and appreciation – by the number of negative ones, like sarcasm, disapproval or cynicism. If the result is below one, it is an indication that a relationship is on the rocks. The marriages that last longest tend to have a ratio above five, which means at least five experiences of positive feedback for every negative one. The same goes for parenting, work or coaching. More positive comments than negative ones make for a far nicer environment.

One of the reasons gratitude helps our social relationships is that it has a positive effect on our wellbeing. Happy people tend to attract others towards them, and wellbeing increases with gratitude because it makes us feel better connected and more aware of our accomplishments. When we are grateful, we tend to see things with the same rose-tinted glasses that confidence gave us in Chapter 5 – we regard the world as a friendlier and more hospitable place and can perform better in whatever sphere we wish to excel in.

Lucy sees this in sport and with her cancer patients. 'I think being grateful just makes life better in every single sense. So, you can sit in a busy oncology clinic in a heatwave, sweating, thirsty, looking out of the window and wishing you were outside, and it is very easy to feel extremely negative. Or you can sit in exactly the same clinic and remind yourself that you have got your twenty minutes in the sunshine at lunchtime and that, actually, you are not one of the patients who is waiting to speak to you to be told that their cancer has got worse. And that you are going to have a lovely bike ride home in the sunshine because it is such a sunny day.' By focusing on the great bits rather than the negative, Lucy highlights that the same experience can be felt completely differently.

This positive wellbeing increases our life satisfaction. A study in 2004 found gratitude to be in the top three of twenty-four personality strengths that affect life satisfaction and suggested that it can explain about 18.5 per cent of the difference in people's happiness. When we add happiness to the vitality we get from gratitude, we become the type of person other people are attracted to – and this creates a positive feedback loop of wellbeing and an improved sense of belonging.

Gratitude doesn't just improve our wellbeing in the present – it also affects how we think about our past. We usually think of our memories as being fixed, yet when we examine them through a new filter they turn out to be quite flexible. You might have had a wonderful wedding day, but if you get divorced, your memories of it will be tainted. Equally, though, there can be a positive change. The day we are made redundant feels dreadful at the time, but if we go on to get a better job, it might feel more like a stepping stone that we remember far more positively over time. In this way, gratitude can take the sting out of negative memories and turn them into positive ones.

As well as improving our positive feelings, gratitude can significantly reduce our negative ones, making us less likely to suffer from depression, anxiety, stress and drug and alcohol dependence. When researchers from Florida State University studied gratitude in athletes, they found that it decreased psychological distress and reduced the risk of burnout. Studies have demonstrated that it helps us deal better with negative states like stress and depression, because when we have a grateful outlook we tend to use more helpful coping mechanisms. Instead of hiding away and avoiding people when we are stressed, we might seek out social support to feel less alone, get other perspectives and feel better equipped to cope with our worries.

The role of perspective is important here. Finding reasons to be grateful can be a good way to reflect upon change, whether that means the sunny days after a long, cold winter, the tasty meal after fasting or a day off after a long period at work. After Hurricane Andrew tore through Florida in 1992, survivors were grateful that, although they had lost a great deal, they had not lost a loved one. They were able to see the bigger picture, which helped them cope.

Another reason our wellbeing improves with gratitude is that it improves our sleep, reducing the time it takes us to fall asleep and increasing how long we stay asleep for. Negative thoughts just before sleep are unhelpful, and this rumination is reduced when we focus on positive thoughts, such as gratitude for what we have. When a study asked sixty-five people suffering from chronic pain to keep a daily gratitude diary, those who completed the task slept for half an hour longer each night than the control group.

This improved sleep, positive feelings and support from other people all improve our physical health. Studies have found that people who feel more gratitude visit their GP less often, have lower blood pressure and a lower risk of mental health problems. It is thought that gratitude activates our parasympathetic nervous system (the system that controls our rest and relaxation), reducing our stress levels and helping our body to function effectively. It is also possible that being thankful for what we have makes us more likely to focus on helpful health behaviours, such as keeping fit and watching what we eat. An American study found that when people kept a weekly gratitude journal, they exercised for forty minutes more per week.

Our wellbeing increases alongside our self-esteem, and the self-esteem of those with high levels of gratitude seems to be higher for two reasons. Firstly, the deeper relationships it brings help people feel more secure and supported. A study of athletes found that when they really trusted their coach, their self-esteem increased along with their gratitude; having a supportive coach gave them a reason to be grateful and more confident. The second reason our self-esteem gets a boost is that, when we focus on what we have, we can't focus on what we don't have. While envy can pique our senses and help us focus on what we might like to achieve, too much makes us feel inferior and insecure. Researchers have found that gratitude is an effective control on envy because the two things are so incompatible. Our brain literally cannot process both emotions at the same time. When we feel grateful for what we have, we stop wanting what other people have. We stop feeling inadequate, which removes the sting of comparisons.

As an oncologist, Lucy knows that every day she gets to do good, but that feeling increases when others are grateful for her help. 'Generally you will get some recognition from somewhere – someone – that you've done something to make their life or day a little bit better. You do get thanked every single day.'

Alongside improving our self-esteem, gratitude also helps us feel more optimistic. A study found that keeping a weekly gratitude journal made individuals between 5 and 15 per cent more optimistic. This happens because gratitude is about focusing on the good in life; when we feel good about where we are, we are more likely to see good in our future.

But while optimism involves being forward-looking, gratitude stops us getting ahead of ourselves and helps us focus on another one of our pillars: the importance of being process-driven (see Chapter 6). We spend significant time in life looking forward and preparing for what hasn't happened, but being thankful for what we have keeps us in the here and now and gives us some perspective. When we remember what we are good at, we approach things more positively and are more creative in resolving problems. It keeps us tapped into the processes, which helps our performance.

We already know that belonging, a sense of wellbeing and being process-driven help us to be more successful, but gratitude has some additional benefits that improve our performance, too.

In studies of students, gratitude has been found to increase academic engagement and improve exam results, serving as motivation to work harder. It has also been found to help with the persistence needed in tough times. After university students were asked to think about gratitude, fewer dropped out of their courses. In a study set up to help people improve their body image, those who were taught to be grateful were twice as likely to stick with the programme. Another study asked participants to write down all the things they wanted to achieve over the next few months; half of them were also asked to keep a gratitude journal. Those who kept the journal made greater progress with their goals; the awareness of their successes boosted their feelings of accomplishment.

All these beneficial elements of gratitude combine to improve performance. Teri McKeever is the head coach of the swimming team at the University of California, and previously coached the US Olympic team. In 2015, she gave a speech explaining how gratitude had contributed to her athletes' success. Before some practice sessions, she would hand out pens and paper and ask the swimmers to write down ten things they were grateful for. The athletes shared their lists with each other before jumping into the pool. 'Those practices are always more productive, cohesive and enjoyable for all of us,' McKeever said in her Grateful Athletes video presentation. Her approach doesn't just help athletes feel more positive; sharing things that might be personal helps them connect with those around them and focus on the moment.

Gratitude can also be shown to have a positive effect on performance within organizations. It improves how colleagues interact, builds stronger connections and improves the well-being of the company. When staff feel valued by the leaders of their organization, they are more committed and productive. They also tend to have fewer competitive rivalries – the working environment feels safe rather than aggressive, and they are better able to express themselves. People feel that taking risks will lead to them being valued or rewarded, rather than sneered at or penalized. They also have more autonomy, the pillar we explored in Chapter 3 – they have a choice and a voice. And staff increase their mastery – another pillar (see Chapter 2); as they are praised for their strengths, they become more aware of them and able to utilize them better.

Gratitude helps the organization externally, too, as it contributes to the retention of customers. It is much more expensive to attract a new customer than it is to retain an old one, so organizations spend millions on developing loyalty schemes. Understanding how gratitude influences loyalty is vital to stimulate a stronger customer relationship, and it can be a great marketing tool. My mum has loyally bought Persil washing powder for the last fifty years because, when she was first married, she put a red top in the washing machine with one of my dad's white shirts. Dad's shirt came out pink. She posted the shirt to Persil, who not only fixed the shirt but also refunded the postage cost, and her gratitude has kept her a loyal customer ever since. That one interaction has netted Persil several thousand pounds of sales. It illustrates how gratitude is important in business; if we are able to build a good relationship with customers and they feel grateful to us, they are more likely to come back time and time again.

Finally, one of the real benefits of gratitude to performance is that people who are naturally grateful tend to use growth-focused coping – while gratitude doesn't make us immune to bad days, it does help us bounce back from them faster. If we employ a grateful mindset, after going through a tough time we can reflect that it has given us an opportunity to grow. It isn't the experience that creates growth, but the skills we learn in response to it and the perspective it offers us.

In its promotion of adaptive coping and personal growth, gratitude can give us a different perspective on tough times and setbacks, making us see them as learning opportunities. When we grow through adversity, we can reinterpret difficult events in a more positive way, learning from them so we have a better outcome in the future. A study on military veterans found that those who felt a stronger sense of gratitude were those who were less likely to develop post-traumatic stress disorder after returning from combat. Similarly, it is the kidney transplant recipients who have the most gratitude towards the donor and surgeon who report the highest quality of life following their transplant.

Our recovery from these hardships can be influenced by how well we are able to attach benefit to the experience, and gratitude is a key part of this. Those who are able to feel grateful report increased levels of wellbeing after a negative experience. Having undergone trauma and reflected on the process with gratitude, they might report that they want to live life more fully and get more out of each day.

Writing about difficult events with gratitude also encourages a positive response to trauma. In one study, when participants wrote about a traumatic event, they required significantly fewer visits to the medical centre for as long as five months after they had written about it. Writing about events is thought to help people reframe negative memories so they feel less harmful. For example, someone who lost their job as a result of the COVID-19 lockdowns might reframe the situation as a good opportunity to spend time with their children, who they had missed while they were working.

Why Gratitude Is Great

One idea why gratitude is so powerful is that it helps to balance out our biases. Our brains have been found to give three times more weight to bad experiences than good, and for a good reason: we need to stay safe. With our brain alert to danger, we can react more quickly to threats and avoid them. But as most of the threats we face in modern life are to our self-esteem rather than our physical survival, this inclination towards negativity tends to cause us stress and misery. Alongside this, our brains don't just give more weight to the negatives, they remember them more strongly too – they want to keep the information on what can hurt us at the front of our mind so we avoid it. This may be theoretically helpful, but it gives a negative slant to our thoughts – known as negativity bias. We need to actively brighten our thoughts, and we can do this by using gratitude to perceive difficult situations differently, to remember the positives about our lives and to devote more resources to cope with them.

We call this 'reframing' – trying to see negative things in a more positive light to give us a better sense of coherence. This might be one of the reasons why we sometimes develop as a result of managing a trauma – it lets us see something previously viewed as negative in a more positive light. That might be an opportunity to learn something new, gain a new skill or strengthen a relationship. This positivity develops into a schema of gratitude that uses more effective coping strategies. Gratitude is also a good coping mechanism itself; we build up more positive thoughts, increase our focus on the benefits we have in life and reduce negative emotions like envy.

With this reframed perspective we can seek out more effective coping mechanisms, replacing negative ones like self-blame, avoidance or substance abuse with those that seek emotional support or deal with issues, like chatting to a friend, going for a walk or writing a plan of action. A student who has just failed an exam and is unable to find any gratitude might get angry with themselves, berate their ability or go and get drunk. A grateful student, on the other hand, might be able to see the failed exam as preparation for how to do better next time and proactively learn from that experience. They might seek support from their friends who could put their failure into perspective and ask for advice on how they could study differently in the future. The athletes I have worked with who set out to achieve incredible challenges and break records don't sulk when they fail the first time; instead, they see it as a brilliantly specific dress rehearsal for their next attempt. The students who fail an exam may be frustrated if it was a final, but in the future they will reflect positively on what the experience taught them. These examples show that when we use gratitude effectively, rather than burying our heads in the sand and hoping the problem will go away, there is awareness, acceptance and proactivity. And this means that we can cope so much better. Lucy's cancer patients remind her of this when their diagnosis triggers them to evaluate what is really important to them.

'I had a young man who got diagnosed when he was eighteen and died in his very early twenties. He was just so grateful that he'd had two years of starting university and travelling a little bit. And most people would find that really hard to see, but he was just so grateful that he had crammed in as much as he possibly could have done in those two years since he was diagnosed. I think when you know that time is short, you live life with a bit more urgency and you appreciate things that perhaps you wouldn't normally. And perhaps realize what is important and what's not important.'

This more positive outlook also flows through one of the other theories on why gratitude is so effective: it helps us to broaden our approaches to life. While negative emotions narrow our attention on the problem at hand, positive emotions stretch our perspective and motivate us to create solutions that we might need in the future – as a result, we can see more opportunities around us. Positive emotions open us up to opportunities and move us away from the threat or fear that accompanies negative emotions. We can see this if we consider someone who has just started exercising. With negative emotions such as fear, they may feel that they are not good enough or that they will be laughed at. But when they become grateful for the fact that their body is working well enough to exercise, they will instead focus on what they are enjoying about it and how it makes them feel. The possibility of someone laughing at them suddenly holds far less power.

Positive, gratitude-inspired emotions improve our brain functioning so we find it easier to develop stronger skills and relationships. This approach extends our thoughts and behaviours that use both emotional and practical support, and in doing this we build up long-term physical, mental and social resources, like problem-solving strategies and support from people we feel close to. All this extends our cognitive resources, helping us deal with whatever stressful thing comes our way.

The final theory on why gratitude is so effective has to do with the connections it helps us make with others. As we learned in Chapter 1, our sense of belonging is fundamental to our success. Our brain's risk-regulation system helps us navigate conflicts, especially potential rejection, and encourages greater intimacy. The more we feel valued, the more we feel able to push for greater intimacy, which in turn enhances our social relationships and allows us to function more effectively. When this idea has been tested among groups of friends, researchers have found that, when they express gratitude to each other, their friendships intensify.

Growing Gratitude

Gratitude can be a trait that we are born with or an automatic response to something lovely, but it is also a mindset that we can develop. We can think of it as an emotional muscle that we need to strengthen to get the most from it. In fact, even the process of finding things to be grateful for brings us benefits. In training ourselves this way, we internalize the process of noticing and responding to kindness, turning gratitude into a habit. As we develop a sense of justice and responsibility, gratitude becomes part of our moral personality.

If we have children, we are probably guilty of encouraging them to say thank you from an early age. This is a great habit to get into, but studies have found that we can't genuinely feel gratitude until we are at least seven years old – before that, we don't have the theory of mind to understand that someone else has given up something for us. As gratitude is a complex emotion, it is thought that children are unlikely to have a deep understanding of it before the age of ten.

However, that doesn't mean that we can't start early. Studies have found that cracking down on entitled behaviour in children helps develop gratitude, with the caveat that they also need to see their parents modelling gratitude. Infusing parenting with gratitude and having regular conversations about it can work well. These efforts to encourage gratitude have instant benefits; when children can draw on it, they can also establish a sense of belonging as they become teenagers and start to develop their sense of independence.

In some American universities, the importance of gratitude is such that student athletes are asked to attend 'attitude of gratitude' workshops, in which they learn the best ways to express gratitude to improve their sporting performances. These workshops teach different ways to boost their gratitude and increase the social support they feel, to enjoy their sport and be less likely to hit burnout.

In a similar way, we can develop our personal levels of gratitude. As gratitude builds gratitude, once we start looking for it, we get into a positivity loop and find more things to become grateful for. There are three techniques that we can employ to find something that will resonate and feel worthwhile: daily listings, contemplation and behavioural expressions.

Write a gratitude list

There are a few different types of lists you can try. The most common is a gratitude list, where each day you write down things for which you are grateful. Unlike many nerve-racking psychological activities, most people enjoy this one. One effective way is to simply write down three good things about your life each day. This increases happiness and reduces levels of depression; studies have shown these benefits last months after the list-writing took place. It is a particularly good activity to do before bed, as it can help quieten the brain and calm sleep-sapping rumination. Even if you don't fancy making lists every day, just thinking about and 'counting your blessings' once a week was found in a 2007 study to help significantly lower the blood pressure of people with hypertension.

Lucy used to write a race week plan to help her get excited and grateful to be racing. 'I'd include things to help me to get excited and think, "Wow, I'm so lucky to be racing" and I think actually, for me, going back to work as an oncologist (I carried on racing professionally for three years afterwards), I had some of my best results despite working part time. On paper I shouldn't have kept on winning races because I wasn't training like everyone else was. But having training as a release from work, having racing on the weekend, for me, was just a pure bonus, pure joy, pure fun, pure no-pressure. There were so many things that I was grateful about.'

Practise grateful contemplation

A nice way to practise bringing more gratitude into your life is to work on one of these lists in your head (no need to write it down) while you are doing something boring or tricky. Playing a game in your head where you think about the things you could be grateful for can be a good distraction, and a way to practise that positivity. When we move into grateful contemplation, we are doing more than just writing lists; we are reflecting on our lives.

Another way we can consider what we are grateful for is to contemplate how things might have been. We can call the process of imagining what our life would be like without the things we are grateful for 'mental subtraction'. This is not something that needs to be planned; it might be regarded as daydreaming, comparing where you are now to where you could have been. You might also daydream about the people in your life who inspire you. What have you learned from them and how have they changed your aspirations? Reflecting on these people can help you feel grateful that they are in your life.

Having seen patients go through setback after setback, through no choice of their own, Lucy uses comparisons to feel thankful for what she has. 'When I'm racing and it's hurting, I will remind myself that suffering is a privilege and that I'm really lucky to be able to have a body that is letting me push that hard to make myself hurt that hard. People with cancer don't get that opportunity.'

Another nice way to regularly contemplate is to write two prompt cards for yourself, saying 'I'm glad...' and 'I'm thankful...'. If you leave them somewhere where you will see them regularly, every time you spot them you should complete the sentence. It might be something like, 'I'm glad that I got up early so I could see the sunrise as I walked the dog' or 'I'm thankful for the coffee I'm about to drink.' Little moments like this can help you bring more gratitude into your life in a quick and easy way.

Make gratitude a habit

Finally, there are some behavioural techniques that are more formal, but very effective in helping us to develop a grateful mindset. The most traditional way is through a gratitude journal, in which we reflect on all the things that have happened each day. It can be as big as a promotion at work or as small as someone slowing down to let you cross the road in busy traffic. We jot down these actions and how they made us feel. The idea is to be as specific as possible and to highlight different things each time. The process of reflection can put us into a more grateful mood.

Journaling like this is an effective way to develop gratitude because it becomes a habit, and knowing we have to complete the journal each night encourages us to look for things to feel grateful for during the day. It can take a month or so for the benefits to be felt, but after a while these journals can be really effective. In a 2003 study titled 'Counting blessings versus burdens', it was found that keeping a gratitude journal led to 16 per cent fewer physical symptoms, 19 per cent more time exercising, 10 per cent less pain and 8 per cent more sleep. A later study found that maintaining a gratitude journal could reduce depressive symptoms by up to 30 per cent, and others have found that wellbeing measures improve by up to 10 per cent.

A less widely used method is gratitude visits, where we go to see someone who has previously helped us to thank them for their kindness. One study found that gratitude visits helped reduce depressive symptoms of sufferers by up to 35 per cent, while another found that the happiness of people who made visits rose by 10 per cent in the short term and were higher even a month later.

The prospect of a gratitude visit might feel daunting, but writing a gratitude letter can feel far safer – especially as you get the benefits even if you don't post it. When different activities were tested in a study, it was the letter that saw the biggest positive change in happiness among the participants. A University of California, Berkeley study asked participants who were struggling with their mental health to write a gratitude-focused letter, but not to send it. Four weeks after writing the letters, the participants' mental health had improved, and some of the improvements remained up to eight weeks later.

A few years ago, Lucy wrote to her former biology teacher. 'I wanted to let him know that I'm grateful and he played a role in where my life has ended up. I had no idea whether it would ever get there, but just that whole process of writing it made me realize I was grateful to him.' The letter arrived safely and she got a lovely message back. 'I think it is just nice to tell people when they've helped you.'

Gratitude in Business

It is not only about individuals; organizations can also benefit from showing gratitude. Understanding the power of gratitude and incorporating it into what they do can be a powerful way to unite teams, grow business and secure support. It is used particularly effectively by charitable organizations. Instead of an annual report, some charities create a 'gratitude report' that they share with their donors, highlighting the benefits created by their money or time. Other charities try to connect their staff to beneficiaries or share feedback from them to boost engagement and remind people of their purpose.

Frame feedback with gratitude

In all organizations, feedback can lead to benefits when it is framed with gratitude. Feedback is often focused on specific objectives, such as numbers to hit or projects to deliver. Softer feedback that might concern how someone is to work with or how supportive they are of other people is often not included in discussions about an employee's performance, yet when managers show appreciation for these behaviours, it can hugely benefit motivation and increase an employee's dedication to the organization. One survey suggested that up to 70 per cent of people don't feel that discussions about their performance at work take these meaningful elements into account. When they are incorporated, employees are better able to develop new skills and have a much clearer understanding of their own trajectory – it signals that their personal and professional wellbeing is important, which increases their own gratitude.

Create appreciation programmes

These can be effective in building gratitude within organizations. When people who go above and beyond to help others are rewarded in some way, it creates a cycle of gratitude and a more appreciative environment. The acknowledgement that their actions have been noticed ensures that they do not feel taken for granted and the additional public recognition boosts their positive feelings – in addition, seeing that these meaningful elements are recognized encourages others to increase their engagement, too.

Some companies ask staff to send their HR department a note when they are grateful to specific colleagues, with those nominated being entered into a prize draw or celebrated in a newsletter. Studies tracking the impact of such incentives have found that they tend to double employee engagement levels. The key is to celebrate success and support on an individual basis, not in comparison to others, as comparison can build resentment rather than gratitude.

Every message Lucy gets from a patient is treasured. 'Patients don't realize perhaps how a tiny little gesture or a card – or even just saying thank you – can literally make my week. And because I know what a difference a tiny gesture makes to me, I find it really rewarding to give out gestures to other people. By remembering to do that, I like to think that improves relationships with work colleagues enormously.'

Gratitude can help anyone be successful, whether we are a leader in a business, a student revising for exams or, like Lucy, an athlete with a competition approaching. Gratitude also helps us sustain our other pillars of success. The other pillars provide the foundations, but being grateful for them will get you into a successful mindset. Try it now. Think back over your day and pull out three things for which you are grateful. See if this gives your mood a lift. Now, from this positive platform, you can start plotting how to bring one of the other pillars to life and take the next step in securing your success.

GRATITUDE TOOLKIT

Comparison crushing

Our brain is unable to process gratitude and envy at the same time - so focusing on being thankful helps stop comparisons and reduces feelings of inadequacy.

Think about three people you sometimes compare yourself to and feel inadequate against. For each person complete the sentence:

I am envious of:

_____

because they have:

_____

however, I am grateful that instead I have:

_____

Thank you for the failure

Gratitude allows us to reframe our negative thoughts in a more positive light so failures just become a dress rehearsal for the next time we try to broaden the approaches we take to life.

Below, write three failures you have experienced and, for each, add something you are grateful that you learned from that experience:

Failure	Lesson learned
1.	
2.	
3.	

Reasons to be grateful

Each day, before falling asleep we can consider things to be grateful for. It is a lovely way to end the day. On tough days it can be hard to know where to look for gratitude, so here are ten areas to look through:

1. Reason to be grateful in day-to-day life:

2. Reason to be grateful in the long term:

3. Reason to be grateful within my family:

4. Reason to be grateful with my friends:

5. Reason to be grateful in my sport/exercise:

6. Reason to be grateful about where I live:

7. Reason to be grateful in my education:

8. Reason to be grateful within my talents:

9. Reason to be grateful in my body:

10. Reason to be grateful with my mindset:

Conclusion

A University of California study suggests that each day we receive up to thirty-four gigabytes of information via TV, radio, books, podcasts, adverts and communications from other people – enough to fill a laptop within a week. And how much of that do we remember? We tend to take away just one thing from each interaction, whether it be an advert we notice, a podcast we listen to or a TV show we watch. One single thing is all that stands any chance of making it into our long-term memory.

Each of the success stories in this book has offered a wealth of insightful anecdotes, advice and expertise, but if I had to, I could select one key takeaway from each. Colonel Dame Kelly Holmes, MBE (mil) said that it wasn't her Olympic medals that made her successful, but rather the relationships she has been able to build because of them. I will always remember Maxine Peake as the girl who couldn't get a part in a college play, but kept going until she landed a place at RADA. Sean Conway's story resonated because he did what many of us have dreamed of – quit his job to travel the world. What I took away from my interview with him was that he carried on after his initial goal became impossible; deciding that there was more than one way to climb a mountain.

The powerful sense of purpose Damian Hall used to drive himself forward highlighted the fact that tiny charms, like an acorn from his daughter, can remind us of our connections to the people who matter most. And Emma Wiggs, MBE reminded me that we can cultivate confidence through sheer hard work and focus, and we can be proud of our efforts when we reach the start line, not just the finish line.

The thing that stuck in my mind about Caspar Berry was that he was able to see success in terms of the 'big picture' rather than being swayed by what was happening in the moment. Stunt performer Bobby Holland Hanton reminded me that practice gives us the courage to do scary things, like jumping off balconies, but can also help us recover from serious setbacks.

I began the chapter on optimism by talking about Tigger from *Winnie the Pooh*, and Drew McOnie is definitely a real-life Tigger. His advice can help us give ourselves permission to spend time daydreaming about the best possible outcomes. Sara Pascoe's insight – that we should never start an interaction with a negative – provided a light-bulb moment I wish I'd had years ago. And finally, I can't forget hearing Lucy Gossage's voice crack when she talked about how working with cancer patients reminds her that she is privileged to be able to compete in high-level sport. It helps her feel grateful for the things that feel hard when times are tough.

I wonder what it was that you took from each success story. What might you do differently as a result of hearing about their journeys?

I asked each of my interviewees a final question: how do they define success? Their answers show that the truth rarely lies in the medals, world records, fortune and fame we see glamorized in the media. Between them, they achieved all these things, but these achievements have given them the perspective to see that true success is deeper and far more personal.

Dame Kelly Holmes, Sean Conway, Damian Hall and Sara Pascoe were all clear that, despite the fact that they have been up against others to win medals, set records or get new contracts, they cannot measure their success against anyone else's. Sean sums it up succinctly: 'If you are judging your success on other people's success, that inevitably leads you down the path you didn't want to go down in the first place.'

Bobby Holland Hanton admitted that he used to measure his success by how much money he made, but he was forced to reassess his life when he went through spinal surgery. He realized that success to him is being surrounded by friends and family. Emma Wiggs's version of success is similar – most definitely based on performance, but about enjoying the journey that takes you to the start line, and enjoying it as part of a team.

Having a dual career in sport and oncology would suggest that Lucy Gossage might have two versions of success, and yet she doesn't. In both her triathlons and with cancer patients, she sees success as the support and inspiration she might be able to give to others.

When Maxine Peake gives us her version of success, we see that these high achievers, just like us, are simply trying to spend as much as they can of their lives doing what they love. She says she will always remember her first agent telling her: 'Maxine, a star is somebody who does what they do and makes a living from it. I don't mean big bucks, but being able to get through doing what you love.'

All our success stories have basically pointed to this importance of doing what you love, surrounded by people you love, reaching towards the things you love. Drew McOnie and Caspar Berry pull them all together into a single word: contentment. Drew said: 'When I was young, my definition of success was what Hollywood told me it was. I was chasing this dream of stability – financial stability and accolades – but they come and go so quickly. So, I no longer pursue happiness; I pursue contentment, because the feeling of contentment is the best kind of analogy for success for me.'

Through all these perspectives, we have heard that success is not about medals, world records or having your name up in lights. Success is personal and has no single definition. For some people it's about bringing others together, while for other people it is about meeting their purpose. Some see success as inspiring others or showing them how much they matter. For many, it is about fulfilling their potential and spending their days doing the things they love.

My initial impression, after I had finished speaking to our success stories, was that I had made an excellent selection. They embody 'their' pillar so closely and have used their skills to create lives that are really worth living. They use 'their' pillar to build strength in other areas so they become more resilient, more content, more successful in ways that work for them and their ambitions. However, with a little more reflection, I realized that this was less down to my perception skills and more due to how each one of us, whoever we are, embodies one of these pillars. We each have a pillar to act as our super-strength, our go-to tool to help push us forward and maintain our motivation until we become successful. When we have this pillar in place, and then slowly add other pillars, we create our own toolkit and build ourselves a strong and robust platform for long-term success.

As we say goodbye, think about your current super-strength and decide which pillar you want to build next. It might take time. It will certainly take effort and patience. But with this pillar in mind, your stage is set, your stunts can be practised and the race will be on; go out with all you have learned and live the purposeful and motivated life that you deserve.

Acknowledgements

Researching a book can sometimes feel like a lonely process; on long days tapping away at a laptop or trawling academic libraries, there is a craving for others. In writing and bringing it into production, those others – professionals, friends, family and clients – slowly reappear in your life as they all leave their mark upon the final text. When I reflected on the process and looked back at who helped bring this book to life, it struck me that, not only were many people involved, but that they all, in some way, embodied the pillars of success:

Belonging

This is the pillar I value the most. In feeling like I belong with my family – my husband Paul and daughter Hattie (her half-eaten fruit makes an appearance in Chapter 9), my mum (her washing powder loyalty appears in Chapter 10) and dad (whose pink shirt accidently inspired the washing powder loyalty) – I feel safe in the world and able to strive for my version of success.

Mastery

Any writer with an academic background has been lucky enough to stand on the shoulders of giants. My sport psychology peer support group (Jo, Matt, Charlotte, Clare, Darren, Hugh, James, Julie, Ross, Sophie, Woody, Sarah and Tom) offered brilliant support; Nichola Pearl offered help with tricky subject matter; and my supervisor Tim Holder helped me begin my psychology journey.

Autonomy

I must thank two previous bosses who, by offering it, taught me the power of autonomy: Heather Rogers-Hutton and Jaine Clarke.

Purpose

Eddie Brocklesby (featured in Chapter 4) is an absolute force of nature who lives every moment of her life with purpose, in a way that we can all learn from, and I regularly do... usually over a bottle of wine!

Confidence

The confidence to bring *The Ten Pillars of Success* to life came from the wonderful 'success stories' featured in each chapter. Colonel Dame Kelly Holmes, MBE (mil), Maxine Peake, Sean Conway, Damian Hall, Emma Wiggs, MBE, Caspar Berry, Bobby Holland Hanton, Drew McOnie, Sara Pascoe and Lucy Gossage were not only fab to work with, but truly brought the theories to life, offering insightful and enlightening stories that we can all benefit from.

Process

The book publishing world is complex and you need brilliant people alongside you. I have really valued the expertise and guidance of Ed Faulkner and Kate Ballard at Allen & Unwin, and Julia Kellaway for her editing excellence. Additionally, thanks to Alice Morgan, Harry Scrobble and Alex Curran at Audible; Pam Rutherford and Alex Rayment at ID Audio; and Nick Humphrey and Gaby Drinkald at Midas for bringing *The Ten Pillars* to life originally; and to Hayley Carruthers for reading an early version for me.

Courage

As we learn in the chapter on courage, we need people behind us to help us believe that our goals are possible. For this, I have to give a huge amount of thanks to both Victoria Marshallsay and James Spackman.

Optimism

The ten pillars and the knowledge which fed into the book all comes from the clients I am lucky enough to work with. Whether in sport, on the stage, working in medicine or running businesses, as therapists we learn alongside our clients and they shape the person, and writers, we become, and every session I have leaves me feeling optimistic at the possibilities that performance psychology enables.

Internal insight

There are many stories included within the pages of this book and I want to thank all those who have lived their lives in such a way that we get to learn from them: Michael Jordan, Kathy Sullivan, Michael Phelps, Eddie Brocklesby, Darell Hammond, James MacDonald, John Lunt, Dame Sarah Storey, DBE, Brian Tracy, Malala Yousafzai, Rose McGowan, Scott Weinberg, Diane Coutu, Anthony Menendez, Kim Liao, Els Visser, Sir

James Dyson, Diana Nyad, Ed Jackson, Nik, Harry and Archie Robinson, Oprah Winfrey and Teri McKeever.

Gratitude

In my professional life I am grateful to all those who work in the research side of psychology, creating the information, knowledge and interventions included here. In my real life: Michelle Greig, Maryka Semarka, Jenny Edenborough and Maria Lee – thank you for keeping my head healthy and my belly laughing.

Index

abortion, 185, 187
achievements, owning of 57
addiction, 25, 27, 192, 209
adrenaline, 155, 167
agreeableness, 99
Alcoholics Anonymous, 27, 209
alter egos, 200–201
Alzheimer's disease, 102
amygdala, 100, 154–60, 172–3,
  198
analysis of losses, 171, 173–4
anomie, 17–28
appreciation, 85, 292
Aristotle, 178
Arnold, Dave, 12
asylum seekers, 25
Athens Olympics (2004), 8, 13,
  15, 134, 136
attachment theory, 9–11, 31–3
Australia, 220–21, 229
authentic leadership, 73–4
autonomy, 4, 65–92, 162
  building of, 85–8
  courage and, 187
  education and, 70
  mastery and, 69
  others and, 71–8
  parenting and 70, 71, 72
  pressure points, 78–85

purpose and, 102, 104, 106,
  107

babies, 195, 237
basketball, 40, 41, 43, 152, 167
belonging, 4, 7–35, 45, 162
  anomie, 17–28
  attachment theory, 9–11,
    31–3
  businesses and, 15–16
  courage and, 187–8
  demographics of, 23–6
  development of, 26–35
  education and 16–17, 24–5
  gratitude and, 274–5
  hereditary element, 23
  mastery and, 45
  optimism and, 214–15
  purpose and, 104
  support and, 12–17
Berry, Caspar, 5, 148–9, 151,
  155–6, 157, 161, 164, 168,
  170, 298, 299
best friends, 12
best possible self, 109, 225–6,
  231
blind spots, 246
blood transfusions, 181
body language, 135, 144

brain drain, 197, 226
brain gratitude and, 279, 283, 286
brain threat response, 100–101, 153–60, 166–9, 171–3, 198, 283
brave list, 194–5, 205
breaking things down 171
Brocklesby, Edwina, 97, 102
Brownlee, Alistair and Jonathan, 76
business
  autonomy and, 77–8
  belonging and, 15–16
  gratitude and, 291–2
  purpose and, 93
  self-awareness and, 248
  whistle-blowers in, 190–91
Button, Jenson, 76
Byker Grove, 149
bystander effect, 12

cancer, 209, 211, 270, 276, 284
cards, 1
cheerleaders, 68
Chicago, 208
China, 177, 179, 235
chronic pain, 278
chunking, 171
Churchill, Winston, 208
Cicero, 269–70
Cigna, 23
circadian rhythm, 227, 232
coaching, 12, 30, 70, 71, 72, 77, 80–81, 83, 152
colourful breathing, 169, 172–3
Comaneci, Nadia, 39
comfort zones, 125–6, 177–9, 187, 190, 192, 194–6, 200–201, 204

comparisons, 157–8
competencies, 238, 241
confidence, 4, 82, 119–46
  body language and, 135, 144
  boosting of, 136–43
  cards, 143, 145–6
  faking of, 133–6
  lack of, 132–3
  mastery and, 124–6
  overconfidence, 131–2
  preparation and, 119, 120, 126–8
  supporting sources, 128–31
  types of, 123
  vicarious, 129, 142, 157
confidence jars, 139–40, 144–5
confirmation bias, 57
Confucianism, 179
conscientiousness, 99
control, 3, 40, 81–5, 90, 138–9, 152–60, 169–70
control mapping, 90, 170
Conway, Sean, 66–7, 68–9, 71, 73, 75, 79, 82, 297, 298
coping strategies
  autonomy and, 81
  confidence and 128
  gratitude and, 277, 282, 284
  internal insight and, 240–41, 256, 261, 263
  optimism and, 216–20, 224–5
  purpose and, 100, 105
  unhelpful, 21–2, 24, 33, 47, 53, 62
core self, 238–9
Cornell University, 51
cortisol, 79, 135, 155
courage, 4, 177–206
  autonomy and, 187
  belonging and, 187–8

development of, 191–201
four-step process, 189–91
moral, 179–80, 182
physical, 179–80, 181
sources of, 186–9
Coutu, Diane, 188
COVID-19 pandemic, 28, 94, 138, 273, 283
Craig, Daniel, 181
cycling, 76, 79, 127, 161, 228

Dame Kelly Holmes Trust, 8
death reflection, 109
death, fear of, 100–101
defensive pessimism, 224
delegation, 86
depression, 21–2, 102, 182
depressive realism, 250
Dinnerladies, 38
Disney, 149
divorce, 21, 25, 209, 214, 228, 275, 277
Donne, John, 7
doormen, 192
Dunbar, Robin, 26–7
Dunning-Kruger effect, 51, 249
Durkheim, Émile, 21
Dyson, James, 212

eating the frog, 167
Edelman, Marek, 193
Edison, Thomas, 37, 40, 43, 212
education
autonomy and, 70
belonging and 16–17, 24–5
gratitude, 280, 284
mastery and, 41, 47–8
purpose and, 108
Eeyore, 207

Einstein, Albert, 51
Elf at Work, 8
emotional control 152–60
emotional intelligence, 241
emotional literacy, 241
emotional stability, 99
English Housing Survey, 18
envy, 279
ethical boundaries, 192–4
exams, 41, 48, 156, 280, 284
expectations, 158
explanation, 86
explanatory style, 210–11
Extraction (2020 film), 180, 196
extroversion, 99

failure
analysis of, 171, 173–4
autonomy and, 76
confidence and, 119, 120
gratitude and, 294
mastery and, 40, 50, 51, 58, 61, 62
Farah, Mohamed, 150
feedback, 11
autonomy and, 71–3, 75–8
confidence and, 125, 134, 143
courage and, 188
gratitude, 291–2
internal insight and, 244
mastery and, 45, 48
process and, 151–2, 175
purpose and, 113
financial crisis (2008), 223
five-step process, 160
Florida State University, 277
football, 73, 122, 135, 162–3
Frankcom, Sarah, 42, 45
free writing, 110

Friender, 27
Froome, Christopher, 76

Galea, Dermot, 148
gambling, 211, 223
Generation Z, 23
Gibran, Kahlil, 208
goal setting, 175–6
golf, 125–6, 200
Good Citizens, 220–21
GoodGym, 28
Gossage, Lucy, 270–71, 273, 276–7, 279, 284, 288, 292–3, 298, 299
Grateful Athletes, 281
gratitude, 4, 269–95
  belonging and, 274–5
  development of, 286–93
  envy and, 279
  journals of, 278
  relationships and, 275–6
  types of, 271–4
  wellbeing and, 269, 276–83

Hall, Damian, 94–6, 98, 103–4, 115, 116, 297, 298
Halliburton, 193
Hamlet (Shakespeare), 38
Hammond, Darell, 105
Harvard Business Review, 188
Harvard University, 248
Hawaii, 101, 270–71
Hayes, Stuart, 147
Hemsworth, Christopher, 184, 196
Hesmondhalgh, Julie, 42
HGV drivers, 192
Holland Hanton, Bobby, 180, 181, 183–6, 191, 196, 199–200, 298, 299

Holmes, Kelly, 8, 10–11, 12, 13–15, 21–2, 28, 136, 297, 298
hot hands, 125
'how' vs 'what', 152, 164–6
Hurricane Andrew (1992), 278

identifying emotions, 257–9
if-then planning, 112
imposter syndrome, 51–4, 81
Indonesia, 198–9
inner voice, 167–8
Insights Discovery, 207
Instagram, 28
internal dialogue, 54–5
internal insight, 4, 235–67
  development, 250–60
  lack of, 248–50
  leadership and, 246–8
interpersonal complementarity, 275
introversion, 133
Ireland, 185
Ironman Triathlon, 97, 102, 229, 270
isolation, 17–23
IVF (in vitro fertilisation), 178

'jack of all trades' saying, 44–5
Jackson, Ed, 218
James Bond movies, 180, 181
Japan, 96, 101
Jekyll & Hyde, 219
Jesus Christ Superstar, 208
Johnson, Dwayne, 200
Jordan, Michael, 40, 41, 43

KaBOOM!, 105–6
Kelly, John, 94
Kennedy, John Fitzgerald, 7

key emotions, 238
Kickstarter, 221
kidney transplants, 282
King Kong, 208
Komodo, Indonesia, 198–9
Kona, Hawaii, 270–71
Korean War (1950–53), 186, 230
Korn Ferry, 246

Lao Tzu, 235
Las Vegas, Nevada, 5, 149, 155–6, 157
Liao, Kim, 194–5
life crafting, 115–16
life satisfaction, 100, 108, 214, 269, 277
Linköping University, 30
Lombok, Indonesia, 198
loneliness, 17–28
Losada ratio, 276
Lysistrata (Aristophanes) 38

mantras, 114–15
marathon running 94–6, 98, 103–4, 115, 116, 195
Mariana Trench, 43
marriage, 21, 24, 25, 209, 214, 228, 275, 277
mastery, 4, 37–64, 162
  autonomy and, 69
  belonging and, 45
  climates of, 46–7
  confidence and, 124–6
  purpose and, 99
  showing, 56–61
  undermining of, 48–56
McGowan, Rose, 184–5, 187
McKeever, Teri, 280–81

McOnie, Drew, 208–9, 210, 211, 219–20, 221–2, 225, 230, 298, 299
medicine, 85
Melbourne, Victoria, 229
Mencius, 179
Menendez, Anthony, 193
mental imagery, 140–42
mentoring, 111
#MeToo campaign, 184
Military in Motion, 8, 28
mindfulness, 59, 252–5
Miramax, 149
mistakes, confrontation of, 60–61
Montreal Olympics (1976), 15
motivation
  autonomy and, 65, 66, 70, 73, 74, 75, 77, 80, 83, 85, 88, 150
  belonging and, 11, 29, 31
  confidence 120–21, 137, 142–3
  internal insight and, 238, 240, 244
  mastery and, 44, 47, 49, 50, 54, 56
  optimism and, 219, 222
  process and, 150, 161–3
  purpose and, 93, 95–6, 103–4, 112–13
motivational intensity, 244
muscle memory, 200
Myers-Briggs Type Indicator, 207

National Aeronautics and Space Administration (NASA), 7, 43
negative self-appraisal bias, 250

negativity bias, 139, 140, 283
Nike, 40
Nyad, Diana, 212

Obama, Michelle, 51
Old Vic theatre, London, 219
Olympic Games, 121, 280
    1976 Montreal 39
    2004 Athens, 8, 13, 15, 134,
    136
On Camp with Kelly, 14
On The Town, 208
openness to experience, 99
optimism, 4, 207–34
    belonging and, 214–15
    bias, 211
    careers and, 215–16
    coping strategies, 216–20
    development of, 224–30
    health and, 213–14
    heritability of, 212–13
    risks of, 211, 222–4

Paralympic Games, 81, 119,
    124, 138, 140, 160–61
    2016 Rio, 140
    2021 Tokyo, 138, 142
parenting
    attachment theory, 9, 32
    autonomy and 70, 71, 72
    loneliness and, 27
    purpose and, 98
Parks, Rosa, 177
Pascoe, Sara, 236, 242–5,
    246–7, 298
pay, 49
Peake, Maxine, 38–9, 41–2, 44,
    45–6, 49, 51, 52, 297, 299
Peanut, 27
Pennine Way, 94, 103, 115

perfectionism, 55–6, 102,
    158–60
performance climates, 46–7
Persil 269, 281
personality tests, 207
personality traits, 4, 99, 138,
    186, 272–3
perspective
    autonomy and, 79, 89, 90
    confidence and, 124, 143
    gratitude and, 278
    internal insight and, 235
    optimism and, 216, 226, 228
    process and, 151, 159, 161,
    167, 168
Perth, Australia, 151
Phelps, Michael, 49–50
poker, 5, 149, 155–6, 157, 161,
    164, 170
Poland, 26
post-traumatic stress disorder
    (PTSD), 282
power posing 135, 144
pragmatic optimism, see
    optimism
process, 4, 147–76
    development of, 163–71
    emotional control 152–60
    learning and, 160–61, 173–4
    maintaining motivation
    161–3
Psychological Bulletin, 23
Puller, Lewis 'Chesty' 230
purpose, 4, 93–118
    autonomy and, 102, 104, 106,
    107
    belonging and, 104
    establishment of, 110–13
    identification of, 106–10
    mastery and, 99

mental health benefits, 100–101
personality traits and, 99
physical health benefits, 101–3
poisonous purposes, 106
psychological safety, 104–5
success, definition of, 103
sustainment of 113–16
Putin, Vladimir, 178

Quantum of Solace (2008 film), 181

racism, 192
rape culture, 184
reflection, 259–60
reframing thoughts, 57–9, 217, 220, 228–30, 233–4, 283
refugees, 25
religion, 269
Rio Paralympic Games (2016), 140
Robinson, Nik, 220–21
role models, 33, 73, 80, 108, 142–3, 145
Ronaldo, Cristiano, 135
Roosevelt, Theodore, 180
Rotterdam School of Management, 115
routine, 166–7
Royal Academy of Dramatic Art (RADA), 39, 44, 52, 297
Royal Exchange Theatre, 42, 45
Royal Navy, 242
rugby, 218
Rush Memory and Aging Project, 102
Russian Federation, 177, 188

Salford College of Technology, 38
self-awareness, 237, 241–50
self-esteem
    autonomy and, 76
    belonging and, 9–10, 14, 17, 20, 23, 31
    courage and, 179
    gratitude and, 279
    internal insight and, 248–9
    mastery and, 38, 46, 52
    process and, 156
self-harm, 21–2
Serenity Prayer, 209
sexism, 192
Shameless, 38
Shedd, John, 178
shyness, 133
Silk, 38
skim-learning, 47
sleep, 214, 278
smiling, 227–8
smoking, 211
Snapchat, 24
social competence, 30–31
social connectivity, 27–30
social loafing, 13
social media, 9, 24, 27, 106, 116, 189
social sense, 238, 239–40
spinal cord injuries, 151
Sport England, 129
Stanford University, 248, 275
Storey, Sarah, 160–61, 171
Strictly Ballroom the Musical, 208
stunt performers, 180, 181, 183, 184, 185–6, 191, 196, 199–200
success, definition of, 59–60, 103

suffragettes, 106
suicide, 21
Sullivan, Kathy, 43
superstitions, 135–6
Sweden, 212
swimming, 49–50, 70, 280–81

Taliban, 177
taxation 68
technology belonging and, 20,
    27
teenagers, 24, 98, 107, 237
telecommunications industry, 49
tennis, 135
ThinkImpact, 24
thinking aloud, 255–7
This Girl Can campaign (2015),
    129
Thor franchise, 180
thoughts, reframing of, 57–9,
    217, 220, 228–30, 233–4,
    283
threat zone, 100–101, 154–60,
    168–9, 171, 172, 173, 198
Tiananmen Square protests
    (1989), 177
Tigger, 207–9, 210, 224, 228,
    298
Tokyo Paralympic Games
    (2021), 138, 142
Tracy, Brian, 167
transformational leadership, 73
triathlons, 97, 102, 114, 147,
    229, 270–71, 273, 276–7,
    279, 284, 288, 292
triggers, 168–9
trust, 87–8

Ukraine, 177, 188
unhelpful thoughts, reframing
    of, 57–9, 217, 220, 228–30,
    233–4, 283
United Kingdom
    belonging in, 18, 22, 23, 24–5
    car safety in, 113
    student athletes in, 81
    This Girl Can campaign
        (2015), 129
United States
    belonging in, 15, 24
    civil rights movement (1954–
        68), 177
    Hurricane Andrew (1992),
        278
    Korean War (1950–53), 186,
        230
    purpose in, 105
    student athletes in, 80
University of California, 21,
    152, 275
University of Chicago, 23
University of Pennsylvania, 13
upstream reciprocity, 275

values 1, 3, 10, 26, 250
    autonomy and, 68, 69, 80, 84,
        89
    belonging and, 26
    courage and, 178, 179,
        182–3, 186, 190, 192, 193,
        201
    internal insight and, 239,
        250–52
    purpose and, 97, 100, 103–4,
        106, 107, 110, 116
vicarious confidence, 129, 142,
    157, 228
Visser, Els, 198–9
visualization, 109, 117, 226,
    231

Walters, Julie, 38
Warsaw Uprising (1944), 193
weightlifting, 134
Weinberg, Scott, 185
Weinstein, Harvey, 184–5
wellbeing, 2, 4
  autonomy and, 65, 66, 73, 77,
    78, 79, 80, 83
  belonging and, 22, 29, 31
  gratitude and, 269, 276–83
  mastery and, 44, 54
  optimism and, 214, 216
  purpose and, 100
Wharton School, 13
what-if planning, 197–200,
  205–6
whistle-blowers, 190–91
Wiggs, Emma, 119, 120, 124,
  126, 130, 133, 135, 137–8,
  142, 298, 299
Wikipedia, 110, 116

Williams, Serena, 135
Wilson, McLandburgh, 208
Windsor, Berkshire, 147
Winfrey, Oprah 269, 270
Winnie the Pooh series (Milne)
  207–8, 298
winning 2, 3
  mastery and, 48
  process and, 163
  win or learn approach,
    160–61, 171, 173–5, 221
WIT (Edson) 42
Wood, Victoria, 38
Wooden, John, 152
Woods, Tiger, 200

yawn tracker, 232
YouGov, 23
Yousafzai, Malala, 177

Zelensky, Volodymyr, 177